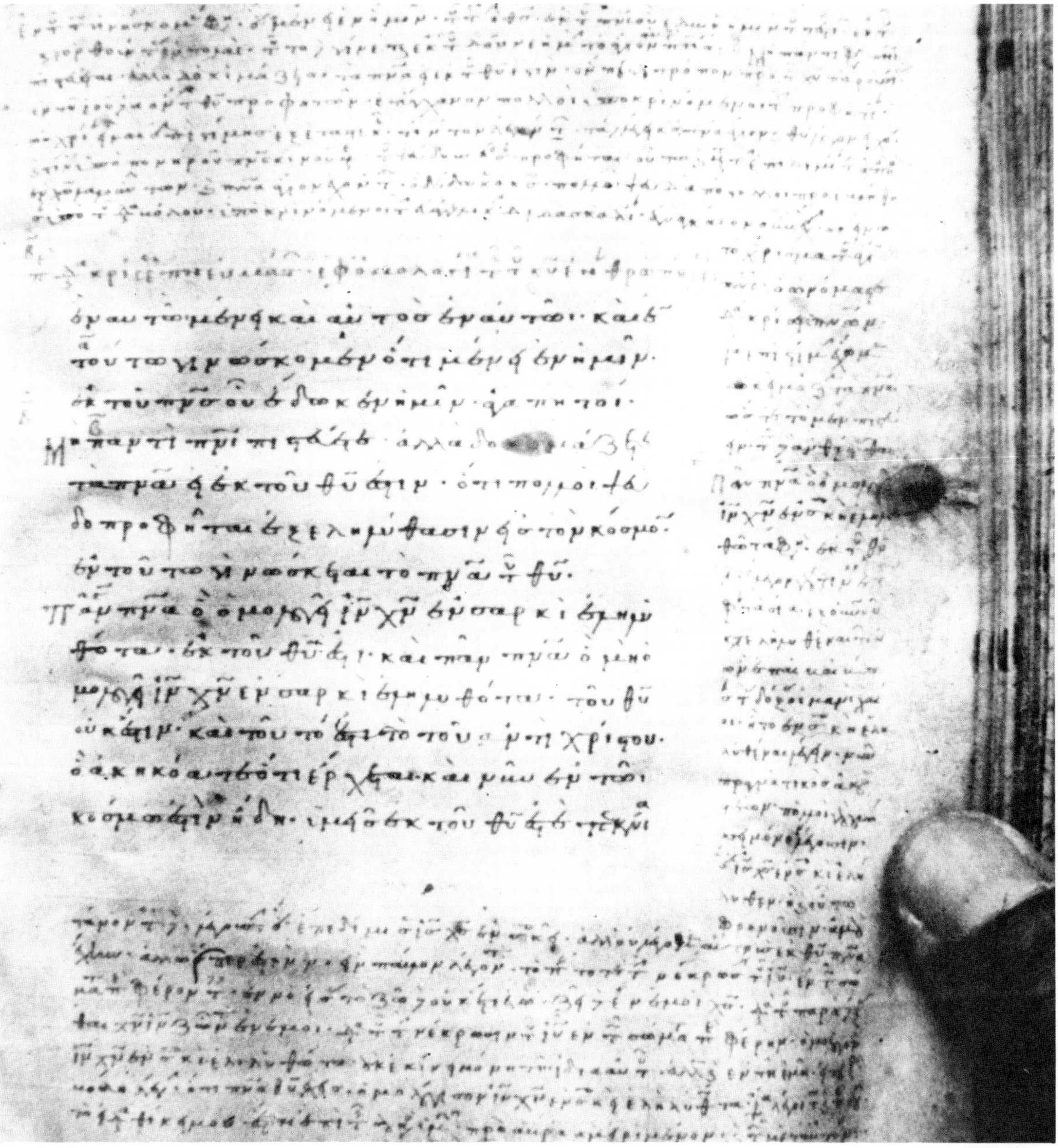

hermeneia

**Hermeneia
—A Critical
and Historical
Commentary
on the Bible**

The Johannine Epistles

A Commentary on
the Johannine Epistles

by Rudolf Bultmann

Translated by
R. Philip O'Hara with
Lane C. McGaughy and
Robert W. Funk

Edited by
Robert W. Funk

**Fortress
Press**

Philadelphia

Translated from the German *Die drei Johannesbriefe*
(2nd edition) by Rudolf Bultmann. Kritisch-Exegetischer
Kommentar über das Neue Testament begründet von
Heinrich August Wilhelm Meyer, Vierzehnte Abteilung—
Achte Auflage. © Vandenhoeck & Ruprecht, Göttingen,
1967.

Library of Congress Catalog Card Number 75-171510
ISBN 0-8006-6003-X

Printed in the United States of America

Type set by Maurice Jacobs, Inc., Philadelphia

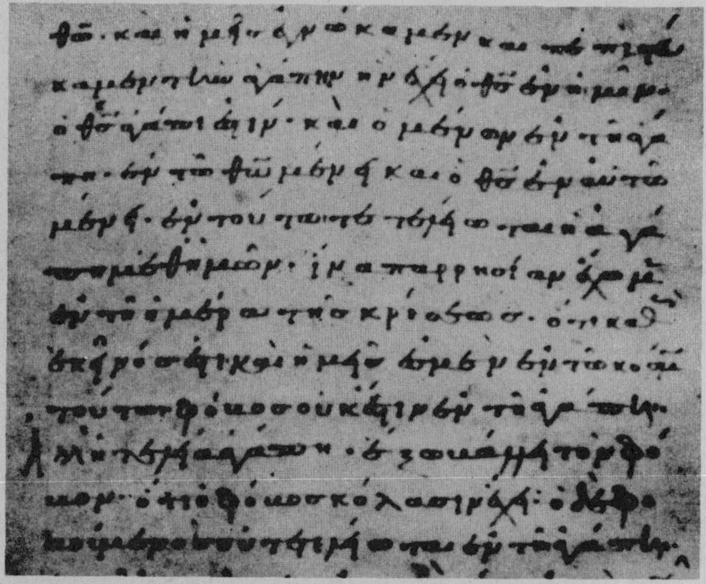

1 John 4:16–18

Rudolf Bultmann was Professor of New Testament and
Early Christian History at the University of Marburg
until his retirement. His best known works include *History
of the Synoptic Tradition* (English translation, 1963),
Jesus and the Word (English translation, 1934), *The Gospel
of John* (English translation, 1971), *Theology of the New
Testament* (English translation, 1955), and his contri-
butions to *Kerygma and Myth*. Throughout his highly
productive and provocative career, Professor Bultmann
has given steady attention to the study of the Johannine
literature. His earlier commentary on the Gospel of
John (first published in 1941; English translation, 1971)
is here complemented by a commentary on the Johannine
Epistles.

Contents

The name *Hermeneia*, Greek ἑρμηνεία, has been chosen as the title of the commentary series to which this volume belongs. The word *Hermeneia* has a rich background in the history of biblical interpretation as a term used in the ancient Greek–speaking world for the detailed, systematic exposition of a scriptural work. It is hoped that the series, like its name, will carry forward this old and venerable tradition. A second, entirely practical reason for selecting the name lay in the desire to avoid a long descriptive title and its inevitable acronym, or worse, an unpronounceable abbreviation.

The series is designed to be a critical and historical commentary to the Bible without arbitrary limits in size or scope. It will utilize the full range of philological and historical tools including textual criticism (often ignored in modern commentaries), the methods of the history of tradition (including genre and prosodic analysis), and the history of religion.

Hermeneia is designed for the serious student of the Bible. It will make full use of ancient Semitic and classical languages; at the same time, English translations of all comparative materials—Greek, Latin, Canaanite, or Akkadian—will be supplied alongside the citation of the source in its original language. Insofar as possible, the aim is to provide the student or scholar with full critical discussion of each problem of interpretation and with the primary data upon which the discussion is based.

Hermeneia is designed to be international and interconfessional in the selection of its authors; its editorial boards were also formed with this end in view. Occasionally the series will offer translations of distinguished commentaries which originally appeared in languages other than English. Published volumes of the series will be revised continually, and, eventually, new commentaries will replace older works in order to preserve the currency of the series. Commentaries are also being assigned for important literary works in the categories of apocryphal and pseudepigraphical works of the Old and New Testaments, including some of Essene or Gnostic authorship.

The editors of *Hermeneia* impose no systematic–theological perspective upon the series (directly, or indirectly by its selection of authors). It is expected that authors will struggle to lay bare the ancient meaning of a biblical work or pericope. In this way the text's human relevance should become transparent, as is always the case in competent historical discourse. However, the series eschews for itself homiletical translation of the Bible.

The editors are heavily indebted to Fortress Press for its energy and courage in taking up an expensive, long–term project, the rewards of which will accrue chiefly to the field of biblical scholarship.

The first draft of the translation of this volume was prepared by R. Philip O'Hara. Owing to the press of time and the inhibiting power of distance, Lane C. McGaughy assisted Robert W. Funk in preparing the final version of the text here presented. Eldon Jay Epp, Raymond E. Brown, and James W. Dunkly greatly assisted the translators on points both large and small.

The editor responsible for this volume is Robert W. Funk of the University of Montana.

May 1973

Frank Moore Cross, Jr.
For the Old Testament
Editorial Board

Helmut Koester
For the New Testament
Editorial Board

1. Sources and General Abbreviations

Abbreviations used in this volume for sources and literature from antiquity are the same as those used in the *Theological Dictionary of the New Testament*, ed. Gerhard Kittel, tr. Geoffrey W. Bromiley, vol. 1 (Grand Rapids, Michigan, and London: Eerdmans, 1964), xvi–xl. Some abbreviations are adapted from that list and can be easily identified.

Common abbreviations employed in this volume include the following:

ad loc.	*ad locum*, at the place or passage under discussion
ANF	*The Ante-Nicene Fathers: Translations of the Writings of the Fathers down to A.D. 325*, ed. Alexander Roberts and James Donaldson (Buffalo: The Christian Literature Publishing Company, 1885–97; reprinted Grand Rapids, Michigan: Eerdmans, 1951–56)
BZ	*Biblische Zeitschrift*
cf.	confer, compare with
col(s).	column(s)
Corp. Herm.	*Corpus Hermeticum*
ed.	editor, edited by
[Ed.]	Editor of this volume of Hermeneia
ET	English translation
FRLANT	Forschungen zur Religion und Literatur des Alten und Neuen Testament
HTR	*Harvard Theological Review*
idem	the same (person)
item	also, in addition
JBL	*Journal of Biblical Literature*
JTS	*Journal of Theological Studies*
KEK	Kritisch-exegetischer Kommentar über das Neue Testament begründet von Heinrich August Wilhelm Meyer
LCC	The Library of Christian Classics (Philadelphia: Westminster Press, and London: The SCM Press)
Loeb	The Loeb Classical Library, founded by James Loeb, ed. E. H. Warmington (Cambridge, Mass.: Harvard University Press, and London: Heinemann, 1912ff)
n.	note
NGG	Nachrichten von der Gesellschaft der Wissenschaften zu Göttingen
NTS	*New Testament Studies*
p. (pp.)	page(s)
RAC	*Reallexikon für Antike und Christentum*, ed. Theodor Klauser (Stuttgart: Hiersemann, 1950)
RGG	*Die Religion in Geschichte und Gegenwart: Handwörterbuch für Theologie und Relitionswissenschaft*
RSV	Revised Standard Version of the Bible
scil.	*scilicet*, it is permitted (to supply)
s.v.	*sub verbo* or *sub voce*, under the word (entry)
TDNT	*Theological Dictionary of the New Testament*, ed. Gerhard Kittel and Gerhard Friedrich, tr. and ed. Geoffrey W. Bromiley (Grand Rapids, Michigan, Eerdmans, 1964–)
ThLZ	*Theologische Literaturzeitung*
ThR	*Theologische Rundschau*
tr.	translator, translated by, translation
[trans. by Ed.]	translated by editor of this volume of Hermeneia
TU	Texte und Untersuchungen zur Geschichte der altchristlichen Literatur
v (vss)	verse(s)
v.l.	*varia lectio*, variant reading
vol.	volume(s)
ZNW	*Zeitschrift für die neutestamentliche Wissenschaft und die Kunde der älteren Kirche*
ZThK	*Zeitschrift für Theologie und Kirche*

2. Short Titles of Frequently Cited Literature

In instances where two editions of the same work have appeared, the pagination of both versions is cited in the order in which they are listed in the short title bibliography below (the second in brackets [ ]).

Bauer
Walter Bauer, *Griechisch–Deutsches Wörterbuch zu den Schriften des Neuen Testaments und der übrigen urchristlichen Literatur* (Berlin: 1958), or: Walter Bauer, *A Greek–English Lexicon of the New Testament and Other Early Christian Literature*, tr. and adaptation W. F. Arndt and F. W. Gingrich from the 4th ed. (Chicago: University of Chicago Press, and Cambridge: Cambridge University Press, 1957).

Bergmeier, "Zum Verfasserproblem des II. und III. Johannesbriefes"
Roland Bergmeier, "Zum Verfasserproblem des II. und III. Johannesbriefes," *ZNW* 57 (1966): 93–100.

Blass–Debrunner
F. Blass and A. Debrunner, *A Greek Grammar of the New Testament and Other Early Christian Literature*, tr. and rev. Robert W. Funk (Chicago: University of Chicago Press, 1961).

Braun, "Qumran und das Neue Testament"
Herbert Braun, "Qumran und das Neue Testament: Ein Bericht über 10 Jahre Forschung (1950–1959)," *ThR* 28 (1962): 97–234; J. C. B. Mohr [Paul Siebeck] (1964): 101–17; now in *Qumran und das Neue Testament* (Tübingen:, 1966), I:290–306.

Braun, "Literar–Analyse"
Herbert Braun, "Literar–Analyse und theologische Schichtung im ersten Johannesbrief," *ZThK* 48 (1951): 262–92; now in *Gesammelte Studien zum Neuen Testament und seiner Umwelt* (Tübingen: J. C. B. Mohr [Paul Siebeck], 1962), 210–42.

Bultmann
Rudolf Bultmann, *The Gospel of John: A Commentary*, tr. G. R. Beasley–Murray, with R. W. N. Hoare and J. K. Riches (Oxford: Blackwell, and Philadelphia: Westminster, 1971), or: Rudolf Bultmann, *Das Evangelium Johannes*. Kritsch–exegetischer Kommentar über das Neue Testament, Zweite Abteilung (Göttingen: Vandenhoeck & Ruprecht, 1964), with *Ergänzungsheft* (1966).

Bultmann, "Analyse des ersten Johannesbriefes"
Rudolf Bultmann, "Analyse des ersten Johannesbriefes," *Festgabe für Adolf Jülicher* (Tübingen: J. C. B. Mohr [Paul Siebeck], 1927), 138–58.

Bultmann, "Die kirchliche Redaktion"
Rudolf Bultmann, "Die kirchliche Redaktion des ersten Johannesbriefes," *In Memoriam Ernst Lohmeyer*, ed. Werner Schmauch (Stuttgart: Evange-lisches Verlagswerk, 1951), 189–201.

Charles
R. H. Charles, ed., *The Apocrypha and Pseudepi-grapha of the Old Testament in English, with Introductions and Critical and Explanatory Notes to the Several Books*, vols. 1 and 2 (Oxford: Clarendon Press, 1913).

Conzelmann, " 'Was von Anfang war' "
Hans Conzelmann, " 'Was von Anfang war'," *Neutestamentliche Studien für Rudolf Bultmann*, ed. W. Eltester. Beihefte zur *ZNW* 21 (Berlin: Alfred Töpelmann, ²1957), 194–201.

Dodd
Charles Harold Dodd, *The Johannine Epistles*. The Moffatt New Testament Commentary (London: Hodder & Stoughton, 1946).

Funk, "The Form and Structure of II and III John"
Robert W. Funk, "The Form and Structure of II and III John," *JBL* 86 (1967); 424–30.

Haenchen, "Neuere Literatur"
Ernst Haenchen, "Neuere Literatur zu den Johannesbriefe," *ThR* 26 (1960): 1–43, 267–91; now in *Die Bibel und Wir: Gesammelte Aufsätze, Zweiter Band* (Tübingen: J. C. B. Mohr [Paul Siebeck], 1968), 235–311.

Holtzmann
H. J. Holtzmann, *Evangelium, Briefe und Offenbarung des Johannes*, 3rd ed., ed. Walter Bauer. Hand–Kommentar zum Neuen Testament 4 (Tübingen: J. C. B. Mohr [Paul Siebeck], 1908).

Jonas, *Gnosis und spätantiker Geist*
H. Jonas, *Gnosis und spätantiker Geist, Erster Teil: Die mythologische Gnosis, mit einer Einleitung zur Geschichte und Methodologie der Forschung*. FRLANT 51 (Göttingen: ³1964).

Käsemann, "Ketzer und Zeuge"
Ernst Käsemann, "Ketzer und Zeuge," *ZThK* 48 (1951): 292–311, reprinted in *Exegetische Versuche und Besinnungen* I (Göttingen: Vandenhoeck & Ruprecht, 1960), 168–87.

Nauck, *Die Tradition und der Charakter des ersten Johannesbriefes*
Wolfgang Nauck, *Die Tradition und der Charakter des ersten Johannesbriefes* (Tübingen: J. C. B. Mohr [Paul Siebeck], 1957).

O'Neill, *The Puzzle of 1 John*
J. C. O'Neill, *The Puzzle of 1 John* (London: S.P.C.K., 1966).

Schnackenburg
Rudolf Schnackenburg, *Die Johannesbriefe*. Herders Theologischer Kommentar zum Neuen Testament 13, 3 (Freiburg i. B.: Herder, ³1965).

Windisch–Preisker
Hans Windisch, *Die Katholischen Briefe*, 3rd ed., rev. Herbert Preisker. Handbuch zum Neuen Testament 15 (Tübingen: J. C. B. Mohr [Paul Siebeck], ³1951).

The English translation of the Johannine Epistles printed at the head of each section of this Commentary is from the *Revised Standard Version of the Bible*, copyrighted 1946, modified in accordance with the exegetical decisions of the commentator. Translations of the Greek text in the body of the Commentary are customarily derived from the RSV; occasionally, however, the translator has translated words, phrases, and even whole sentences afresh, depending on the contours of the discussion and the requirements of lucidity. The translators and editor are responsible for all translations of other biblical texts, but they have followed the RSV wherever possible.

Translations of ancient Greek and Latin texts are taken from the *Loeb Classical Library* wherever possible. Translations made by the translator or editor are so indicated.

Whenever available, recent scholarly works are cited in their published English versions. Bultmann's *The Gospel of John: A Commentary*, which is frequently cited, is referred to by English page, with the page of the German original following in brackets [ ], for the benefit of those accustomed to using the original version. Works appearing in two forms are cited in both forms wherever possible.

The Bibliography has been augmented considerably, principally with articles and works of recent vintage.

The endpapers of this volume are reproduced from Codex No. 207 of the National Library, Athens, Greece. This twelfth-century manuscript, which contains the text, with commentary, of Acts and the Pauline and Catholic epistles, is Minuscule 1360 in the list established by C. R. Gregory. For the commentary on 1 John, see J. A. Cramer, *Catena in Epistolas Catholicas* (Oxford, 1840), pp. 105–45. The front endpaper contains 1 John 3:15–24 and 3:24–4:4*a*; the back endpaper contains 1 John 4:4*a*–9*a* and 4:16–20. The reproduction on page v is a detail. The photographs and identifications are provided through the courtesy of Gerhard Krodel, The Lutheran Theological Seminary, Philadelphia, Pennsylvania.

The English translation of the Johannine Epistles printed at the head of each section of this Commentary is from the *Revised Standard Version of the Bible*, copyrighted 1946, modified in accordance with the exegetical decisions of the commentator. Translations of the Greek text in the body of the Commentary are customarily derived from the RSV; occasionally, however, the translator has translated words, phrases, and even whole sentences afresh, depending on the contours of the discussion and the requirements of lucidity. The translators and editor are responsible for all translations of other biblical texts, but they have followed the RSV wherever possible.

Translations of ancient Greek and Latin texts are taken from the *Loeb Classical Library* wherever possible. Translations made by the translator or editor are so indicated.

Whenever available, recent scholarly works are cited in their published English versions. Bultmann's *The Gospel of John: A Commentary*, which is frequently cited, is referred to by English page, with the page of the German original following in brackets [ ], for the benefit of those accustomed to using the original version. Works appearing in two forms are cited in both forms wherever possible.

The Bibliography has been augmented considerably, principally with articles and works of recent vintage.

The endpapers of this volume are reproduced from Codex No. 207 of the National Library, Athens, Greece. This twelfth-century manuscript, which contains the text, with commentary, of Acts and the Pauline and Catholic epistles, is Minuscule 1360 in the list established by C. R. Gregory. For the commentary on 1 John, see J. A. Cramer, *Catena in Epistolas Catholicas* (Oxford, 1840), pp. 105–45. The front endpaper contains 1 John 3:15–24 and 3:24–4:4*a*; the back endpaper contains 1 John 4:4*a*–9*a* and 4:16–20. The reproduction on page v is a detail. The photographs and identifications are provided through the courtesy of Gerhard Krodel, The Lutheran Theological Seminary, Philadelphia, Pennsylvania.

In this introduction I will not present a summary of exegetical results, since these should be derived from the exegetical work to which the commentary is designed to lead. Nor will I deal here with questions that are treated by the so-called Introductions to the New Testament, such as the dating of the texts and the person or persons of the author. For these questions I may refer, apart from the Introductions to the New Testament, to the detailed discussion of Ernst Haenchen in his review article, "Neuere Literatur zu den Johannesbriefen," as well as to the introduction to Rudolf Schnackenburg's commentary on the Johannine Epistles.

The question of authorship needs to be dealt with here only insofar as it concerns the relationship of the Johannine Epistles to the Gospel of John and the interrelationship of the three Epistles. These questions will of course also have to be considered in the commentary itself. A preliminary orientation is nevertheless a useful introduction to the reading of the commentary and can pave the way for understanding certain exegetical problems.

The question of the relationship of the Epistles to the Gospel is basically the question of how 1 John is related to the Gospel. The close affinity in language and content between the two books makes it understandable that the identity of the authors has often been asserted and is frequently asserted even today. I cannot agree with this supposition. The decisive argument against this identification, as Haenchen has correctly observed,[1] is the following: the Gospel of John and 1 John are directed against different fronts. Whereas the Gospel is opposed to the "world," or to the Jews who are its representatives, and therefore to non-Christians, the false teachers who are opposed in 1 John are within the Christian community and claim to represent the genuine Christian faith. This shows that 1 John originates in a period later than the Gospel. I will omit here the details that confirm this chronology; they will have to be considered in the commentary. The relationship between 1 John and the Gospel rests on the fact that the author of 1 John had the Gospel before him and was decisively influenced by its language and ideas. He used it, however, as Haenchen rightly says, "not slavishly, but rather in line with the church tradition in which he lived."[2]

So far as the relationship of the three letters to each other is concerned, complete clarity, in my opinion, is not possible. It can be said with certainty only that 2 John is dependent upon 1 John, indeed, that 2 John is definitely a secondary work and is evidence for an evolving "early Catholicism" (*Frühkatholizismus*). The letter form should probably be taken as a fiction.[3] The justification for this judgment must be given in the commentary.

The determination of a precise historical context for 3 John is completely uncertain. In any case, this docu-

---

1   "Neuere Literatur," 35f [273].
2   "Neuere Literatur," 29 [267]. On the question of the linguistic relationship of the letters to the Gospel of John, apart from C. H. Dodd, "The First Epistle of John and the Fourth Gospel," *Bulletin of the John Rylands Library* 21 (1937): 129–56; W. F. Howard, "The Common Authorship of the Johannine Gospel and Epistles," *JTS* 48 (1947): 12–25; W. G. Wilson, "An Examination of the Linguistic Evidence Adduced against the Unity of the First Epistle of John and the Fourth Gospel," *JTS* 49 (1948): 147–56; cf. also Frederick C. Grant, *The Gospel of John in the King James Version, with critical introduction and notes*, II, Harper's Annotated Bible Series (New York: Harper, 1956), 41–3.
3   Emmanuel Hirsch, *Studien zum vierten Evangelium. Text, Literarkritik, Entstehungsgeschichte* (Tübingen: Mohr, 1936), declared all three Johannine letters to be fictional; cf. M. Dibelius, "Johannesbriefe," *RGG²*, 3:348f. In *Geschichte der urchristlichen Literatur*, I (Berlin: W. de Gruyter & Co., 1926), 61–5 (*A Fresh Approach to the New Testament and Early Christian Literature* [London: Ivor Nicholson & Watson, 1936], 209–13), Dibelius vacillates.

ment is a genuine letter, which one particular person addressed to another. Individual expressions are reminiscent of the language of the Gospel and of 1 John. It is clear that the Epistle was written in an actual situation which can be characterized as the period of conflict between the old, specifically Johannine tradition and the initial development of ecclesiastical organization. The chronology cannot be fixed more exactly. One can probably say only that this Epistle presupposes 1 John. The basis for this judgment must be deferred to the commentary as well.

In order to lighten the burden of the commentary and to prepare for the exegesis presented therein, the problem of the literary unity or the literary critical analysis of 1 John may be briefly discussed. For this problem I can again refer to Ernst Haenchen.[4]

In *Festgabe für Adolf Jülicher*,[5] I presented an analysis of 1 John to which I still adhere, apart from some modifications. I am of the opinion that a prior written Source (*Vorlage*) underlies the text of 1 John, which the author annotated. I need not repeat the analysis here, since I carry it out in the commentary. My hypothesis was accepted, although in a form modified at many points by Herbert Preisker in his revision of Hans Windisch's commentary on the Catholic Epistles, and, above all, by Herbert Braun.[6] It was also accepted in a peculiar, though in my opinion untenable, way by Wolfgang Nauck.[7] Nauck acknowledges that the author of the Epistle used a Source, but he thinks that the Source stems from the author himself. The most recent hypothesis of J. C. O'Neill is also original.[8] He wishes to demonstrate that, in 1 John, Jewish sources have been reworked, and indeed by a member of a Jewish sect who, having become a Christian, wants to lead his Jewish comrades to faith in Jesus as the Messiah. O'Neill distinguishes

Christian additions from the Jewish Source. Even if this construction is unconvincing, O'Neill nevertheless must be credited with showing that 1 John presupposes the Jewish language–tradition and thought–world. In addition, I also want to mention that, although Otto A. Piper maintains the unity of 1 John, he does not deny the use of older Christian tradition.[9]

In the volume in honor of Ernst Lohmeyer,[10] I have carried further my analysis of 1 John by attempting to demonstrate that the text of 1 John was reworked to bring it into conformity with ecclesiastical tradition. My thesis proceeds from the fact that the Proemium of 1 John imitates the usual prescript of a letter and thus suggests that 1 John really is a letter. If that is the case, then one also expects a conclusion that imitates the usual epistolary conclusion. In fact that appears to me to be the case in 5:13. It follows that 5:14–21 is to be imputed to a later redaction. For this, as well as for the redactional glosses in 1:5–5:13, I refer to the commentary.

In addition to my earlier analysis, however, I must deal with a further question which concerns the unity of 1 John. It is the question whether 1 John 1:1–5:13, as a document in which a Source is used and commented upon, is a unified composition. (Naturally here the ecclesiastical redaction is to be disregarded.) The question of a unified train of thought and the question of structure have often been discussed, but none of the attempts to demonstrate unity and a sequence of thought is satisfactory. One has the impression that the Epistle could have been concluded with 2:27, and I think that 1:5–2:27 was originally, in fact, an independent writing, or perhaps more appropriately, a rough draft. Following this are individual sections which deal essentially with the same themes already dealt with in 1:5–2:27. These themes are sometimes modified and expanded, but

4   "Neuere Literatur," 1–43 [235–82].
5   "Analyse des ersten Johannnesbriefes."
6   "Literar-Analyse."
7   *Die Tradition und der Charakter des ersten Johannes-briefes.*

8   *The Puzzle of 1 John*, 2–7.
9   "1 John and the Didache of the Primitive Church," *JBL* 66 (1947): 437–51.
10 "Die kirchliche Redaktion."

without benefit of a structured context. One is driven to the conclusion that here pieces have been combined which were originally conceived as individual units. The analysis of 2:28–5:12 is given in the commentary at 2:28ff. Haenchen considers the problem of a unified theology in 1 John, but not that of literary unity. O'Neill sees the second problem; he denies the unity, without, however, giving an analysis of the composition.

I must here forego discussing the relationship of the Johannine letters to the Old Testament and to Judaism, as well as to Gnosticism. These are themes which Schnackenburg, in the introduction to his commentary, and Haenchen, in his research summary, have dealt with extensively. The relationship to the Qumran texts in particular has been dealt with by Herbert Braun, carefully and with critical examination of the various hypotheses.[11] Naturally, all these questions will be discussed in detail in the commentary.

11 "Qumran und das Neue Testament."

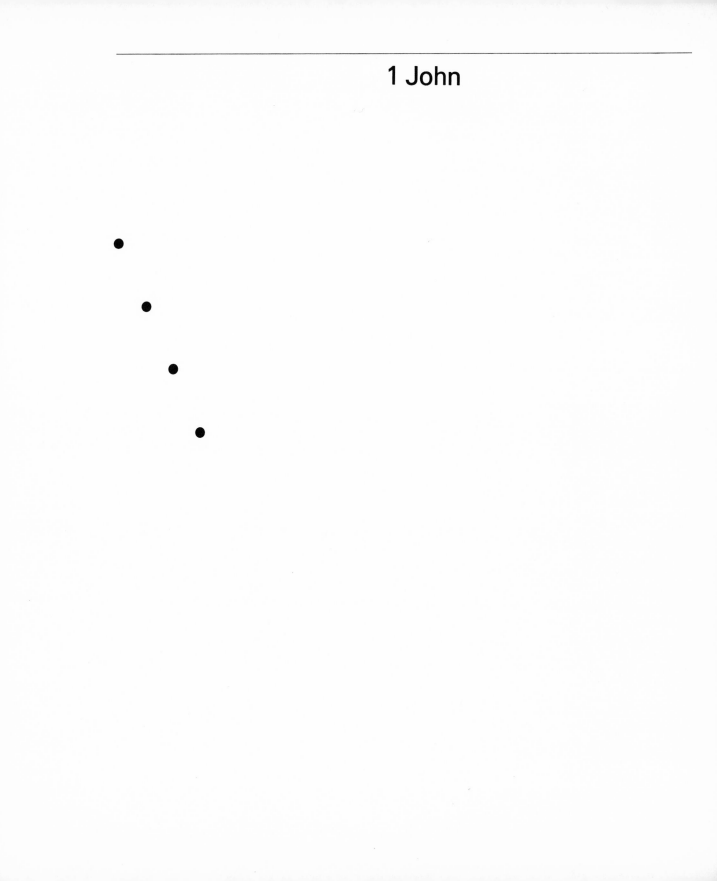

1   Proemium

1   That which was from the beginning, which we have heard, which we have seen with our eyes, which we have looked upon and touched with our hands, concerning the word of life—2/ the life was made manifest, and we saw it, and testify to it, and proclaim to you the eternal life which was with the Father and was made manifest to us—3/ that which we have seen and heard we proclaim also to you, so that you may have fellowship with us; and our fellowship is with the Father and with his Son Jesus Christ. 4/ And we are writing this that our joy may be complete.

■ 1 Ἀπαγγέλλομεν καὶ ὑμῖν ("we proclaim also to you," v 3) is the phrase that grammatically supports the proemium. Yet the structure of the proemium is complicated by the fact that the ἀπαγγέλλομεν of v 3, which one properly expects to be the continuation of v 1, is already inserted in the parenthesis of v 2, i.e., in μαρτυροῦμεν καὶ ἀπαγγέλλομεν ("we testify and proclaim").[1] Thus the construction is disrupted.[2] It is clear, however, that the object of the (double) ἀπαγγέλλομεν is stated initially in v 1 by the four relative clauses.[3] All four relative clauses, of course, intend one and the same object, viz., the content of the ἀγγελία ("message"). The first expression, ὃ ἦν ἀπ᾿ ἀρχῆς ("which was from the beginning") apparently means nothing other than

---

1   Both verbs denote Christian proclamation. Ἀπαγγέλλειν (bear or communicate a message) had no more become a *terminus technicus* for Christian proclamation than had ἀγγελία (v 5), but μαρτυρεῖν very likely had. The latter initially described testimony in the legal sense, based on knowledge, especially the testimony of an eyewitness; in Christian usage it then came to mean (like μαρτυρία and μάρτυς) the Christian message (see Bultmann on Jn 1:6, pp. 50f n. 5 [30 n. 5], and Strathmann, *TDNT*, *s.v.*). That the message depends upon an eyewitness can be indicated in each case by the context (as in 1 Jn 1:2).

2   One is inclined to ask, of course, whether v 2 is a redactional insertion (E. Schwartz, "Aporien im vierten Evangelium I." *NGG*, 1907:342–372). However, the verse with its double ἐφανερώθη ("made manifest") expresses an interest of the author that penetrates the whole Epistle, so that it is difficult to

accept this assumption. Furthermore, acceptance of this verse as an insertion would doubtless require that the conclusion of v 1, περὶ τοῦ λόγου τῆς ζωῆς ("concerning the word of life"), be considered an insertion, as well as the phrase, ὃ ἑωράκαμεν καὶ ἀκηκόαμεν ("that which we have seen and heard") at the beginning of v 3, which resumes the perfect verbs of v 1.

3   The ὅ of the first relative clause is nominative, whereas the three subsequent relative clauses begin with the accusative ὅ, which in each case is dependent on the verb. Ὃ ἦν ἀπ᾿ ἀρχῆς ("That which was from the beginning"), however, is also considered an object; τοῦτο ("that") is obviously to be understood.

what Jn 1:1 expresses in the form ἐν ἀρχῇ ἦν ὁ λόγος ("In the beginning was the word"), and there can be no doubt that the Johannine Prologue served as the model for vss 1–4. But why (as in the following three relative clauses) is the neuter formulation chosen instead of the masculine, as is also the case in 2:13f? The answer in the first instance must be: under discussion here is the *subject matter*, the content of the ἀγγελία ("message"),[4] as indicated by the phrase περὶ τοῦ λόγου τῆς ζωῆς ("concerning the word of life").[5] The fact that subject matter and person are basically identical becomes evident at the end of v 3, where it is disclosed that the κοινωνία ("fellowship") is μετὰ τοῦ πατρὸς καὶ μετὰ τοῦ υἱοῦ αὐτοῦ Ἰησοῦ Χριστοῦ ("with the Father and with his Son Jesus Christ").[6] What is significant, however, is that subject matter and person are identical in a unique fashion: to speak of the subject matter is to speak at the same time of the person.

■ **2** The phrase, ἡ ζωὴ ἐφανερώθη (v 2, "the life was made manifest"), names the subject matter which is designated in what immediately follows as ζωὴ αἰώνιος ("eternal life"), and thus as salvation, for which the readers (as well as all men) strive. When the text speaks of ζωή ("life") as ἐφανερώθη ("made manifest"), then it also speaks of the subject matter; but, without a doubt, ἐφανερώθη refers to the historical event in which the subject matter has its origin.[7] The clauses ὃ ἀκηκόαμεν... ὃ ἐθεασάμεθα καὶ αἱ χεῖρες ἡμῶν ἐψηλάφησαν ("which we have heard... which we have looked upon and touched with our hands") also refer to this event, and therefore to the historical appearance of the logos of Jn 1:1.[8] When it is then said of ζωὴ αἰώνιος ("eternal life") (v 2): ἥτις ἦν πρὸς τὸν πατέρα ("which was with the Father"), this statement corresponds to the statement in Jn 1:18: ὁ ὢν εἰς τὸν κόλπον τοῦ πατρός

---

4   Cf. Conzelmann, "'Was von Anfang war,'" 196: the Epistle, "unlike the Gospel, is oriented not primarily to the *person*, but to the *subject matter*...." Cf. Braun, "Literar-Analyse," 282 [232].

5   Dodd is correct: περὶ τοῦ λόγου τῆς ζωῆς ("concerning the word of life") is the theme. The relative clauses indicate the content, namely: with regard to the λόγος τῆς ζωῆς, we proclaim to you what was from the beginning. Dodd would understand λόγος τῆς ζωῆς as the gospel. In fact "logos" is to be understood primarily as "word"; λόγος τῆς ζωῆς would then be the word that deals with life (objective genitive). But why does the author not simply say: τὸν λόγον τῆς ζωῆς? Is not the meaning of "Logos" as divine person also echoed in the term λόγος? Then τῆς ζωῆς would be a qualitative or epexegetical genitive (i.e., concerning the Logos, which is life).

6   The historical φανερωθῆναι ("made manifest") of the Son is also mentioned in 3:5 and 8, and his having come or his coming ἐν σαρκί ("in flesh") in 4:2 and 2 Jn 7. It is clear from the broader context that vss 1 and 2 are spoken in opposition to Gnosis. Schnackenburg, p. 62, points to the dissimilarity to Paul, for whom the cross stands at the center of the Christian proclamation, not the incarnation.

7   Φανερωθῆναι appears often in John and 1 John. It designates revelation as an occurrence, an event, not as instructive enlightenment, although this meaning can also emerge. Ἀποκαλύπτειν ("reveal"), which is used by Paul along with φανεροῦν, is lacking (cf. Bultmann on Jn 17:6, p. 497 n. 2 [380 n. 2], and Schnackenburg, p. 62, n. 1).

8   The vacillation of tense between the perfect (which denotes the continuation of past occurrence) and the aorist (which denotes the occurrence as past) is without significance. Cf. the change from ἠκούσατε (2:18) to ἀκηκόατε (4:3), or from ἀπέσταλκεν (4:9) to ἀπέστειλεν (4:10), from ἔδωκεν (3:24) to δέδωκεν (4:13), from ἔγνωκεν (3:6) to ἔγνω (4:8). That the sequence of ἀκηκόαμεν and ἑωράκαμεν in v 1 and v 3 varies is likewise of no significance. Nevertheless, one may say that ἀκηκόαμεν comes first in v 1 because, with respect to revelation, "the appropriate stance is above all hearing" (Schnackenburg), and that in v 2 ἑωράκαμεν alone is used and precedes ἀκηκόαμεν in v 3, because ὁρᾶν corresponds to φανερωθῆναι (Schnackenburg).

("the one in the bosom of the Father").[9] Thus ἡ ζωὴ ἐφανερώθη ("the life was made manifest") corresponds to καὶ ὁ λόγος σὰρξ ἐγένετο ("and the word became flesh") in Jn 1:14.

Yet there is a peculiar difference. Subject matter and person are not directly identical; rather, one must speak of a paradoxical identity, which consists in the fact that a historical event is at the same time the eschatological event—not, however, in the same way as in the Gospel of John. In the Gospel the coming and going of Jesus is understood simply as the eschatological event (3:19; 5:25; 9:39; 12:31; etc.). For 1 John, on the other hand, it is characteristic that the eschatological event is further realized in the proclamation. From this point of view it is understandable that it is ἀπ᾿ ἀρχῆς and not ἐν ἀρχῇ, as in Jn 1:1; therefore, "from the beginning," not "in the beginning." Hence what is spoken of here is not the preexistent Logos, but its "manifestation," its "incarnation," which is the object of ἀκηκόαμεν ("we have heard"), etc., and thus the origin of the ἀγγελία ("message").[10]

If the ἀγγελία ("message") has its origin in φανερωθῆναι ("made manifest"), then the question arises: who are the "we" who have perceived the φανερωθῆναι and thus can say ὃ ἀκηκόαμεν, etc.? The fact that τοῖς ὀφθαλμοῖς ἡμῶν ("with our eyes") is appended to ὃ ἑωράκαμεν ("we have seen") and that καὶ αἱ χεῖρες ἡμῶν ἐψηλάφησαν ("and our hands touched")[11] follows ὃ ἐθεασάμεθα ("we looked upon"), show that these verbs denote sense perception. It cannot be a matter of spiritual perception as in Acts 17:27, in the sense of Stoic pantheism.[12] The basic difference is thereby already made clear: the ἐφανερώθη ἡμῖν ("made manifest to us") of v 2 cannot be taken in the sense of a Stoic or mystical pantheism.

The question, however, remains: who are the "we," who can say ἀκηκόαμεν ("we have heard"), etc.? The verbs denoting sense perception give the impression that the "we" are the ear and the eyewitnesses of the historical Jesus. In this case it certainly could not be a matter of sense perception as such, for this possibility was open also to the unbelieving Jewish contemporaries of Jesus, without leading to ἀπαγγέλλειν ("proclaim") and μαρτυρεῖν ("testify"). It must therefore mean perception on the part of believing eyes, which, although bound to sense perception, perceive the φανερωθῆναι ("mani-

---

9 Πατήρ is a familiar designation for God in 1 Jn (1:2f; 2:1, 13, 15f, 22–24; 3:1; 4:14) and is used continually in John.

10 Therefore ἀρχή ("beginning") has this meaning and does not, as it is often interpreted, refer to creation. It refers to the origin of the historical event "made manifest" (φανερωθῆναι), and not the temporal ἀρχή or given time at which the Christian message encountered the readers (or the believers). If the author can also use ἀρχή in the latter sense (2:7, 24; 3:11; 2 Jn 5f), then the paradoxical identity of the origin and the historic fulfillment of the proclamation is simply finding expression in the double meaning of ἀρχή. Cf. especially Conzelmann, " 'Was von Anfang war,' " 194–201.

11 Ψηλαφᾶν ("touch") can refer in this context only to the historical figure of Jesus (the "incarnated one") and not to the resurrected one, as in Lk 24:39; cf. Jn 20:24ff. So also Schnackenburg, p. 53.

12 In such a way the *Corp. Herm.* V.1f can even speak of λάβεσθαι αὐταῖς ταῖς χερσίν ("lay hold on it with your hands") in order to express the fact that the ἀφανὴς θεός ("invisible God") is visible for the νόησις ("mind") in the cosmos. Cf. also Dio Chrysostomos, *Or.* 12.60, where ἅπτεσθαι ("to lay hold of") of the θεῖον ("deity") is mentioned. Further, Plutarch, *De genio Socratis* 20 p. 589b: τῷ γὰρ ὄντι τὰς μὲν ἀλλήλων νοήσεις οἷον ὑπὸ σκότῳ διὰ φωνῆς ψηλαφῶντες γνωρίζομεν ("For in very truth our recognition of one another's thoughts through the medium of the spoken word is like groping in the dark . . .").

festation") of the $\zeta\omega\acute{\eta}$ ("life").

But are the contemporaries of the historical Jesus really intended? There is a difficulty with this view: 1 John (like the Gospel of John upon which it is dependent) was written in such a late period that it is scarcely possible that "a rather large circle of ear– and eyewitnesses was still alive."[13] The difficulty may be obviated and the question of the "we" answered by distinguishing contemporaneity with the historical event from contemporaneity with the eschatological event; in other words, by recognizing the paradox that an historical event can be, or

in this case really is, at the same time an eschatological event. The "we," therefore, are the "eschatological" contemporaries of Jesus. They can say $\dot{\alpha}\kappa\eta\kappa\dot{o}\alpha\mu\epsilon\nu$ ("we have heard"), etc., as those in whom the historical $\dot{\alpha}\kappa\eta\kappa\dot{o}\alpha\mu\epsilon\nu$, etc., is further effected—the historical $\dot{\alpha}\kappa\eta\kappa\dot{o}\alpha\mu\epsilon\nu$ from which the eschatological is not severed.[14]

It has often been noted that it is not unusual for people of a later generation to speak of the history (i.e., of events) of an earlier time as if they had experienced it themselves. The sentences quoted by Windisch from the Paschal–liturgy (H. Freedman, tr., and I. Epstein, ed., *Hebrew–English Edition of the Babylonian Talmud: Pesaḥim* [new ed.; London: Soncino Press, 1967], p. 116b) are particularly impressive: "In every generation a man is bound to regard himself as though he personally had gone forth from Egypt, ... He brought *us* forth from bondage into freedom, ..." Cf. Amos 2:10f: "I brought you up out of the land of Egypt, and led you forty years in the wilderness," and Joshua 24:7: "Your eyes saw what I did to Egypt." But also cf. Tacitus, *Agric.* 45: "A little while and our hands it was which dragged Helvidius to his dungeon" (mox nostrae

duxere Helvidium in carcerem manus).

Here is expressed the consciousness of the solidarity of succeeding generations with past history, in whose continuation we ourselves stand and through which, therefore, the present is determined (in blessing or guilt). But this is not a real analogy to 1 Jn 1:1–3, as Schnackenburg (p. 55) correctly discerns, whereas H. Seebass, "Kirchliche Verkündigung und die sogen. Entmythologisierung," *Kerygma und Dogma* 11 (1965): 158, fails to recognize the distinction. For the event, of which the ear and eyewitnesses speak here, is the eschatological event, which, although it does signify that the eternal has become historical, nevertheless is not an event that produces a further effect in the history of a historical community, i.e., a nation or a people. The tradition that mediates the eschatological event to later

---

13 So Schnackenburg, p. 56. He rightly emphasizes: "A predominantly historical interest in eyewitnesses ($\alpha\dot{v}\tau\acute{o}\pi\tau\alpha\iota$, Lk 1:2) and personal companions of Jesus (Acts 1:21) is not present in 1 John; rather, there is a religious interest" (p. 53). He senses the difficulty, however, and comes finally to the conclusion that "a pupil and representative of John the son of Zebedee could nevertheless be counted among the circle of 'apostolic' witnesses, who, through their association with the Son of God who appeared on earth 'in the flesh,' " bear a unique and exclusive witness to faith in him (p. 57). To me that seems to be a counsel of despair.

14 Cf. Conzelmann, " 'Was von Anfang war,' " p. 199

n. 20: "The accumulation of catchwords indicates the total scope of the transferral of historical salvation to the believers. The supporting elements are eyewitness accounts, proclamation, connection with the bearers of the tradition ('community'). The present community has a historical foundation, and the historical extends into contemporary society." Cf. my explanation of Jn 1:14 (Bultmann, pp. 67–70 [44–46]).

generations is, therefore, not the tradition passed on in history, but rather comes to pass in (legitimized) ἀπαγγέλλειν ("proclaim") and μαρτυρεῖν ("testify"). It could rather be asked whether Irenaeus, *Adv. haer.* V. 1:1, is not written in the sense of 1 Jn 1:1–3: ". . . and, again, we would not be able to know, unless we had seen our master and had heard his voice with our own ears . . ." (neque rursus

nos aliter discere poteramus nisi magistrum nostrum videntes et per auditum nostrum vocem eius percipientes) [trans. by Ed.].

For this reason, the verbs employed here indicate sense perception. One could say that they are spoken as a bold stroke, and that they had to be spoken in opposition to those who also call themselves believers, but who sever the present eschatological revelation from the historical φανερωθῆναι ("made manifest")—therefore in opposition to the gnosticizing Christians against whom the whole letter is directed, because they deny that the Son of God has come ἐν σαρκί ("in the flesh," 4:2; cf. 2 Jn 7), and yet consider themselves to be Christians (2:19).[15]

In a sense one could also say that the plural "we" is the ecclesiastical plural of Jn 1:14. There is a certain difference here, however, because in the ἐθεασάμεθα ("we beheld") of Jn 1:14 evidently the totality of believers speaks, whereas the "we" of 1 Jn 1:1–5 is distinguished from the "you" and can thus represent only a part of the community of believers. Which part is easily identified: it is those to whom the task of the ἀπαγγέλλειν and the μαρτυρεῖν falls, viz. the bearers of the tradition. As the "we," they address the congregation as the "you," and indeed for this purpose: ἵνα καὶ ὑμεῖς κοινωνίαν ἔχητε μεθ᾽ ἡμῶν ("in order that you may have fellow-

ship with us," v 3).[16]

When, in the ensuing verses, in place of the plural γράφομεν ("we write") (1:4), which is to be expected after vss 1–3, the singular γράφω (2:1, 7f, etc.) or ἔγραψα (2:14, 21, etc.) appears, one sees that the author of this Epistle is conscious of himself as having a personal authority, i.e., as being a representative of the bearers of the tradition.[17] Precisely out of this consciousness he addresses the readers as τεκνία μου ("my children," 2:1) or simply as τεκνία ("children") (2:12; 3:7; 4:4); or as παιδία ("children," 2:18). Since he can address them as ἀγαπητοί ("beloved") as well (2:7; 3:2, 21), it is evident that he is conscious of a fraternal fellowship with them. Indeed, since he even can say (2:7) that he does not write a new commandment to them, but rather that ἣν εἴχετε ἀπ᾽ ἀρχῆς ("which you had from the beginning"), then even those addressed are in some sense bearers of the tradition. Vss 2:13f illustrate the same point, particularly when ἐγνώκατε τὸν ἀπ᾽ ἀρχῆς ("you know him who is from the beginning") is said of the πατέρες ("fathers"), and the same follows from 2:19–21, especially from οἴδατε αὐτήν ("you know it") (*scil.* τὴν ἀλήθειαν, "the truth"), 2:21.

---

15 So, too, Schnackenburg, pp. 53f. Cf. also Conzelmann, " 'Was von Anfang war,' " 200 (n. 20 to p. 199): "It is no longer a question simply of a decision for or against the proclamation, but rather for or against a certain form of it; thereby, too, for or against certain bearers of it. The letter thereby falls into the circle of other post-apostolic writings." Concerning the contemporary situation of 1 John, cf. Dodd, pp. 9–16, and Wilbert Francis Howard, *Christianity according to St. John* (London: Duckworth,

[2]1947), 54f.

16 That does not alter the fact that the author, in the further course of the Epistle, includes himself along with the readers in the "we." Cf. 2:28; 3:1f; and the "we" of οἴδαμεν in 3:2 (see below).

17 I cannot see that the author is speaking in the style of a prophetic revelation in the initial words of the Epistle (Haenchen, "Neuere Literatur," 14). He speaks with the consciousness of a representative of the tradition that goes back to the revelation.

Verses 2:19–21 illuminate the situation and thereby the initially dubious relationship of the "we" and the "you." To be sure, the "we" are, in the first instance, the transmitters, who function authoritatively for the "you." But on the other hand both the "we" and the "you" belong to a fellowship to which vss 2:7, 19–21 appeal; and this fellowship is clearly expressed in 3:1f.[18] That the "we" and the "you" stand within the same continuity of tradition is also expressed by the fact that the author can say to the readers: ὑμεῖς ὃ ἠκούσατε ἀπ᾽ ἀρχῆς ("what you heard from the beginning," 2:24), or ἣν [scil. τὴν ἀγγελίαν] ἠκούσατε ἀπ᾽ ἀρχῆς ("which [message] you heard from the beginning," 3:11), although ἀρχή here does not mean the origin of the proclamation, but rather the temporal point at which the readers came to faith (cf. above, p. 9 n. 10).

■ **3** Just as vss 1 and 2 stated the object of the Christian proclamation, so this is once again taken up in v 3a (ὃ ἑωράκαμεν καὶ ἀκηκόαμεν, "what we have seen and have heard"); and when v 3 again takes up the (μαρτυροῦμεν) καὶ ἀπαγγέλλομεν ("[we testify] and proclaim") of v 2 with ἀπαγγέλλομεν καὶ ὑμῖν[19] ("we also proclaim to you"), the aim of the whole Epistle is announced: ἵνα καὶ ὑμεῖς κοινωνίαν ἔχητε μεθ᾽ ἡμῶν ("in order that you may have fellowship with us"). Naturally this sentence is spoken with a view to the threatening cleavage between the true believers and the heretics.[20] The κοινωνία ("fellowship") is the union in common faith brought about by the proclamation.[21] On the basis of what precedes, one could perhaps expect the author to write κοινωνία μετ᾽ αὐτοῦ: with that which we proclaim, or with him whom we proclaim. And the explanatory sentence in fact shows that κοινωνία μεθ᾽ ἡμῶν is also κοινωνία μετὰ τοῦ πατρὸς ("with the Father") καὶ μετὰ τοῦ υἱοῦ αὐτοῦ Ἰησοῦ Χριστοῦ ("and with his Son Jesus Christ"). However, there is fellowship with the latter (i.e., Father and Son) only by virtue of the former, i.e., by virtue of the legitimate tradition.[22] With this explanation (in which ἐστίν is to be supplied)[23] the mystery is solved (cf. above, pp. 7f). Whereas up to this point only the subject matter was mentioned directly and the person of the revealer only alluded to, now this person is named explicitly: Ἰησοῦς Χριστός ("Jesus Christ").[24] And whereas in v 2 it was said of the ζωὴ αἰώνιος ("eternal life") that it was πρὸς τὸν πατέρα ("with the Father"), it is now stated that the

---

18 The "we–sentences" which have an admonitory character and articulate the criterion of genuine faith (as, for example, 4:6; 5:2) are to be distinguished from the "we" in οἴδαμεν ("we know") in 3:2, 14, in which the author includes himself with the readers, as in 4:14, 16. Nonetheless, the distinction is fluid, as for instance in 4:6. In still another way is the "we" in 1:6–10 to be understood; it has the sense of "one" or "someone." See above, 9f, 11 n. 16.

19 The textually uncertain καί before ὑμῖν has no significance for the theme.

20 So Dodd, and see above, p. 11 n. 15.

21 Substantive parallels for this meaning of κοινωνία are e.g., Phil 1:5; 2:1; Phlmn 6. Concerning the many nuances in meaning of κοινωνία, see H. Seesemann, *Der Begriff* Κοινωνία *im neuen Testament* (Giessen: 1933); Bauer, *s.v.* In John both substantive and verb are lacking. It occurs in 1 John, apart from 1:3, only in 1:6f. Κοινωνία μετά is not normal Greek although it occurs in the LXX: Job 34:8; cf. *Corp. Herm.* XIII.9.

22 Holtzmann, 240, appropriately quotes Bede's comment on this point: "For whoever desires to have fellowship with God ought first to be joined to the fellowship of the church" (quia quicunque societatem cum deo habere desiderant, primo ecclesiae societati debent adunari [MPL 93: 86]).

23 Καὶ ἡ κοινωνία δὲ ἡ ἡμετέρα [ἐστίν]: The δέ that belongs with the καί is lacking in some manuscripts, but it is indispensable for clarifying the thought "but also" or "what is more"; cf. Blass–Debrunner §447 (9).

24 Ἰησοῦς Χριστός occurs only seldom in John (1:17; 17:3); in 1 John it occurs more frequently: 2:1; 3:23; 4:2; 5:6, [20]; also 2 Jn 7.

κοινωνία is fellowship with the Father and his Son Ἰησοῦς Χριστός.[25] Father and Son are bound together in a unity in 1 Jn 2:22–24; 2 Jn 9, as in the Gospel of John, e.g., 14:9; 17:3, 10f. The κοινωνία with the Father is at the same time κοινωνία with the Son; whoever denies the Son also denies the Father (2:22–24; cf. 4:8, 15; 5:10–12). When the κοινωνία μετὰ τοῦ πατρὸς καὶ μετὰ τοῦ υἱοῦ αὐτοῦ . . . is designated as ἡ ἡμετέρα ("ours"), then the clause ἵνα καὶ ὑμεῖς κοινωνίαν ἔχητε μεθ᾽ ἡμῶν ("in order that you may have fellowship with us") is understood to mean that this is not a mere (profane) fellowship between human beings—that with it is given fellowship with the Father and the Son.

The term κοινωνία ("fellowship") is encountered only here and in vss 6f, but the motif runs throughout the whole Epistle in a series of different expressions that speak of being in God (2:5; [5:20]) or of remaining in God (2:6, 24), and in the reciprocal formula: we in God and he in us (3:24; 4:13). All such expressions characterize the believers' relationship to God not as mysticism, but rather as a mode of life. For as vss 5ff immediately indicate, the relationship to God involves the keeping of God's commandments.[26]

■ 4 In v 4 ἀπαγγέλλομεν ("we proclaim") is replaced by ταῦτα γράφομεν ἡμεῖς ("we write these things"),[27] which applies to the whole Epistle and thus to every-thing following, without the necessity of excluding what is expressed in vss 1–3. The statement of intent, too, is now differently formulated, in that it reads ἵνα ἡ χαρὰ ἡμῶν ᾖ πεπληρωμένη ("in order that our joy may be complete") instead of ἵνα . . . κοινωνίαν ἔχητε ("in order that you may have fellowship," v 3). The ἡμῶν ("our") is noteworthy, not only after the statement of purpose in v 3, which contains the wish for the readers, but also because an ὑμῶν ("your") would better correspond to the traditional formulation of the wish at the end of the prescript. It is understandable, therefore, that in some manuscripts and translations, the ἡμῶν has been changed to ὑμῶν. Nevertheless, ἡμῶν is the correct reading (so also Schnackenburg), when one considers that according to v 3 the κοινωνία ("fellowship") of the author with the readers is at the same time the κοινωνία with the Father and the Son. Just as the latter is included in the former, so also the χαρά ("joy") of the readers and the author is the same.

The χαρά ("joy") is nothing other than the salvation that is given with the κοινωνία ("fellowship") with

25 Jesus is the Son of God as in John (cf. 1:3, 7; 2:22f; 3:8; 5:10, 15, and elsewhere). The designations thus alternate as υἱὸς θεοῦ ("Son of God"), υἱὸς τοῦ πατρός ("Son of the Father"), and simply υἱός ("Son"), with the same meaning.

26 Schnackenburg, in an extensive excursus (pp. 66–72), has informatively articulated the peculiarity of the Johannine idea of the fellowship with God in distinction from the Old Testament view, and similarly from the philosophical (Stoic), fanatical, and Gnostic views. His notion that one can speak of a "mysticism of being" appears to me to be off the mark. He does emphasize correctly, however, that in 1 John fellowship with God is, in its essence, con-nected with ethics. In John, as well, one cannot speak of mysticism; cf. Bultmann, pp. 69 [45], 380f [290f], 435 [333], 541 [416], 612f [473f]; concerning εἶναι ("be in") or μένειν ἐν ("abide in"), pp. 321 n. 1 [243 n. 2], 535 n. 1 [411 n. 3]; regarding the reciprocal relationship, 380f [290].

27 Ἡμεῖς ("we") has been altered in some MSS and translations to ὑμῖν ("to you"). The explication of ταῦτα is ἵνα κτλ., as is often the case after a demonstrative (2:1; 3:[1], 8, 11, 23; 4:9, 17, 21; 5:3, 13).

the Father and the Son: the eschatological salvation.[28] But the χαρά is present without losing its eschatological sense, because the believers are freed in faith from the world that is pressing in upon them,[29] as stated in 5:13: ταῦτα ἔγραψα ὑμῖν ἵνα εἰδῆτε ὅτι ζωὴν ἔχετε αἰώνιον ("I write this to you that you may know that you have eternal life"). 3:14, too, says that the ζωή ("life") is present: ἡμεῖς οἴδαμεν ὅτι μεταβεβήκαμεν ἐκ τοῦ θανάτου εἰς τὴν ζωήν . . . ("We know that we have passed out of death into life . . ."). However, as certainly as this eschatological joy can be present, it is just as

certainly only a provisional joy, whose fulfillment is still pending.[30] Thus the wish: ἵνα ἡ χαρὰ ἡμῶν ᾖ πεπληρωμένη, i.e., that our joy may be complete. It is complete in the fellowship that already exists between the author and the readers in conjunction with the Father and the Son, and yet it is not.[31] For the being of the believer is no static being, but is always in the process of becoming, a περιπατεῖν ("walking") (see 1:5, etc.), because he stands under the claim of the commandment. That is demonstrated immediately in 1:5–2:11, and basically in the whole Epistle.

---

28 Joy is the divine gift that is experienced in the cultic celebrations in the Old Testament and in the mystery religions, as well as in the cognition and vision of Gnosis and mysticism. It can be expected as an eschatological gift from the future, but can also be experienced in present devotion. Cf. Jn 17:13 (Bultmann, pp. 505f n. 4 [387 n. 1]; generally, pp. 505–7 [386–8] and pp. 541f [416f], 579–85 [446–51]). See further E. Gulin, *Die Freude im Neuen Testament. 2. Das Johannesevangelium* (Helsingfors: 1936). The fact that the way to χαρά leads through λύπη ("sorrow" Jn 16:20–24) is not a theme in 1 John; for the front against which 1 John is directed is not lack of faith but false faith, false teaching. See above, pp. 2f. Χαρά occurs only here in 1 John, but appears in 2 Jn 12 in a similar context.

29 The wish has its substantive parallel in Jn 15:11: ταῦτα λελάληκα ὑμῖν ἵνα ἡ χαρὰ ἡ ἐμὴ ἐν ὑμῖν ᾖ καὶ ἡ χαρὰ ὑμῶν πληρωθῇ ("These things I have spoken to you, that my joy may be in you, and that your joy may be full"); 17:13: ταῦτα λαλῶ ἐν τῷ κόσμῳ ἵνα ἔχωσιν τὴν χαρὰν τὴν ἐμὴν πεπληρωμένην ἐν ἑαυτοῖς ("These things I speak in the world, that they may have my joy fulfilled in themselves"). Those who have received this gift are not any more ἐκ τοῦ κόσμου ("of the world" Jn 17:6, 16), and they have received what the world cannot give (Jn 14:27). The gift can also be called εἰρήνη

("peace" Jn 14:27), a concept which does not occur in 1 John, but which does occur in the epistolary wishes of 2 Jn 3; 3 Jn 15.

30 Πληροῦσθαι is different from τελειοῦσθαι insofar as τελειοῦσθαι means the attainment of the end (cf. Jn 19:28, τετέλεσται, and in addition, Bultmann, pp. 674f [523]), whereas πληροῦσθαι designates fulfillment (Schnackenburg: "the actualizing of a possibility"). Nevertheless, the distinction is not always sharp, as 2:5 and Jn 3:29 show. Regarding πληροῦν in John, cf. Bultmann, pp. 505f [387], 541f [417]. Adolf Schlatter wants to explain πεπλήρωται (Jn 3:29) in accordance with Hebrew שָׁלֵם, which has the meaning of "being complete, being whole" (*Die Sprache und Heimat des vierten Evangelisten*, Beiträge zur Förderung christliche Theologie, 6:4 [Gütersloh, 1902], 51f).

31 Gulin, *Die Freude im Neuen Testament*, 2:65, wants to avoid the paradox by explaining ἵνα . . . ᾖ πεπληρωμένη thus: in order that the object of joy be realized, namely that the readers return again to the true faith. This is as unconvincing as Schnackenburg's explanation that the fulfillment of joy exists in the fact that the circle of those joined to God expands and "becomes stronger."

1   Fellowship with God and Walking
          in the Light

5   This is the message we have heard from
      him and proclaim to you, that God is
      light and in him is no darkness at all. 6 / If
      we say we have fellowship with him
      while we walk in darkness, we lie and do
      not live according to the truth; 7 / but if
      we walk in the light, as he is in the
      light, we have fellowship with one an-
      other, and the blood of Jesus his Son
      cleanses us from all sin. 8 / If we say we
      have no sin, we deceive ourselves, and
      the truth is not in us. 9 / If we confess
      our sins, he is faithful and just, and
      will forgive our sins and cleanse us from
      all unrighteousness. 10 / If we say we
      have not sinned, we make him a liar, and
      his word is not in us.

2
1   My little children, I am writing this to you
      so that you may not sin; but if any
      one does sin, we have an advocate with
      the Father, Jesus Christ the righteous;
      2 / and he is the expiation for our sins,
      and not for ours only but also for the sins
      of the whole world.

■ **5** The author now begins to develop the ἀπαγγέλλομεν ("we proclaim") of vss 2f in a concrete setting:
καὶ ἔστιν αὕτη ἡ ἀγγελία . . . ὅτι ("This is the message . . . that," v 5).[1] Ἀγγελία ("message") is characterized as ἣν ἀκηκόαμεν ἀπ' αὐτοῦ ("which we have
heard from him").[2] But who is meant by "him"? The
(Christian) reader of course knows that the "Son" is intended, but the self-explanatory occurrence of αὐτός
("him") is nevertheless surprising. To be sure, it was discernible in vss 1–3 that the eternal became historical
in the person of Jesus, but in vss 1–3 he was referred to as
the object of ἀκούειν ("hear") and of the proclamation,
but he was not spoken of as its author. Also in v 3,
where υἱός ("Son") was spoken of together with πατήρ

---

1   The construction is almost identical in 2:25; 3:11;
    5:11 (cf. Jn 1:19). The author is fond of the antici-
    patory demonstrative with ὅτι following: here and
    in 4:9, 10; 5:9, 11, 14; or with ἵνα following: 3:8,
    11, 23; 4:17, 21; 5:3; 2 Jn 6. And then καί takes
    on the meaning "and so, that is, namely" (explica-
    tive, particularizing: Bauer *s.v.* I.3; epexegetical:
    Blass-Debrunner §442[9]) here, as in 2:25; 3:23;
    5:11, 14.
2   It is usually ἀκούειν παρά in Greek; nevertheless,
    ἀκούειν ἀπό is also possible: Blass-Debrunner
    §§173(1); 210(3). Perhaps ἀπό is chosen here be-
    cause παρά could be taken to mean that it is a mat-
    ter of words heard directly from the historical Jesus.

That the text here reads ἀναγγέλλομεν instead
of ἀπαγγέλλομεν, as in vss 2f, scarcely makes a difference. Even if ἀναγγέλλειν originally meant
"repeatedly to report something heard," it is nevertheless often used in the sense of "to preach the
Gospel" (Bauer *s.v.*); it can mean specifically "to
proclaim" when said, e.g., of a κῆρυξ ("herald")
(Schniewind, *TDNT* I, 62 [I, 61.31ff].

("father"), "Son" was not characterized as the one who commissioned ἀπαγγέλλειν ("proclamation"). And so the self-evident way in which he is introduced here remains surprising. It is to be explained by the fact that the author has the false teachers in mind, in opposition to whom he appeals to the authority that lies behind ἀγγελία ("the message"), and for the Christian readers this authority need be cited only as αὐτός ("him").[3]

The content of the proclamation is stated initially in vss 5–7. The first clauses formulated in parallelism (vss 6, 7) are presumably derived from a Source. It remains uncertain whether the ὅτι–clause ("that . . .") in v 5 also belongs to this Source. Its two parts do not form *parallelismus membrorum*, but rather are two clauses joined by καί ("and"); in terms of subject matter, however, they stand in antithesis to each other.

Ὁ θεὸς φῶς ἐστιν ("God is light"): this sentence no more defines the nature of God as he is in himself than does ὁ θεὸς ἀγάπη ἐστίν ("God is love," 4:8, 16) and πνεῦμα ὁ θεός ("God is spirit," Jn 4:24).[4] It rather expresses what God means for man. In the Old Testament too, in Judaism as well as in Hellenism, and most fully in Gnosis, "light" is used to designate God, God's nature, and the sphere of the divine. In all its variations, however, the ultimate underlying notion is that the real meaning of light is the luminosity man needs in order to find his way in his daily as well as his spiritual life.

The illumination of existence belongs of necessity to "life" in such a way that, always and everywhere, light and life, darkness and death belong together. And just as the idea of the ἀγαθόν ("good") can be described by Plato as φῶς, so "light" can in general be a designation of salvation, especially of eschatological salvation.[5]

It follows from 2:8 that also for 1 John (as for John) φῶς is a characteristic of salvation. For, in the sentence ἡ σκοτία παράγεται καὶ τὸ φῶς τὸ ἀληθινὸν ἤδη φαίνει ("the darkness is passing away and the true light is already shining"), ἀληθινόν ("true") indicates that the desire of all men is for "light," but that perception of the genuine light can be mistaken.[6] Ἡ σκοτία παράγεται ("the darkness is passing away") and ἤδη φαίνει ("already shines") thereby show that salvation is conceived eschatologically, in the sense of τὸ φῶς ἐλήλυθεν εἰς τὸν κόσμον ("the light has come into the world," Jn 3:19). Now in 1:5 the demanding character of light is emphasized rather than its salvation character, as is made clear in v 6, just as the sentence in 2:8 serves as the basis for ἐντολή ("commandment"). It is characteristic for 1 John (as for John) that the eschatological salvation which is given to faith as a gift is not a possession, but rather includes the demand that the believer is never a finished man (of faith) but rather is always on the way. In other words, that God is light does not mean that one can possess him in a vision, but rather that he is,

---

3   Braun, "Literar-Analyse," 283f [232f], rightly shows that ἀπ' αὐτοῦ does not refer to the words of the historical Jesus. Ἀγγελία naturally has its origin in Jesus' "having come" in history, but reference to this history (in 1 John) is not concrete.

4   On Jn 4:24 cf. Bultmann, pp. 191f [141]. The sentence cannot be turned around to read τὸ φῶς (ἡ ἀγάπη or τὸ πνεῦμα) θεός ἐστιν ("the light [love, spirit] is God").

5   Concerning this point, cf. Bultmann, pp. 40–45 [22–26] on Jn 1:4, also pp. 157 n. 5 [113 n. 6], 339f [258], 342f [260f]. In addition, Windisch-Preisker on 1 Jn 1:5 and Schnackenburg, pp. 76–79, 80 n. 4. Concerning light and darkness in the Qumran texts, see

Herbert Braun (below n. 7). On light symbolism in antiquity, see Bultmann, "Zur Geschichte der Lichtsymbolik im Altertum," *Philologus* 97 (1948): 1–36, reprinted in *Beiträge zum Verständnis der Jenseitigkeit Gottes im Neuen Testament* (Darmstadt, 1965), pp. 7–42. W. Beierwaltes, *Lux intelligibilis. Untersuchung zur Lichtmetaphysik der Griechen*, Unpub. Diss. (Munich: 1957).

6   Cf. Jn 1:9: ἦν τὸ φῶς τὸ ἀληθινόν ("the light was the true [light]").

7   In ordinary Gnosis, light and darkness are mutually exclusive antitheses. Light designates the nature or sphere of the divinity. Cf. especially among the Mandaeans, *Ginza R.* 1.3.10 (Lidzbarski, pp. 6,26–

or should be and can be, a mode of human existence. To this correspond the expressions ἐν τῷ φωτὶ περιπατεῖν ("to walk in the light," v 7) (see above p. 14 on v 4, and cf. Jn 8:12; 13:35), and ἐν τῷ φωτὶ μένειν ("to abide in the light," 2:10).

Just as περιπατεῖν ἐν τῷ σκότει ("to walk in darkness," v 6; 2:11) corresponds, antithetically, to the phrases just cited, so καὶ σκοτία ἐν αὐτῷ οὐκ ἔστιν οὐδεμία ("and in him is no darkness at all") follows from ὁ θεὸς φῶς ἐστιν ("God is light"). There can be little doubt that this expression is directed against the false teaching. It is not directed, however, against a Gnostic teaching of a mixture of light and darkness in the godhead,[7] but rather against the assertion of gnosticizing false teachers that they are in the light, which does not tally with the fact that they are actually in darkness, viz. in their mode of living, in their περιπατεῖν ("walking"). For, σκοτία ("darkness") characterizes a mode of existence, a περιπατεῖν, just as φῶς ("light") does. That this is the case may be demonstrated by the fact that the false teachers have no κοινωνία μετ᾽ ἀλλήλων ("fellowship with one another," v 7) and hate their brothers (2:9, 11), or that they assert their sinlessness (v 8) and deny the revealer's incarnation (2:22; 4:2f).

1 John has its dualistic terminology in common with Gnosis.[8] But whereas in Gnosis the terminology rests on a genuine cosmological dualism, i.e., on the notion of light and darkness as two cosmic powers, in 1 John, as in John, darkness is not a cosmic power that stands opposed to the divine power, but is the way men are closed against God—a closure indeed that becomes a power ruling the individual, precisely as the "world" to which every man intrinsically belongs and which he jointly constitutes in his individual closure.[9] But since the revelation of light opens the possibility for man to come into the light out of his confinement in darkness, a dualism of decision arises out of the cosmological dualism. Insofar as the decision between "walking in the darkness" and "walking in the light" is concerned, the cosmological dualism has been historicized: the decision of faith is the choice between two possibilities of self–understanding offered by the proclamation.

■ **6** The consequences of v 5b are developed in what follows, primarily in 1:6–2:17. In this section the author evidently employs a Source which is stylistically related to the Revelatory Discourse Source used in John. The text of the Source, which is commented upon and expanded by the author and by the ecclesiastical redactor, was probably as follows.[10]

7,2): "He (*scil.* the "high king of light") is light, in which there is no darkness; living, in which there is no death; good, in which there is no evil . . . ." According to Gnostic ideas, judgment lies in the separation of light and darkness; cf. Bultmann, pp. 156f [113], on Jn 1:19. The antithesis of the ways of light and darkness appears in the Qumran *Manual of Discipline*. Cf. Braun, "Qumran und das Neue Testament," p. 194 [98] on Jn 1:5ff.; pp. 218f [122–4] on Jn 8:12; pp. 101f [290f] on 1 Jn 1:5–7.

8   The Johannine dualism does not have its roots in the Old Testament, but rather in Gnosis. The influence of Gnostic dualism was indeed already operative in later Judaism, as is demonstrated by the

Testaments of the XII Patriarchs and as is now attested by certain portions of the Qumran texts. Some Johannine formulations have their parallels in these texts. That, however, in no way proves the dependence of the Johannine writings on the Qumran community, but, insofar as there are no direct Gnostic influences present, Johannine dependence on a syncretistic Judaism. Nothing is thereby said about the place of composition of the Johannine writings.

9   Cf. Bultmann, pp. 54f [33f] on Jn 1:10.

10   The reconstruction of the putative Source is somewhat different from what I attempted to give in "Analyse des ersten Johannesbriefes," 157. There I showed, by means of stylistic features that differen-

1:6 ἐὰν εἴπωμεν ὅτι κοινωνίαν ἔχομεν μετ᾽ αὐτοῦ
καὶ ἐν τῷ σκότει περιπατῶμεν
ψευδόμεθα καὶ οὐ ποιοῦμεν τὴν ἀλήθειαν.

1:7 ἐὰν δὲ ἐν τῷ φωτὶ περιπατῶμεν,
ὡς αὐτός ἐστιν ἐν τῷ φωτί,
κοινωνίαν ἔχομεν μετ᾽ αὐτοῦ.

[7b]

1:8 ἐὰν εἴπωμεν ὅτι ἁμαρτίαν οὐκ ἔχομεν
ἑαυτοὺς πλανῶμεν,
καὶ ἡ ἀλήθεια οὐκ ἔστιν ἐν ἡμῖν.

1:10 ἐὰν εἴπωμεν ὅτι οὐχ ἡμαρτήκαμεν,
ψεύστην ποιοῦμεν αὐτόν,
καὶ ὁ λόγος αὐτοῦ οὐκ ἔστιν ἐν ἡμῖν.

[—]

2:4 ὁ λέγων ὅτι ἔγνωκα αὐτόν,
καὶ τὰς ἐντολὰς αὐτοῦ μὴ τηρῶν
ψεύστης ἐστίν, καὶ ἐν τούτῳ ἡ ἀλήθεια οὐκ ἔστιν.

2:5 ὃς δ᾽ ἂν τηρῇ αὐτοῦ τὸν λόγον
ἀληθῶς ἐν τούτῳ ἡ ἀγάπη τοῦ θεοῦ τετελείωται.

2:9 ὁ λέγων ἐν τῷ φωτὶ εἶναι
καὶ τὸν ἀδελφὸν αὐτοῦ μισῶν,
ἐν τῇ σκοτίᾳ ἐστὶν [? ἕως ἄρτι].

2:10 ὁ ἀγαπῶν τὸν ἀδελφὸν αὐτοῦ
ἐν τῷ φωτὶ μένει,
καὶ σκάνδαλον ἐν αὐτῷ οὐκ ἔστιν.

2:11 ὁ δὲ μισῶν τὸν ἀδελφὸν αὐτοῦ
ἐν τῇ σκοτίᾳ ἐστὶν
καὶ ἐν τῇ σκοτίᾳ περιπατεῖ.

1:6 If we say we have fellowship with him
While we walk in darkness
We lie and do not live according to the truth.

1:7 But if we walk in the light,
As he is in the light,
We have fellowship with him.

[7b]

1:8 If we say we have no sin
We deceive ourselves,
And the truth is not in us.

1:10 If we say we have not sinned,
We make him a liar,
And his word is not in us.

[—]

2:4 He who says "I know him"
But disobeys his commandments
Is a liar, and the truth is not in him.

2:5 But whoever keeps his word
In him truly love for God is perfected.

2:9 He who says he is in the light
And hates his brother,
Is in the darkness [? still].

2:10 He who loves his brother
Abides in the light,
And in him there is no cause for stumbling.

2:11 But he who hates his brother
Is in the darkness
And walks in the darkness.

[RSV modified]

The Either/Or is clearly formulated in vss 6–7a: The claim[11] to have fellowship with God[12] is a lie when it is combined with a wandering in darkness. Ψευδόμεθα has initially the simple meaning: "we speak falsehood";

---

tiate the author from the Source, the difference between the Source and the additions of the author. Here I only point to the fact that the sentences of the Source form parallel members, composed, in each case, of three lines; in addition, without exception the three-membered periods form antitheses. This style differs from the *parallelismus membrorum* and the antitheses of the Old Testament style. In distinction from the prosaic style of the author, the language of the Source can be characterized as poetical. The peculiarities of the author's style will be pointed out at appropriate points in what follows. Concerning the discussion of the question of sources, see Haenchen, "Neuere Literatur," 9f; Braun, "Li-

terar-Analyse," 262–71 [210–20].

11 The "we" of εἴπωμεν in vss 6–10 is of course not the same as that in v 5, but rather has the general meaning of "one" or "someone." In the same sense, ὁ λέγων in 2:4, see above, p. 12 n 18.

12 According to v 6 μετ᾽ αὐτοῦ naturally means "with God."

13 There is no difference between the two words for "darkness": σκότος (only here and in Jn 3:19) and σκοτία (2:9f, etc.). See Bultmann, p. 320 n. 4 [242 n. 5] on Jn 8:44, and the excursus of W. Bauer, *Johannesevangelium* on 8:44 regarding the dualism of truth and falsehood.

but what follows, καὶ οὐ ποιοῦμεν τὴν ἀλήθειαν ("and we do not live according to the truth") shows that ψεύδεσθαι connotes an even deeper meaning. "Lying" (ψεύδεσθαι) is not simply accidental, but is rather a characteristic of "walking in the darkness." According to 2:4, the "liar" (ψεύστης) is the one in whom "truth is not." The dualism of "truth" and "liar" corresponds to the dualism of "light" and "darkness."[13] Just as God is "light" (v 5), so is he also "truth," and just as "light" is (is intended to be) the mode of human existence, so also is "truth."[14] For, as in John, "truth" does not mean the revelatory unveiling of things in the cognitive act, in the Greek sense, but rather the reality of God.[15] Therefore, there are the various synonymous expressions of the "being" of the truth "in us" (1:8; 2:4), of our "being of the truth" (2:21, 3:19; Jn 18:37), of "walking in the truth" (2 Jn 4), of "knowing" and "being on familiar terms with" the truth (2:21; 2 Jn 1; Jn 8:32).

Ποιεῖν τὴν ἀλήθειαν ("doing the truth") must also be understood from this perspective,[16] but that scarcely excludes doing good deeds, for τηρεῖν τὰς ἐντολάς ("keeping the commandments") attests that the truth is "in" a man.[17] This only proves, however, that all these expressions designate the mode of life, since the mode of life works itself out in conduct also. Consequently, "doing the truth" can also be described as essential, real conduct. The antithesis, "lying" (ψεύδεσθαι), desig-

nates the futility of life. For, if "truth" (ἀλήθεια) designates the authentic reality, then "lie" (ψεῦδος) is the inauthentic, the unreal, nothingness, basically even death, just as he who does not love his brother but hates him, is a liar (4:20)—one who, according to 2:11, remains in darkness, and according to 3:14, remains in death. Conversely, "truth," "light," and "life" belong together, as the whole Epistle demonstrates (cf. Jn 14:6). All lies stem from the devil who, as the liar (Jn 8:44), is ἀνθρωποκτόνος ἀπ᾿ ἀρχῆς ("a murderer from the beginning"). Whoever does not acknowledge Jesus as the Christ, and consequently denies the "life" revealed in him (1:2), is a liar (2:22) and asserts that God is a liar (5:10). It is thus clear that to lie and not to do the truth means to cut oneself off from reality and become futile.[18]

■ 7 Verse 7a shows that doing the truth is a mode of life that is realized in conduct: ἐὰν δὲ ἐν τῷ φωτὶ περιπατῶμεν . . . κοινωνίαν ἔχομεν μετ᾿ ἀλλήλων ("but if we walk in the light . . . we have fellowship with one another").[19] One might expect "fellowship with him" (μετ᾿ αὐτοῦ), in accordance with v 6. In all likelihood, that is what stood in the conjectured Source, but the author of the Epistle probably changed it to "with one another" with the thought that the reader needs to know in what walking in the light, as opposed to walking "in the darkness" (v 6), consists. What is the

---

14 Cf. Schnackenburg, p. 81 nn. 2 and 3 regarding the correlation of φῶς and ἀλήθεια; on "truth" in the Qumran texts in particular, Schnackenburg, p. 81 n. 1, and Braun "Qumran und das Neue Testament," 101f [290f].

15 Cf. Bultmann, *TDNT* I:245–7 [245.23ff] and Bultmann, pp. 433ff [332ff] on Jn 8:31f. So also Schnackenburg, pp. 84f, where parallels from the Qumran texts are cited.

16 It has a deeper meaning than the Hebrew אֱמֶת עָשָׂה, which means "to prove faithful, to deal righteously." Cf. Bultmann, *TDNT* I:242 [243.6ff] and Bultmann, p. 162 n. 3 [117 n. 6]. It appears that the expression "to do the truth" is also attested in

the Qumran texts in this (moralistic) sense; cf. Braun, "Qumran und das Neue Testament," 208f [112f].

17 Just as φαῦλα πράσσειν ("do evil") is the antithesis of "do the truth" in Jn 3:20f.

18 Braun, "Qumran und das Neue Testament," 220 [124f], on Jn 8:37–44, shows that the antithesis truth/falsehood cannot be derived from the Qumran texts.

19 Περιπατεῖν ("walk") in the metaphorical sense of "conduct" is found already in Hellenistic Greek and in the LXX, and also in the New Testament. It occurs frequently in Paul with ἐν ("in"): Rom 6:4; 2 Cor 4:2 (so also 1 Jn 1:6f; 2:11; 2 Jn 4), or

criterion? The answer is given by "we have fellowship with one another." The inference, "we then have fellowship with him,"[20] can be omitted (similarly 2:4f, see below), because this is obviously given with walking in the light. Basically it is contained in the clause, "as he is in the light" (i.e., corresponding to the fact that . . .). It may come as a surprise that the text reads "as he [God] is *in* the light" and not simply "as he [God] is light," as in v 5. The meaning is in fact the same, for the phrase "to be in" ($\epsilon \hat{\iota} \nu \alpha \iota \, \dot{\epsilon} \nu$)[21] characterizes the being of that same person who is said "to be" ($\epsilon \hat{\iota} \nu \alpha \iota$) light in v 5.

It is a foregone conclusion for the author (or for his Source) that walking in the light is grounded precisely in the fact that God's nature is light, just as it is also for him (or for his Source) a matter of course that as God is "light" so is he also "love" ($\dot{\alpha} \gamma \dot{\alpha} \pi \eta$) (4:8, 16), and thus that $\dot{\alpha} \gamma \alpha \pi \hat{\alpha} \nu \, \dot{\alpha} \lambda \lambda \dot{\eta} \lambda o \upsilon \varsigma$ ("love one another," 4:7f) is grounded in the nature of God as "love." The question may be asked what kind of fellowship is intended by $\kappa o \iota \nu \omega \nu \dot{\iota} \alpha \, \mu \epsilon \tau' \, \dot{\alpha} \lambda \lambda \dot{\eta} \lambda \omega \nu$ ("fellowship with one another"). If in 4:7 the imperative $\dot{\alpha} \gamma \alpha \pi \hat{\omega} \mu \epsilon \nu \, \dot{\alpha} \lambda \lambda \dot{\eta} \lambda o \upsilon \varsigma$ ("let us love one another") is directed at the $\dot{\alpha} \delta \epsilon \lambda \phi o \dot{\iota}$ ("brethren"), then one is tempted to interpret "fellowship with one another" as the brotherly relationship of the believers among themselves, as is $\dot{\upsilon} \mu \epsilon \hat{\iota} \varsigma \, \dot{\alpha} \gamma \alpha \pi \hat{\alpha} \tau \epsilon \, \dot{\alpha} \lambda \lambda \dot{\eta} \lambda o \upsilon \varsigma$ ("you love one another") in Jn 13:34.[22] The

formulations of the antithetical attitude in 2:11, 4:20, however, make it probable that "with one another" is to be referred to human fellowship in general.

Before the conjectured text of the Source is again taken up in v 8, a sentence is inserted in v 7b, which is probably an addition of the ecclesiastical redactor. Not only does its prose contrast with the surrounding poetical style, but it is also disturbing to the content.[23] In v 7a, "to have fellowship with one another" is mentioned as the characteristic of "walking in the light." The sentence $\kappa \alpha \dot{\iota} \, \tau \dot{o} \, \alpha \hat{\iota} \mu \alpha \, \kappa \tau \lambda.$ ("and the blood . . .") does not, however, characterize "walking in the light," so that it can be taken together with "having fellowship with one another." Whoever wrote v 7b understood "and the blood . . ." as the consequence of "having fellowship with one another": "and then (i.e., when we have fellowship with one another) the blood of Jesus cleanses us from all sin."[24] That, however, is a poor continuation of the "if-then" of v 7a. Moreover, the idea that "having fellowship with one another" is the condition for purification stands in contradiction to v 9, where the condition is the confession of sin. It all amounts to this: the sentence, the blood of Jesus cleanses from sin, corresponds, indeed, to the ecclesiastical theology, but not to Johannine thought.[25]

■ 8 The sentence, with which v 8 begins, comes initially as a surprise, because the protasis $\dot{\epsilon} \dot{\alpha} \nu \, \epsilon \check{\iota} \pi \omega \mu \epsilon \nu \, \ddot{o} \tau \iota \, \dot{\alpha} \mu \alpha \rho$-

---

with $\kappa \alpha \tau \dot{\alpha}$ ("according to"): Rom 8:4; 14:15; 1 Cor 3:3; 2 Cor 10:2 (so also 2 Jn 6; 3 Jn 3f). Cf. Eph 5:8: $\dot{\omega} \varsigma \, \tau \dot{\epsilon} \kappa \nu \alpha \, \phi \omega \tau \dot{o} \varsigma \, \pi \epsilon \rho \iota \pi \alpha \tau \epsilon \hat{\iota} \tau \epsilon$ ("walk as children of light").

20   Some witnesses read $\mu \epsilon \tau' \, \alpha \dot{\upsilon} \tau o \hat{\upsilon}$ ("with him"), which Schnackenburg, p. 82 n. 1, rightly rejects in opposition to my earlier opinion in "Analyse des ersten Johannesbriefes."

21   $E \hat{\iota} \nu \alpha \iota \, \dot{\epsilon} \nu$ ("to be in") can be used, in the same sense, of the inclusion of a person in a thing (1:7; 2:5, 9, 11; 4:4f [5:20]; TestNapht 2:10; *Corp. Herm.* IX 4b; XIII 11b), and of the inclusion of a thing in a person (1:8, 10; 2:4, 10; 3:5; Jn 1:47; 2:25; 7:18; 8:44; 11:10; 15:11; Herm Man V 2:5; VII 8). The reciprocal relationship occurs also in Jn 14:10f;

17:21.

22   On this question, cf. Bultmann, pp. 528f [405f].

23   Schnackenburg, p. 73 n. 1, thinks that if I delete v 7b, I overlook the fact that the key word of vss 8–10 occurs here: $\dot{\alpha} \mu \alpha \rho \tau \dot{\iota} \alpha$ ("sin"). I consider the reverse to be the case: the interpolator was led astray by vss 8–10 so as to introduce $\dot{\alpha} \mu \alpha \rho \tau \dot{\iota} \alpha$ prematurely into v 7b.

24   Naturally the meaning is "from every committed sin," as $\dot{\epsilon} \dot{\alpha} \nu \, \dot{o} \mu o \lambda o \gamma \hat{\omega} \mu \epsilon \nu$ ("if we confess") in v 9 confirms, not "from the power of sin, of transgression." Likewise Jn 9:41; 15:22, 24; 19:11.

25   Vss 5:6, 8 speak of Jesus' blood in another sense. In John, the passages which mention Jesus' blood as efficacious in the sacrament also go back to the ec-

τίαν οὐκ ἔχομεν ("if we say we have no sin") corresponds to the ἐὰν εἴπωμεν ... ("if we say ...") in v 6, and accordingly "have no sin" becomes parallel with "walking in the darkness." The sentence, however, is understandable in that vss 5–10 are aimed at the false teachers who assert their sinlessness.[26] This assertion means for the author (as for his Source) walking in darkness. The conclusion ἑαυτοὺς πλανῶμεν ("we deceive ourselves") corresponds exactly to the ψευδόμεθα ("we lie") of v 6. For self-deception does not mean a simple mistake, but rather that misdirected self-understanding which is not aware of its nothingness. And ἡ ἀλήθεια οὐκ ἔστιν ἐν ἡμῖν ("the truth is not in us") corresponds to οὐ ποιοῦμεν τὴν ἀλήθειαν ("we do not do the truth") and designates the futility of such a mode of being.[27] The thought of v 8 is taken up again in v 10, substantially in the same sense, but in a new form.

■ **9** Verse 9 is inserted between these verses and comments on v 8, insofar as the warning about considering oneself sinless includes the admonition to confess one's sins.[28] This explanation was probably inserted in the Source by the author, but it completely accords with the Source.[29] The confession of sins must correspond to "walking in the light" in v 7, and just that is the striking thing about the explanation. Nevertheless, precisely this paradox, that the confession of sin, as well as "having fellowship with one another," belongs together with walking in the light, characterizes Christian existence in contrast to the false teaching of the Gnostics. If the being of a Gnostic is static, then the being of a Christian is dynamic. For the Gnostic, participation in the divine light has become a possession once and for all through his Gnosis, whether it be discovered or acquired. The Christian has never acquired the light as permanent possession through his faith. He must authenticate his faith in περιπατεῖν ("walking"); he is always under way and never stands before God as a finished product,[30] but is rather dependent on forgiveness. He can, however, trust in this forgiveness, for he knows that God πιστός ἐστιν καὶ δίκαιος, ἵνα ἀφῇ ἡμῖν τὰς ἁμαρτίας ("is faithful and just, and will forgive our sins").[31] The continuation καὶ καθαρίσῃ ἡμᾶς ἀπὸ πάσης ἀδικίας ("and cleanse us from all unrighteousness") is probably an addition of the ecclesiastical redactor. It is formulated in the ecclesiastical-cultic terminology that is otherwise

---

clesiastical redactor: 6:53–56; 19:34b, 35 (See Bultmann, pp. 218–20 [161f], 234–7 [174–6], 677f [525f]).

26 Pr 28:13 can perhaps be adduced as a parallel: "He who conceals his transgressions will not prosper, but he who confesses them will obtain mercy." From the proverbs of Amen-em-Opet 18: "Say not: 'I have no wrongdoing,' Nor (yet) strain to seek quarreling. As for wrongdoing, it belongs to the god; It is sealed with his finger." (James B. Pritchard, ed., *Ancient Near Eastern Texts* [Princeton: Princeton University Press, ²1955], p. 423.) In neither case, however, is forgiveness mentioned.

27 See above, on 1:6. On εἶναι ἐν ἡμῖν ("to be in us"), see above on 1:7 (p. 20, n. 21).

28 Ὁμολογεῖν τὰς ἁμαρτίας ("confess sins"), which occurs only here in 1 John, is the articulated confession of personal sins, not a general confession of sins before the congregation and its leader (thus correctly Schnackenburg, p. 85 n. 1 and pp. 86f). Ὁμολογεῖν ("confess") is otherwise used in 1 John for the confession of faith (2:23; 4:2f, 15), in passages, moreover, that are also to be attributed to the author.

29 Braun, "Literar-Analyse," 265 [213], points rightly to the fact that sin is twice spoken of in the plural in v 9. This occurs also in vss 2:2, 12; 3:5; 4:10, which are all to be attributed to the author, whereas the singular occurs in those verses which presumably belong to the Source: in addition to 1:8, also 2:2; 3:4, 8f.

30 Above, p. 14.

31 God is the subject of πιστός ἐστιν καὶ δίκαιος ("is faithful and just"). Πιστός ("trustworthy, faithful") is applied to God in Greek as in the LXX, in Philo, and repeatedly in the New Testament (e.g., 1 Cor 1:9; 10:13); cf. Bauer, *s.v.* Δίκαιος ("just") is a frequent divine attribute in the Old Testament and

foreign to the writing.[32] Since it is a matter of forgiveness, ἀδικία ("unrighteousness") has the sense of a wrong that has been committed (cf. 2 Petr 1:9) and not of doing unrighteous acts (cf., perhaps, 2 Cor 7:1; Jas 4:8).

■ **10** The thought of v 8, and therewith the conjectured Source, is taken up again in another form in v 10: ἐὰν εἴπωμεν ὅτι οὐχ ἡμαρτήκαμεν ("if we say we have not sinned")—up to this point it corresponds completely to v 8a, but the continuation is different. Instead of "we deceive ourselves," it now reads: ψεύστην ποιοῦμεν αὐτόν ("we make him a liar"). We make God a liar (i.e., we declare him to be such), because the assertion of sinlessness does not recognize him as the one who, as πιστὸς καὶ δίκαιος ("faithful and just") in v 9, is the forgiving God. His word that promises and bestows forgiveness is thereby disavowed as God's word. This is the meaning the sentence following must have: καὶ ὁ λόγος αὐτοῦ οὐκ ἔστιν ἐν ἡμῖν ("and his word is not in us"). This sentence corresponds to ἡ ἀλήθεια οὐκ ἔστιν ἐν ἡμῖν ("the truth is not in us") of v 8. God's word is indeed the truth (as Jn 17:17 expressly says). If, however, truth is reality (cf. pp. 18f on 1:6), then it belongs to God's reality that he is a God who bestows forgiveness, and that means, in turn, that he is a God who addresses man, for forgiveness is bestowed by the word[33]—or, more broadly formulated, by revelation. This has occurred in

Jesus, and therefore it can also be said of him who does not believe in the Son of God, that he makes God a liar (5:10).

Now 3:6, 9 (and 5:18) appear to contradict the assertion in vss 8–10 that the claim of sinlessness is a false teaching; this is to be considered below. Provisionally, it need only be said that the admonition to confession of sins goes together as a matter of course with the warning against sin (2:1f).

■ **2:1** provides a clarification. The author begins with a hitherto unused form of address, τεκνία μου ("my little children"), which is employed more frequently in what follows.[34] This shows that here the author himself is speaking, which can also be concluded from the singular γράφω ὑμῖν ("I write to you").[35] Ἵνα μὴ ἁμάρτητε ("so that you may not sin") is intended to prevent the misunderstanding that 1:8–10 implies, viz., that the believer does not need to take transgression seriously. The following καὶ ἐάν τις ἁμάρτῃ κτλ. ("if any one does sin, . . .") clarifies 1:9f, in the sense that we can be certain of God's forgiveness, since παράκλητον ἔχομεν πρὸς τὸν πατέρα, Ἰησοῦν Χριστὸν δίκαιον ("we have an advocate with the Father, Jesus Christ the righteous"). Just as God was designated as "righteous" in 1:9, so Jesus Christ is here given the same designation. He is called παράκλητος ("advocate") as the intercessor (*deprecator*) with God.[36]

---

in Judaism; also occasionally in Hellenism; cf. Bauer, *s.v.* God is repeatedly designated as righteous precisely in statements which express hope in his rule; thus Deut 32:4 (with πιστός ["faithful"] and in connection with ὅσιος ["holy"]); Ps 144:17 (in connection with ὅσιος); 1 Clem 27:1; 60:1 (here with πιστός). The latter two passages are apparently dependent on liturgical language. Cf. Josh 24:14; Nah 9:8, 38 also for the combination of righteousness and faithfulness.

32 Καθαρίζειν ("to cleanse") is used initially for ritual cleansing (as also καθαρισμός); then (already in the Old Testament and in Judaism) in the spiritual sense as cleansing from sin. So 2 Cor 7:1; Tit 2:14;

Heb 9:14; Jas 4:8; 2 Petr 1:9; Acts 15:9 (through baptism Eph 5:26) frequently in the Shepherd of Hermas. Cf. Bauer, *s.v.*

33 Λόγος in v 10 is, of course, not the preexistent Logos (correct, Schnackenburg, pp. 88f).

34 The address "children" (or also "my son") occurs frequently as an address of the wisdom teachers for pupils (or pupil) in Old Testament wisdom and in Judaism. Cf. Bauer, *s.v.*; H. Edmons, *RAC* I:50f *s.v.* "Abt." In the New Testament also Jn 13:33; Gal 4:19 (*v.l.* τέκνα).

35 Ταῦτα γράφω ("I write these things") in the context refers not to the whole letter, but to 1:8–10.

36 Cf. Bauer, *s.v.*, regarding this sense of παράκλητος,

■ **2** The ecclesiastical redactor has appended v 2, which further strengthens the argument: καὶ αὐτὸς ἱλασμός ἐστιν περὶ τῶν ἁμαρτιῶν ἡμῶν κτλ. ("and he is the expiation for our sins, . . ."). It is the notion that Jesus Christ has atoned for sins through his death (his blood), just as it was expressed in the interpolation of 1:7b, and just as it will be repeated in 4:10. This thought, however, does not agree with v 1, where the hope for the forgiveness of sins is based upon the fact that Jesus Christ is our intercessor (advocate) with God. The concept ἱλασμός ("expiation"), which is also foreign to the Gospel of John, belongs to the ecclesiastical theology.[37] Περὶ ὅλου τοῦ κόσμου ("for the whole world") is probably also a traditional expression.[38]

---

as attested in Greek as well as in Judaism; very likely with another meaning in the New Testament, Jn 14:16, 26; 15:26; 16:7; cf. Bultmann, pp. 566–70 [437–39], on Jn 16:7ff. According to O. Moe, "Das Priestertum Christi im NT ausserhalb des Hebräerbriefs," *ThLZ* 72 (1947): 338, Christ is παράκλητος as high priest. Cf. further, Otto Betz, *Der Paraklet: Fürsprecher im häretischen Spätjudentum, im Johannesevangelium und in neu gefundenen gnostischen Schriften*, Arbeiten zur Geschichte des Spätjudentums und Urchristentums, 2 (Leiden: Brill, 1963). Regarding Christ's intercession with God, cf. Rom 8:34; Heb 7:25; 9:24. In Philo, *De migr. Abr.* 122 the logos is ἱκέτης ("intercessor"). Cf., in addition, TestDan 6:2; TestLev 3:5; 5:6.

37 Ἱλασμός has in Greek, in the LXX, and in Philo the sense of "expiation" (then the thing rather than the person would be intended) and of "expiatory sacrifice," which is no doubt here intended, since 1:7b speaks of Jesus' blood. Ἱλάσκεσθαι is used in the same sense in Heb 2:17 and ἱλαστήριον in Rom 3:25, where Paul apparently uses a traditional formulation.

38 In substance, the thought is encountered in Rom 3:23f; 2 Cor 5:19; 1 Tim 2:6. Thus, κόσμος ("world") here does not have the same meaning as in 2:15ff, but rather is the whole of the human world, as in Jn 1:29; 3:16f; 4:42; 12:47.

2

Knowledge of God and Keeping the Commandments

3 And by this we may be sure that we know him, if we keep his commandments. 4/ He who says "I know him" but disobeys his commandments is a liar, and the truth is not in him; 5/ but whoever keeps his word, in him truly love for God is perfected. By this we may be sure that we are in him: 6/ he who says he abides in him ought to walk in the same way in which he walked.

7 Beloved, I am writing you no new commandment, but an old commandment which you had from the beginning; the old commandment is the word which you have heard. 8/ Yet I am writing you a new commandment, which is true in him and in you, because the darkness is passing away and the true light is already shining. 9/ He who says he is in the light and hates his brother is in the darkness still. 10/ He who loves his brother abides in the light, and in it there is no cause for stumbling. 11/ But he who hates his brother is in the darkness and walks in the darkness, and does not know where he is going, because the darkness has blinded his eyes.

■ **3** The theme of fellowship with God is now replaced by the theme of the knowledge of God. It is clear that here, as in 1:6–10, the formulations are directed against the Gnostic false teaching. Ὁ λέγων ("the one who says") in vss 4, 6, 9 corresponds to ἐὰν εἴπωμεν ("if we say") in 1:8, 10, with the same meaning. The author takes the decisive initial sentences in vss 4 and 5 from his Source, but has introduced them with his own words (v 3): καὶ ἐν τούτῳ γινώσκομεν ὅτι κτλ. ("And by this we know that . . .").[1] That the knowledge of God[2] forms a substantive unity with the fellowship with God—one could even say an identity—stems from the fact that the conditions for both are materially the same. Whereas it is κοινωνίαν ἔχειν μετ᾿ ἀλλήλων ("to have

---

1   The formula ἐν τούτῳ γινώσκομεν ("by this we know"), which is characteristic of the author, occurs likewise in 2:5; 3:16, 24; 4:6 (ἐκ τούτου), 13; 5:2 (with the future tense, 3:19). The content of γινώσκειν is explicated, as a rule, by a ὅτι–clause; only in 3:16 and 4:6 by means of an accusative object; and in 4:2 the explication follows in the form of a confession. There is this difference: sometimes τοῦτο refers to what precedes (2:5; 3:19; 4:6), sometimes to what follows (2:3; 3:16, 24; 4:2f, 13). In the latter

case, γινώσκειν is verified by ἐὰν κτλ. (2:3), ὅταν κτλ. (5:2), a prepositional phrase (3:24), or a second ὅτι–clause (4:13), in which ὅτι means not "that" but "because." This construction is analogous to the explication of a demonstrative by means of a ἵνα–clause (1:4, etc.; see p. 15 n. 1).

2   The αὐτός ("him") in ὅτι ἐγνώκαμεν αὐτόν ("that we know him"), on the basis of what precedes, must be God himself. Thus Schnackenburg, p. 75 n. 1, is right in his opposition to me. Jesus is always desig-

fellowship with another") in 1:7, it is τηρεῖν τὰς ἐντολάς ("to keep the commandments") in v 3. "Keeping the commandments" leads, however, immediately to "love of the brother" (ἀγαπᾶν τὸν ἀδελφόν), and thus to the decisive characteristic of "fellowship with one another."

Is it permissible to speak of a condition for the knowledge of God? The if–clause suggests as much. One would then be tempted, however, to understand, as Gnosticism does, that certain conditions have to be met in order for man to be able to come to the knowledge of God, and that, consequently, this knowledge may constitute a direct vision (rather like the 'phenomenon culmination' which is ecstasy). It is doubtless more nearly correct to say that "keeping the commandments" (like "fellowship with one another," 1:7) is not the condition, but rather the characteristic of the knowledge of God. There is no knowledge of God which as such would not also be "keeping the commandments."[3] This is what is made clear in v 4, which lacks an if–clause.

■ **4** Ὁ λέγων ὅτι ἔγνωκα αὐτὸν καὶ τὰς ἐντολὰς αὐτοῦ μὴ τηρῶν κτλ. ("He who says 'I know him' but disobeys his commandments . . ."). What, then, does it mean "to know God"? This sentence makes it clear that knowledge of God is not a theoretical or speculative knowledge, but is rather a relationship to God, in which the one knowing is determined in his existence (and thus also in his "walking," his conduct) by God. It is for this reason that it can be said of someone who is not so determined: ψεύστης ἐστίν, καὶ ἐν τούτῳ ἡ ἀλήθεια οὐκ ἔστιν ("He is a liar, and the truth is not in him"). Both of these sentences say the same thing, for "he is a liar" asserts (as does "we lie," 1:6) not only that such a person says something untrue, but that he is

nothing, since ἀλήθεια ("truth") is reality.[4]

■ **5** This is further substantiated by the reversal in v 5. It is significant that here, instead of "keeping the commandments," the text not only says τὸν λόγον τηρεῖν ("keeps his word"), but also, instead of the expected "the truth is in him," it reads: ἐν τούτῳ ἡ ἀγάπη τοῦ θεοῦ τετελείωται ("in him is the love of God perfected"). It is easily understandable that λόγος ("word") replaces ἐντολαί ("commandments"), since God's "word" is the revelation of his reality and thereby also of his demand (his "commandments") and of his forgiveness as well. In fact, in a certain sense the gift of forgiveness belongs also to the "commandments," insofar as it demands from man the admission of his nothingness.[5] The fact, however, that the text reads "in him is the love of God perfected" shows that God's reality and his love are identical, as is stated in 4:8, 16: ὁ θεὸς ἀγάπη ἐστίν ("God is love"). It is thereby also determined that τοῦ θεοῦ ("of God") is not an objective genitive ("love for God"), but rather a subjective genitive ("God's love for men"). This is confirmed by the fact that man's love cannot be directly oriented toward God (4:20; 5:2f). To be sure, the man who is loved by God is also obliged to love, as vss 10f show, but this loving is oriented directly towards the brother. In the Source utilized by the author and which he takes up again in vss 9–11, brotherly love is understood to be given as part of "God's love" and is included in "is perfected." This means

---

nated as ἐκεῖνος ("that one/he") (2:6; 3:3, 5, 7, 16; 4:17).

3   The expression τηρεῖν τὰς ἐντολάς ("keep the commandments") as in 2:3f; 3:22, 24; 5:2f; Jn 14:15, 21; 15:10; so also in the LXX and Judaism, cf.

Bauer *s.v.* τηρεῖν, and Bultmann, p. 301 n. 5 [227 n. 5] on Jn 8:55.

4   See pp. 18f on 1:6. On εἶναι ἐν see p. 20 n. 21 on 1:7.

5   Cf. p. 22 on 1:10.

that brotherly love is brought to fulfillment,[6] and this is true, of course, only when it is characterized by "keeping his word." In conclusion the author has added: ἐν τούτῳ γινώσκομεν ὅτι ἐν αὐτῷ ἐσμεν ("By this we know that we are in him"). Here, in contrast to its use in 2:3, ἐν τούτῳ ("by this") refers to what precedes (as in 3:19[7]): "Because we keep his commandments (vss 3f), or his word (v 5a), we know that we are in him, namely in God."[8]

■ 6 In a new formulation the author repeats in v 6 the substance of vss 4f: ὁ λέγων (as in v 4) ἐν αὐτῷ μένειν ὀφείλει . . . περιπατεῖν ("he who says he abides in him ought to walk . . ."). Μένειν ἐν ("abide in") here replaces εἶναι ἐν αὐτῷ ("be in him"). There is no perceptible difference between "to be in him" and "abide in

him."[9] The admonition[10] to περιπατεῖν ("walk") takes the place of "keeping the commandments" or "his word." This acquires a more concrete meaning, however, by means of καθὼς ἐκεῖνος περιεπάτησεν ("just as that one walked"): Jesus is thus referred to as the model and the foundation of Christian conduct. There is no doubt that ἐκεῖνος ("that one") refers to Jesus; the fact that it is used here without any preparation, instead of the explicit name, shows that ἐκεῖνος was common as a designation in the circle of the author.[11] The reference to this model[12] is preparation for the fact that the commandments are summed up in the one commandment, the commandment to love, as vss 7–11 immediately indicate.

■ 7 The author begins anew in v 7 with the address ἀγαπητοί ("beloved").[13] He does not, however, begin

---

6   Cf. p. 14 n. 30 on 1:4. The concept of fulfillment or perfection is frequently encountered among the Mandaeans; cf. e.g., *Ginza R.* I,20 (p. 22, 11): "Love one another in faithfulness and bring your love to perfection"; *Ginza R.* I, 18 (p. 20, 5f); III, 78 (p. 77, 13f); IV, 31 (p. 146, 27); XV, 2 (p. 305, 28); XV, 5 (p. 316, 20f). Also cf. *Act. Thom.* 54 (Aa 2:2, p. 171, 10f.): Jesus hands over a virgin to Thomas with the words: "Take thou this woman, that she may be made perfect, and hereafter be gathered to her place." (σὺ ταύτην παράλαβε, ἵνα τελειωθῇ καὶ μετὰ ταῦτα εἰς τὸν αὐτῆς χῶρον συναχθῇ).

7   Cf. p. 24 n. 1 on 2:3.

8   On εἶναι ἐν see p. 20 n. 21 on 1:7a.

9   The term μένειν ("abide") always contains a negative implication: do not yield, do not leave, stay where you are. However, "abide" does not answer the question of place, of where, but rather the question, until when? how long? In oldest Greek usage, it is usually a matter of remaining at an objectively established place, for an objectively determined time, even if this period extends into infinity. A change in linguistic usage occurs when it becomes a matter of persisting in a personal affiliation, whether in relation to a thing or a person. "Abide" then designates faithfulness, as is the case especially in John and 1 John. One can thus think sometimes more of futurity, sometimes more of abiding in the present, especially in the case of those expressions which refer

to the reciprocity of abiding, as 2:24, 27; 3:24; 4:13, 15f, (see Bultmann, p. 267 n. 1 [201 n. 1]). Both are combined in the meaning "be faithful." Schnackenburg, who presents an informative excursus, "Zu den johanneischen Immanenzformeln" ["On the Johannine Immanence Formulas"] (pp. 105–10), deals especially with μένειν in the Johannine writings. It occurs twenty-five times in 1 John, three times in 2 John, forty-one times in John.

10   Ὀφείλειν ("ought, must") as in 3:16; 4:11; 3 Jn 8. All are formulations of the author. See pp. 19f n. 19 (1:7) on περιπατεῖν "walk."

11   Thus, in addition to v 6, cf. 3:5, 7, 16; 4:17; and often in John.

12   Schnackenburg, p. 105 n. 2, points correctly to the fact that it is not a question of discipleship but of imitation; cf. Jn 13:15: ὑπόδειγμα γὰρ ἔδωκα ὑμῖν κτλ. . . . ("For I have given you an example . . ."). There is reference to Jesus also in 1 Jn 2:29; 3:16. Reference to Jesus introduced by καθώς ("just as") as in 3:3, 7 (cf. 4:17); correspondingly οὐ καθώς ("not just as") 3:12. Braun, "Literar-Analyse," 273 [221], emphasizes the ambiguity of καθώς (used for comparison and in a causal sense).

13   The address ἀγαπητοί "beloved" (*v.l.* ἀδελφοί "brethren") is used as in 3:2, 21; 4:1, 7, 11 (in the singular, 2 Jn 2, 5, 11); likewise Rom 12:19; 2 Cor 7:1; etc. Apparently it is a common homiletical form of address.

with a new theme, but rather explains what was already said in vss 3–6, and thereby prepares the way for the understanding of vss 9–11. The theme is the "commandments" of vss 3–6. The fact that the author now speaks of "commandment" in the singular is probably occasioned by the fact that he has a traditional word in mind to which he refers in vss 7f. There is no material difference, for the "commandments" are included in the "commandment" to love, as the interchange of plural and singular in 3:22–24; 2 Jn 4–6 shows.[14]

The sentence οὐκ ἐντολὴν καινὴν γράφω ὑμῖν κτλ. ("I am writing you no new commandment") is presumably motivated by the fact that the author has the false teachers in mind, who do not want to adhere to the παλαία ἐντολή ("old commandment"), but rather want to be progressive (2 Jn 9).[15] Over against them the author emphasizes that no new commandment may be given to the readers. When he designates the old commandment as ἣν εἴχετε ἀπ᾽ ἀρχῆς ("which you had from the beginning") and defines it as the λόγος, ὃν ἠκούσατε ("the word which you heard"), then it is clear that he is thinking of the commandment which is mediated through the Christian tradition, and that ἀρχή

("beginning"), unlike its use in 1:1, means the point within history in which the Christian proclamation was received by the believers.[16]

■ 8 The author, however, is not deterred by the paradox (v 8): πάλιν ἐντολὴν καινὴν γράφω ὑμῖν ("Yet I am writing you a new commandment").[17] In what sense is the old commandment nevertheless a new one? It is not new as a phenomenon in the history of ideas, but rather as an eschatological reality.[18] It is just that which the characteristic ὅ ἐστιν ἀληθὲς ἐν αὐτῷ καὶ ἐν ὑμῖν ("which is true in him and in you") says.[19] According to Jn 13:34, it is grounded in the love which Jesus bestowed upon his own. It has therefore become real[20] in the congregation, which is grounded in the gift of his love. That the commandment is new as an eschatological reality is expressed also in the next clause: ὅτι ἡ σκοτία παράγεται καὶ τὸ φῶς τὸ ἀληθινὸν ἤδη φαίνει ("because the darkness is passing away and the true light is already shining").

Σκοτία ("darkness") and φῶς ("light") designate here not only the essential antithesis of the nondivine and divine spheres, as in 1:5, but also the antithesis of the epochs, which have become clear through the eschato-

---

14 Cf. also the replacement of the singular by the plural in Jn 13:34, as in Jn 14:15, 21; 15:10. In 1 John the plural is usually used: 2:3f; 3:22, 24; 5:2f. The singular appears, in addition to 2:7f; 3:23, also in 4:21. Braun ("Literar-Analyse," 272 [220]) is correct: "The change in number indicates at the outset that one cannot tie the author to the plural in the sense of an atomistic ethic; 'the commandments' are 'the commandment,' 'the word.' "

15 Whether reference is being made to certain concrete "new" commandments on the part of false teachers (so Büchsel) cannot be discovered; see Schnackenburg, p. 100 n. 1.

16 See p. 9 n. 10 on 1:1.

17 Πάλιν meaning "on the other hand," see Bauer s.v.

18 Cf. Bultmann, pp. 526f [404f] on Jn 13:34. When Conzelmann, " 'Was von Anfang war,' " 199, says that in the meantime the "new" commandment itself has become historical and now designates the new-

ness of Christianity in the world, he is indeed correct. It must not be forgotten, however, that Christianity in the world is not a phenomenon of the history of thought but an eschatological phenomenon; see above, p. 9 on 1:1–4.

19 Several MSS read ἐν ἡμῖν ("in us") instead of ἐν ὑμῖν ("in you"). The former is scarcely original, but would not alter the sense: the readers are included in the "us" as members of the congregation.

20 Ἀληθές therefore does not mean "true" in the sense of "correct," but characterizes the "new commandment" as something verifying itself as real. That it verifies itself as real in the congregation is also said in 3:14. Ἐν αὐτῷ ("in him") naturally means in Jesus.

logical event of the revelation as such.[21]

■ **9f** In vss 9–11, the Either/Or, which is given with the present eschatological event, is made emphatic with the words of the conjectured Source—obviously in opposition to the gnosticizing false teachers.[22]

"Whoever maintains that he is in the light
And hates his brother
Is (even yet[23]) in the darkness.
Whoever loves his brother
Remains in the light
And there is no blemish in him."[24]

Just as darkness and light are mutually exclusive antitheses, so, too, are hate and love. Consequently, in this antithesis, the Either/Or of the eschatological event becomes actual. A third possibility, a neutral relationship to one's brother, is excluded. *Tertium non datur.*[25] "Brother" means, as in 3:15 and 4:20, not especially the Christian comrade in the faith, but one's fellowman, the "neighbor."[26]

■ **11** The urgency of this Either/Or is enjoined in v 11, which materially repeats v 9.

---

21 The same view is present here that is expressed elsewhere in the New Testament (as previously in Judaism) in terms of the contrast between the present and coming ages; cf., for example, 1 Cor 1:20; 2:6, 8; Eph 1:21. The identity of viewpoint is also illustrated by Eph 6:12, where "the world rulers of this present darkness" ($\kappa o \sigma \mu o \kappa \rho \acute{\alpha} \tau o \rho \epsilon s \ \tau o \hat{v} \ \sigma \kappa \acute{o} \tau o v s \ \tau o \acute{v} \tau o v$) can also be spoken of, instead of "this present age" ($\tau o \hat{v} \ a i \hat{\omega} v o s \ \tau o \acute{v} \tau o v$). The term $a i \acute{\omega} v$ ("age") is lacking in the Johannine writings. When Dodd says that in the Johannine writings the apocalyptic schema of the two aeons has been converted into the Hellenistic schema of the contrast between eternal and temporal, he is correct only with respect to the terminology. The certainty that the "darkness" is passing away and that the "true light already shines," has its analogies in Rom 13: 11f; 1 Cor 7:29, 31; 1 Thess 5:4–10; Eph 5:8–14, but is nowhere so definitively stated as in 1 John and John (cf. especially 1 Jn 3:14; Jn 3:19; 5:24f). Ἀληθινὸν φῶς is the "true" light in contrast to all earthly light, but, as the author understands it, probably also in contrast to the "light" of which the Gnostics speak (cf. Bultmann, p. 53 n. 1 [32 n. 1] on Jn 1:9). Schnackenburg (pp. 112f) wishes to understand "is already shining" not with reference to the eschatological event, but rather with reference to the historical process which takes place in the "extension of the divine realm of light" in the "victorious advancement of the power of Good." He has thereby very likely misunderstood the paradox that consists of the historicizing of the eschatological event.

22 Dodd, *ad loc.*, sees the contrast to the false teachers in the fact that, for them, the light is the "illumination" or initiation into the knowledge of the transcendent world, while in 1 John it is the newness of life. He may therefore not appreciate that for the Gnostics the light also means a certainty of life.

23 Ἕως ἄρτι is probably an addition of the author to his Source.

24 Schnackenburg (p. 115) considers "blemish" too weak a rendering of σκάνδαλον. His understanding, "there is nothing in him that is scandalous, namely for the others, the brethren," is not convincing. The "snare of sin" which makes a member of the Qumran community accursed may well be an analogy; see Braun, "Qumran und das Neue Testament," pp. 104f [293f] on 1 Jn 2:8–11. O'Neill, *The Puzzle of 1 John*, p. 16, proposes to understand ἐν αὐτῷ as "in light," which is not persuasive.

25 Cf. Bengel, *ad loc.*: "Where there is no love, there is hate; the heart is not empty." (ubi non est amor, odium est: cor non est vacuum) [trans. by Ed.]. 1 Jn 2:9, 11 evidently has nothing in common with the hate directed against everyone outside the community according to 1 QS; cf. Braun, "Qumran und das Neue Testament," pp. 113f [17f], on Matt 5:43f. Schnackenburg (p. 119) is of the opinion, to be sure, that the text has in view the hate of the false teachers for legitimate Christians, their leaders in particular. It more probably refers, however, to hate in general, as in 3:15 and 4:20, which is directed against fellowmen. Cf. Matt 6:24 also for the exclusive contrast of love and hate.

26 The concept ὁ πλησίον ("neighbor") is lacking in the Johannine writings. We do not have here the

"But whoever hates his brother
  Remains in darkness
    And walks in darkness."[27]
The conclusion of v 11 (καὶ οὐκ οἶδεν ποῦ ὑπάγε, ὅτι ἡ σκοτία ἐτύφλωσεν τοὺς ὀφθαλμοὺς αὐτοῦ ["and does not know where he is going, because the darkness has blinded his eyes"]) is perhaps a homiletical expan-

sion of the author, who intends to bring to consciousness the horror of walking in darkness.

concept ἀδελφός ("brother"), used to designate him with whom one is united in religious fellowship, found not infrequently in Judaism and in paganism as well as in the New Testament. Concerning the ethics of brotherhood in Gnosticism, cf. Hans Jonas, *Gnosis und spätantiker Geist*, pp. 169, 171; further, Ernst Käsemann, *Das wandernde Gottesvolk: Eine Untersuchung zum Hebräerbrief* (FRLANT 55, Göttingen, ⁴1961), 90–95. Cf. Schnackenburg, pp. 118f (but

Jn 15:12; 13:34 are probably to be included, where ἀγαπᾶν ἀλλήλους ["love one another"] very likely refers to Christian brothers). Nevertheless, the author can also address his readers in this way, thus 3:13 (ἀδελφοί μου ?) and 2:7 as in 2:1.

27 Jn 12:35 is materially related and agrees in part verbally. For parallels in linguistic usage, see Bultmann, p. 340 n. 4. [258 n. 6] on Jn 9:39. Also cf. Schnackenburg, pp. 116f.

2

Homily and Parenesis

12   I am writing to you, little children, because
your sins are forgiven for his sake. 13/I
am writing to you, fathers, because
you know him who is from the beginning. I am writing to you, young men,
because you have overcome the evil one.
I write to you, children, because you
know the Father. 14/I write to you,
fathers, because you know him who is
from the beginning. I write to you,
young men, because you are strong, and
the word of God abides in you, and you
have overcome the evil one.

15   Do not love the world or the things in the
world. If any one loves the world, the
love of the Father is not in him. 16/For
all that is in the world, the lust of the
flesh and the lust of the eyes and the
pride of life, is not of the Father but is of
the world. 17/And the world passes
away, and the lust of it; but he who does
the will of God abides forever.

[RSV modified]

Since both 1:5–2:2 and 2:3–11 contained an indirect warning against the Gnostic false teaching, it is surprising that the direct polemic against the false teachers does not begin before 2:18. One could indeed understand 1:5–2:11 as preparation for 2:18ff. But how are the homiletical–parenetical passages in 2:12–14 and 2:15–17 to be fitted into the context? Indeed, can one speak of a context at all? A distinction must be made. Whereas 2:15–17 is, in form and content, quite a traditional piece of parenesis, which warns against worldly lust and has nothing to do with the problem of the false teaching endangering the Christian congregation, the homiletical passage, 2:12–14, is by all means precipitated by this problem; it makes the readers conscious of their superiority over the false teaching, indirectly, to be sure, and without expressly mentioning that false teaching. This is done by making the believers conscious of the existential situation that follows from the eschatological character of the present, as it has been delineated in 2:7–11. These verses also, of course, contain the imperative to realize this existential possibility. To this extent, there is certainly a connection between 2:12–14 and what precedes,[1] and also 2:12–14 is preparation for 2:18ff. On the other hand, the parenesis of 2:15–17 interrupts the context, and the question must be raised whether it does not also belong to the ecclesiastical redactor. The position of vss 15–17 can scarcely be justified by the fact that parenesis in 1 John otherwise customarily follows upon dogmatic statements.[2] Moreover, the language of vss 15–17 is characteristically different from

---

1   Schnackenburg sees the connection to lie in the author's wish to comfort the readers because they may be concerned whether they have also walked in the light and lived in fellowship with God. It seems to me more likely that 2:12–14 contains an indirect imperative.

2   See Bultmann, "Die kirchliche Redaktion," p. 191. There I had not yet considered whether 2:15–17 goes back to the ecclesiastical redactor. Cf. Braun, "Literar-Analyse," 277f [226], who senses that there

the language of the author (and his Source), which is to be demonstrated in the detailed exegesis.[3] It could nevertheless be assumed that the author thought it necessary to have a direct admonition follow the indirect imperative contained in vss 12–14. For this purpose he would have made use of traditional parenetical expressions.

The Superiority of the Believers over the World

■ **12–14** The sentences in vss 12–14 are arranged rhythmically: two groups of clauses run parallel to one another, and each is further divided into three parallel lines. The antithetical division characteristic of the assumed Source is not present here; the verses do not therefore stem from this Source, but rather are the author's own creation.

The first group includes three short sentences beginning with γράφω ὑμῖν ("I am writing to you"); the second group, three short sentences beginning with ἔγραψα ὑμῖν ("I write to you"), each of which calls those addressed (ὑμεῖς, "you") by a different name: τεκνία ("children") or παιδία ("children"), πατέρες ("fathers"), and νεανίσκοι ("young men"). This raises first of all the question of the relationship of γράφω to ἔγραψα. Since ἔγραψα can hardly be traced back to an earlier writing (say to 2 John or 3 John, or to a lost letter, at most to the Gospel of John), and scarcely to any of the

preceding passages, the distinction between γράφω and ἔγραψα must be understood simply as a stylistic variation.[4] The other question is, who is intended by those addressed? The address τεκνία designates the readers collectively, as in 2:1, 28 and elsewhere; the same can be said of the address παιδία here and in 2:18. As a consequence, there is no more than a variation in words. In the case of πατέρες and νεανίσκοι, those addressed are differentiated; the author addresses the various age groups.[5] On that basis he writes his readers that[6] the darkness is passing away and that the true light already shines (v 8); he shows them what that means for them. Moreover, the formulations are varied, in part, in the parallel sentences.

Ὅτι ἀφέωνται ὑμῖν αἱ ἁμαρτίαι[7] ("because your sins are forgiven," v 12) and ὅτι ἐγνώκατε τὸν πατέρα ("because you know the Father," v 14a) apply in the first instance to all the readers. Διὰ τὸ ὄνομα αὐτοῦ ("for his name") in conjunction with "because your sins are forgiven" means: because the readers bear his name. His name, since it concerns Christians, is the name Jesus Christ, in whom they believe (cf. 3:23; 5:13).[8] Faith in him and in his name are identical.[9] Essentially both characteristics of the believers are identical. For, just as fellowship with God is realized, according to 1:6–9, through forgiveness (given as a gift for the confession of sins), so also knowledge of the

is a weakening, in 2:15–17, of the paradox expressed in 1:8–10, that confession of sins and being in the truth belong together.

3 Schnackenburg also clearly perceives this difference.

4 Schnackenburg is thus correct, and points to the fact that elsewhere ἔγραψα also occasionally refers to the letter then being written, e.g., 2:21; Phlmn 19, 21; Gal 6:11 (but perhaps not 1 Cor 5:11). Also cf. Bengel: Through the resumption of γράφω in ἔγραψα: "he suggests a very strong admonition" (innuit commonitionem firmissimana). On the contrary, H. H. Wendt, "Die Beziehung unseres ersten Johannesbriefes auf den zweiten," ZNW 21 (1922):

140–6, refers ἔγραψα to 2 John, which was written, in his opinion, prior to 1 John.

5 So also Schnackenburg, who correctly states that it is not a matter of class distinctions, and that 2:12–14 does not contain a *Haustafel* (compendium of household duties) like that in Eph 5:22–6:9; Col 3:18–4:1.

6 The ὅτι–clauses are not explicative but causal, as in vss 8 and 21. Only in this way is there an inner connection with what precedes.

7 On ἀφέωνται instead of ἀφεῖνται, see Blass–Debrunner §97(3).

8 There need not thereby be an allusion specifically to baptism (Schnackenburg, p. 123).

9 Cf. Bultmann, p. 59 n. 2 [37 n. 4] on Jn 1:12.

Father, which is not a theoretical knowledge but the determination of existence through God,[10] means fellowship with him.

Ὅτι ἐγνώκατε τὸν ἀπ᾽ ἀρχῆς ("because you know him who is from the beginning," v 13a and v 14b are formulated identically) applies then to the πατέρες ("fathers"). According to 1:1, Jesus must be understood as τὸν ἀπ᾽ ἀρχῆς ("the one from the beginning"); consequently, the ἀπ᾽ ἀρχῆς can certainly not be the πατήρ ("father") of v 14a. With this recognition, therefore, reference is made to 1:1–3, where the ἀπ᾽ ἀρχῆς is proclaimed to the readers, albeit indirectly, not as a person, but as the subject matter embodied in him.[11]

Finally, ὅτι νενικήκατε τὸν πονηρόν ("you have overcome the evil one") applies to the νεανίσκοι ("young men").[12] The expression is identical in vss 13b and 14c, though in the case of the second, ὅτι ἰσχυροί ἐστε καὶ ὁ λόγος τοῦ θεοῦ ἐν ὑμῖν μένει ("because you are strong, and the word of God abides in you") precedes. The two characteristics mean essentially the same thing. For, in this context ἰσχυροί ἐστε ("you are strong") cannot apply to the physical strength of the young people, but rather belongs with ὁ λόγος . . . μένει ("the word . . . abides . . ."), as it were, in hendiadys: the strength of the "young men" rests on the fact that God's word "abides" in them and determines their existence.[13] Their faithfulness, therefore, is what makes them "strong."

And so it can also be said: "You have overcome the evil one." Πονηρός ("evil one") is the devil, as in 3:13; [5:18], perhaps also in Jn 17:15,[14] and certainly in Eph 6:16; 2 Thess 3:3, whose "works" God's Son came to destroy (3:3). They are victorious over him just as Jesus conquered the world according to Jn 16:33.[15] One may ask whether the victory specifically implies the orthodox faith that triumphs over false teaching; in any case, it is so implied in 4:4.

The Verification of the Superiority over the World

■ **15–17** A parenetical section follows, which has perhaps been inserted by the redactor.[16] As the sequel to vss 12–14, it shows in direct exhortation how what the readers have and are, described in vss 12–14, is to be put to the test. If the theme of vss 12–14 may be designated as the superiority of the believers over the world, then vss 15–17 tell how this superiority is to be verified. The parenesis is a warning against the κόσμος ("world"), and it could have been occasioned by the fact that the the one who wrote it understood the πονηρός ("evil one") of vss 13f as the seductive power of the "world."[17]

What is the meaning of the term "world" that lies behind the exhortation μὴ ἀγαπᾶτε τὸν κόσμον μηδὲ τὰ ἐν τῷ κόσμῳ ("Do not love the world or the things in the world")? That it is not the world as a creation of God,

---

10 See above pp. 24f on 2:3.
11 See pp. 7f on 1:1.
12 Cf. Hans Lewy, *Sobria Ebrietas. Untersuchungen zur Geschichte der antiken Mystik*, BZNW 9 (Giessen: 1929), p. 14 n. 4: "Modes of addressing the young men are peculiar to both the Jewish and Greek literary genre (the προτρεπτικλὶ λόγοι)." Erik Peterson "Die Einholung des Kyrios," *Zeitschrift für systematische Theologie* 7 (1929): 694 n. 5, points out that included among the stated classes at the "reception" (P. Petrie II 45, col. 2, 23–25 [Mahaffy 2:146]; II 45, col. 3, 22 [Mahaffy 2:147]) are also νεανίσκοι, and asks whether the admonition of the νεανίσκοι in 1 Jn 2:13f perhaps presupposes a youth club of the municipal type.

13 The word of God is the reality of God. See above, pp. 25f on v 5. On μένειν ἐν ("abide in") see p. 26 n. 9 on v 6.
14 See Bultmann, p. 508 n. 3 [389 n. 3] on Jn 17:15.
15 Cf. *Act. Thom.* 94 (Aa, 2:2, p. 207.23f; 208.1):
    μακάριοί ἐστε οἱ πραεῖς·
    ὑμεῖς γάρ ἐστε οἱ νικήσαντες τὸν πονηρόν.
    ("Blessed are you meek
    For you are they who have conquered the evil one.") [Hennecke–Schneemelcher, II, 492, modified].
16 See above, pp. 30f, and see the following note.
17 Cf. 5:19: ὁ κόσμος ὅλος ἐν τῷ πονηρῷ κεῖται ("the

32

and that it is also not the world of men, is self–evident. It is the *κόσμος οὗτος* ("this world") of 4:17; Jn 12:31; 16:11; 18:36; 1 Cor 3:19; 5:10; 7:31; Eph 2:2, in the sense of the sphere which is distinguished and separated from God, but not in the sense of an active opposition to God and the believers, as in 3:13; Jn 7:7; 15:18f, 24; 17:14, but rather in the sense of its nothingness, as v 17 shows.[18]

Τὰ *ἐν τῷ κόσμῳ* ("the things in the world") are all transitory things that awaken *ἐπιθυμία* ("lust") and *ἀλαζονεία* ("pride," v 16), and thus mislead man and bind him to transitoriness. They are seductive; thus the exhortation *μὴ ἀγαπᾶτε* ("do not love").[19] The antithesis to *ἀγαπᾶν τὸν κόσμον* ("love the world") is expressed as: *ἐάν τις ἀγαπᾷ τὸν κόσμον οὐκ ἔστιν ἡ ἀγάπη τοῦ πατρὸς ἐν αὐτῷ* ("If any one loves the world, the love of the father is not in him"). Since "love of the father" stands in contrast to "love of the world," the genitive "of the father" (*τοῦ πατρός*) is readily taken as an objective genitive. The fact that, according to 4:20, love cannot be immediately directed to God need not be taken as contrary evidence. For, just as 5:2f speaks of a love indirectly oriented toward God,

consisting of keeping the commandments, so, too, could "love of the father" be understood here as love indirectly oriented toward God, consisting of keeping clear of the "world." Nevertheless, the thought of keeping clear of the "world" is a sign that the one addicted to the "world" has closed himself to the love of God directed toward him. For to love God and to be loved by him are a unity: the former is grounded in the latter.[20] In that case, "of the father" would be a subjective genitive ("the father's love"), as is "of God" in v 5: "in this one God's love is perfected."[21]

■ **16** Verse 16, which provides the basis for v 15, indicates what is brought to mind by the phrase "the things in the world."[22] Above all, it is the *ἐπιθυμία τῆς σαρκός* ("the lust of the flesh"), the lust peculiar to the flesh. "Flesh" is apparently not understood here in the sense otherwise usual in 1 John and John, viz., as the merely negative aspect of the worldly–human (as in 4:2; 2 Jn 7, or even Jn 1:13f; 3:6), but rather with positive force as a power hostile to God—as often in Paul, for whom "flesh" signifies not only the earthly–human, but also functions

---

whole world lies in the power of the evil one"). If the addition of vss 15–17 is caused by the naming of the "evil one" in vss 13f, then the conjecture that vss 15–17 are to be attributed to the redactor is confirmed; for 5:19 certainly stems from him.

18 Cf. the Cosmos-concept of Hellenistic-Gnostic dualism, e.g., *Corp. Herm.* VI 4: ὁ γὰρ κόσμος πλήρωμά ἐστι τῆς κακίας ("For the Kosmos is one mass of evil.") [Scott]; XIII 1: . . . ἀπὸ τῆς τοῦ κόσμου ἀπάτης (". . . from the world's deceptions") [Scott]. *Ginza R.* XVI,5 (p. 390. 17–20) the redeemed one says: "From the day I grew fond of life, from the day my heart grew fond of Kušta, I no longer believed in anything in the world."

19 Naturally ἀγαπᾶν does not mean love in the sense of Christian ἀγάπη but, in accordance with common Greek usage, "Appetitus," to take a fancy to, to place a higher value on, as in Jn 3:19; 12:43; Tim 4:10; etc. See Bauer *s.v.*, also Windisch–

Preisker on 2:15.

20 Schnackenburg, p. 128, puts it well: "Finally . . . love for the father is only the offshoot of the father's love bestowed upon the Christian."

21 See above, pp. 25f on v 5. In this case one would have to assume that, if vss 15–17 stem from the redactor, he imitated the style of the author (or his Source).

22 The formulation, to be sure, is illogical: ἐπιθυμία is awakened by "the things in the world" and "all that is in the world," but does not itself belong to them.

as the origin of sin.[23] Whether and how ἐπιθυμία τῶν ὀφθαλμῶν ("lust of the eyes") differs from ἐπιθυμία τῆς σαρκός ("lust of the flesh") can scarcely be determined. It can refer especially to sexual lust, but can also mean everything that entices the eyes. Ἀλαζονεία τοῦ βίου ("pride of life") is ostentation, boasting,[24] to which worldly góods entice.[25]

The antagonism of man, who makes himself dependent upon the world rather than upon God, is thereby described. This dependence is finally expressed by the characterization that all of this is οὐκ ἔστιν ἐκ τοῦ πατρός, ἀλλὰ ἐκ τοῦ κόσμου ἐστίν ("is not of the father, but is of the world"). This εἶναι ἐκ ("to be of") designates not only the origin, but also what is determined by it, and therefore the being of him to whom it is applicable.[26]

■ 17 What "is of the world" (εἶναι ἐκ τοῦ κόσμου) falls under the judgment of nothingness, v 17: καὶ ὁ κόσμος παράγεται καὶ ἡ ἐπιθυμία αὐτοῦ ("And the world is passing away and the lust of it").[27] Παράγεται ("passing away") does not have the same sense as in v 8. It does not mean that the "world" is (now) passing away (as in 1 Cor 7:31), but that, as "world," it is transitory.[28] In contrast to this, "he who does the will of God abides forever" (ὁ δὲ ποιῶν τὸ θέλημα τοῦ θεοῦ μένει εἰς τὸν αἰῶνα). It is strange that the traditional formulation, "he who does the will of God,"[29] appears here instead of "he who loves God," which is to be expected after v 15. Here μένειν ("abide") does not mean "to remain true" (as in vss 6, 10, 14), but abiding in the sense of enduring, of imperishability, as in 3:15.[30]

---

23 Cf. how Eph 2:3 speaks of ἐπιθυμίαι τῆς σαρκός ("passions of the flesh") and how 1 Petr 2:11; Did 1:4 speak of σαρκικαὶ ἐπιθυμίαι ("fleshly passions"). Cf. Bultmann, *Theology of the New Testament* I, tr. Kendrick Grobel, (New York: Charles Scribner's Sons, 1951), §§ 22, 23. This concept, which is foreign to Old Testament and Jewish thought, has its counterpart in the Qumran texts. Cf. Schnackenburg, p. 129; Braun, "Qumran und das Neue Testament," 105 [201]. Also cf. κοσμικαὶ ἐπιθυμίαι ("worldly passions") Tit 2:12; 2 Clem 17:3. For ἐπιθυμία in the sense of evil desire and lust, see Bauer *s.v.* Vss 15f stand particularly close to Gnostic statements to the effect that concupiscence is the basic trait of human nature; cf., e.g., *Ginza R.* I, 14 (p. 16); II, 4, 67 (p. 62); III, 79 (p. 78). In addition, Jonas, *Gnosis und spätantiker Geist*, I:118; on p. 130 n. 1 note generally the comments on Mandaean parenesis. Cf. also what is said, p. 33 n. 18 (on v 16), concerning the dualistic cosmos–concept.

24 Ἀλαζονεία as in Jas 4:16; Wisd Sol 5:8: τί ὠφέλησεν ἡμᾶς ἡ ὑπερηφανία; καὶ τί πλοῦτος μετὰ ἀλαζονείας συμβέβληται ἡμῖν; ("What did our arrogancy profit us? And what good have riches and vaunting brought us?"). [Charles, I, 542] P. Joüon ("1 Jean 2,16: ἡ ἀλαζονεία τοῦ βίου 'La présomption des richesses,' " *RechSR* 28 [1938]: 479–481) paraphrases: "C'est cette confiance téméraire, cette

présomption, occasionné fatalement par les richesses" ("It is this rash conceit, this overweeningness, made inevitable by riches"). Dodd, *ad loc.*, refers to Theophrastus, *Charact.* 23, where ἀλαζονεία means braggartism.

25 Βίος ("life") here has the sense of worldly goods, as in 3:17; Mk 12:44.

26 Concerning εἶναι ἐκ, cf. 2:21; 4:1–7; 3 Jn 11; Jn 3:31; 18:36; Bultmann, p. 138 n. 1 [97 n. 3]; Schnackenburg, p. 131.

27 Verse 17 is an aphorism, which is perhaps taken from the tradition. The antithetical *parallelismus membrorum* does not correspond to the style of the Johannine antitheses.

28 Cf. 2 Clem 6:6: οἰόμεθα ὅτι βέλτιόν ἐστιν τὰ ἐντάδε μισῆσαι, ὅτι μικρὰ καὶ ὀλιγοχρόνια καὶ φθαρτά ("We think that it is better to hate what is here, for it is trifling, transitory, and perishable . . .") [LCC, I, 195].

29 A common expression in Judaism as in primitive Christianity; see Jn 4:34, Bultmann, p. 194 n. 3 [143 n. 3].

30 On εἰς τὸν αἰῶνα ("forever"), see Jn 4:14, Bultmann, p. 186 n. 4 [p. 137 n. 1].

2   Warning against the False Teachers

18   Children, it is the last hour; and as you have heard that antichrist is coming, so now many antichrists have come; therefore we know that it is the last hour. 19 / They went out from us, but they were not of us; for if they had been of us, they would have continued with us; but they went out, that it might be plain that they all are not of us. 20 / But you have been anointed by the Holy One, and you all know. 21 / I write to you, not because you do not know the truth, but because you know it, and know that no lie is of the truth. 22 / Who is the liar but he who denies that Jesus is the Christ? This is the antichrist, he who denies the Father and the Son. 23 / No one who denies the Son has the Father. He who confesses the Son has the Father also. 24 / Let what you heard from the beginning abide in you. If what you heard from the beginning abides in you, then you will abide in the Son and in the Father. 25 / And this is what he has promised us, eternal life.

26   I write this to you about those who would deceive you; 27 / but the anointing which you received from him abides in you, and you have no need that any one should teach you; as his anointing teaches you about everything, and is true, and is no lie, just as it has taught you, abide in it.

[RSV modified]

Now, finally, the author enters into direct confrontation with the false teachers, a confrontation that indirectly had already determined the preceding exposition.[1] It is not a final confrontation; in 4:1 the theme is taken up again, and it emerges afresh in 5:4. Parenetical expositions are inserted between or are attached; 2:18–27 is a self–contained unit that begins with a new address,

παιδία ("children"), as in v 14. Verse 26, with its retrospective ταῦτα ἔγραψα ὑμῖν ("I write these things to you"), is an obvious closing.

■ 18 Whereas the false teachers are designated as πλανῶντες ὑμᾶς ("those deceiving you") in v 26, in v 18 they are designated as ἀντίχριστοι ("antichrists"). With this designation the author takes up a term of Jewish

1   Dodd, *ad loc.*, thinks he can establish a connection with what precedes: that it is now the "last hour" is connected with the eschatological content of v 17. But does v 17 really have eschatological content?

See above on v 17.

apocalyptic, while reinterpreting it in typically Johannine fashion. He refers to the traditional apocalyptic
expectation (καθὼς ἠκούσατε, "as you have heard")
that the antichrist will appear at the end of time.[2] When
the author then says: καὶ νῦν ἀντίχριστοι πολλοὶ γε-
γόνασιν ("and now many antichrists have come"), he
historicizes the mythical figure;[3] the antichrists are
the false teachers, and everyone who denies that Jesus is
the Christ (v 22), who does not "confess" him (4:3),
who does not acknowledge that Jesus has come in the
flesh (2 Jn 7), is an antichrist. The fact that these antichrists
have arisen is the sign ὅτι ἐσχάτη ὥρα ἐστίν ("that it is
the last hour"). For it is indeed presupposed that Jesus'
coming is the last hour for the κόσμος ("world").[4] It
is just that to which the deniers of Christ indirectly testify. To this extent this assertion has the same meaning
as v 8: "the darkness is passing away and the true light is
already shining." But this is exactly what can and should
be confirmed for the readers by the appearance of the
false teachers.[5]

■ **19** That the false teachers claim to be Christians follows from v 19: ἐξ ἡμῶν ἐξῆλθαν ἀλλ᾽ οὐκ ἦσαν ἐξ ἡμῶν
("they went out from us, but they were not of us"). The

negative assertion shows that the false teachers claim
to belong to the Christian congregation, but unjusti-
fiably so, as the author gives the reader to understand by
the ambiguous sense of ἐξ ("out of/from"): the heretical
teachers belonged to the congregation at one time, for
they emerged from it. That certainly does not mean
that they were excluded (by excommunication, for
instance), nor does it mean that they organized themselves independently (for instance, as a sect). The repeated warnings against them show that they constitute
a present danger to the congregation, and therefore
understand themselves as legitimate members of the
congregation. In the author's judgment, that is a false
assertion: "but they were not of (ἐξ) us," i.e., they doubtless went out of the congregation, but they did not stem
"from" it, in truth they never essentially belonged to
it.[6] For, as v 19b stipulates, had they really, essentially
belonged to the congregation, they would also have re-
mained in it. That of course means, for the author, that
they would have adhered to the orthodox faith. However,
that they did not do so has a peculiar significance (v
19c): ἀλλ᾽ ἵνα φανερωθῶσιν ὅτι οὐκ εἰσὶν πάντες ἐξ
ἡμῶν ("that it might be plain that all are not of us").[7]

---

2   The term ἀντίχριστος is found both in the New
     Testament (only here and in vss 22; 4:3; 2 Jn 7) and
     in the later tradition. Regarding the history of the
     term and above all the figure, see the literature
     cited by Bauer s.v. The first and also primary inves-
     tigation is that of Wilhelm Bousset, *Der Antichrist in
     der Überlieferung des Judentums, des Neuen Testaments
     und der alten Kirche* (Göttingen: 1895). Most recently,
     see Ernst Lohmeyer, "Antichrist," *RAC* I: 450–57,
     and Schnackenburg, Excursus, pp. 145–49.
3   The figure of the antichrist has also been histori-
     cized elsewhere, to be sure, usually with reference to
     a specific individual. In Rev 13:1–8 it appears as
     the Roman empire; in Rev 13:11–18; 2 Thess 2:1–12
     as a false prophet. In this connection cf. Martin
     Dibelius, Excursus to 2 Thess 2:10, in *An die Thes-
     salonicher I/II–An die Philipper*. Handbuch zum Neuen
     Testament 11 (Tübingen, 1937).
4   Cf. Jn 4:23; 5:25; 11:24f. The phrases ἐσχάτη ὥρα

     ("last hour"), ἐπ᾽ ἐσχάτων τῶν ἡμερῶν ("at the
     last days"), and the like stem from Old Testament-
     Jewish apocalyptic. Cf. Schnackenburg, p. 142 n. 2.
5   Schnackenburg (pp. 143f) wants, as do others, to
     maintain that the appearance of the true antichrist
     is yet to come. He therefore contests that the his-
     toricization of the apocalyptic figure is radical; cf.
     especially p. 144 n. 2.
6   It is characteristically Johannine to designate the
     nature of something by reference to its origin, as
     in 2:21; 3:8, 10; etc. Cf., e.g., Jn 3:31; 8:23; etc.;
     Bultmann, p. 138 n. 1 [97 n. 3]; p. 162 n. 3 [117 n. 6].
7   Ἀλλ᾽ ἵνα is elliptical, as in Jn 1:8; 13:18. The for-
     mulation is not entirely logical because two thoughts
     are conflated: ἀλλ᾽ ἵνα φανερωθῇ, ὅτι οὐκ εἰσὶν
     πάντες ἐξ ἡμῶν ("but to make it plain that not all
     are of us"), and ἀλλ᾽ ἵνα φανερωθῶσιν, ὅτι οὐκ
     εἰσὶν ἐξ ἡμῶν ("but that they [viz., the false teach-
     ers] might be made evident, that they are not of us")

"That all are not of us" does not mean: "they all, the false teachers, do not belong to us," but rather: "not all (who so claim) belong to us."[8] The statement permits recognition of the distinction between the empirical and the true congregation: false members are therefore to be found in the empirical congregation. The sentence is thus also an admonition to critical examination and certainly to self–examination as well.

■ 20 As vss 20f show, the author is confident of what bears upon this examination: The readers possess the correct standard for the critical examination: καὶ ὑμεῖς χρῖσμα ἔχετε ἀπὸ τοῦ ἁγίου ("and you have been anointed by the holy one"). Whether God or Jesus Christ is meant by "holy one" is debatable.[9] Since ἀπ᾽ αὐτοῦ ("from him") in v 27a refers to Jesus, and he is mentioned in v 25 as αὐτός ("he"), the latter is probable. The meaning of this sentence is derived from what follows: καὶ οἴδατε πάντες ("and you all know"),[10] which is completed in v 21, where it is certified that the readers know the truth.[11] The meaning of "you all know" is evidently the same as in 1 Cor 8:1: οἴδαμεν ὅτι πάντες γνῶσιν ἔχομεν ("we know that all of us possess knowledge"), and it is curious that the author did not simply say καὶ ὑμεῖς γνῶσιν ἔχετε ("and you possess knowledge"). Instead, he makes reference to the possession of χρῖσμα ("anointing") as the source of γνῶσις ("knowledge"), as v 27 stipulates: τὸ αὐτοῦ χρῖσμα διδάσκει ὑμᾶς ("his anointing teaches you"). On second thought, it is curious that the author did not write ὑμεῖς πνεῦμα ἔχετε ("you possess the spirit"), since in 3:24 and 4:13 knowledge is traced back to the "spirit." That the author mentions "anointing" rather than "spirit" probably owes to the fact that "anointing" played an important role in Gnosticism, viz., as the sacrament of anointing.[12] There is probably also an allusion to baptism; however, it is not primarily the rite of baptism that the author has in mind, since the heretics (who certainly understand themselves as members of the congregation) doubtless also received baptism. The author thus gives a new meaning to the sacrament of anointing, just as he reinterpreted the apocalyptic figure of the antichrist in v 18. To be sure, he does not historicize it in the same way, since anointing does not signify a historically observable process, but he does historicize it to the extent that he interprets it as a real experience, namely, in relation to the reception of the "spirit" on

---

8   Schnackenburg, p. 151, interprets differently.

9   The "holy one" is certainly an epithet of God in the Old Testament, but Jesus, too, can be designated as the holy one, Jn 6:69; cf. Bultmann, pp. 448f [344].

10 Πάντα (accusative: "and you know all things") instead of πάντες (nominative: "and you all know") is not poorly attested, but is nevertheless probably a correction. It is indeed striking that οἴδατε, in that case, has no object, but it was precisely this that prompted the correction to πάντα.

11 Ἀλήθεια and ψεῦδος here bear the simple sense of truth and falsehood, since it is a question of knowledge. This is shown clearly by the formulation in 2:22, where ψεύστης ("liar") is characterized as ὁ ἀρνούμενος ὅτι . . . ("the one denying that . . ."). The overtones "reality" and "nothingness" are thus not present (see pp. 18f on 1:6); however, Schnackenburg, p. 155, seems to think so.

12 Χρῖσμα means oil for anointing; however, the reception of anointing oil naturally means the act of anointing. Verse 20 appears to refer to an anointing as it was connected, in all likelihood, with baptism and the laying on of hands in the primitive church. The designation of baptism as χρῖσμα is first certainly attested in Gregory of Nazianzus. Nevertheless, it is quite possible that baptism was so designated already in primitive Christianity, just as ὁ . . . χρίσας ἡμᾶς κτλ. ("the . . . one anointing us . . .") in 2 Cor 1:21 probably refers to baptism. Cf. Lietzmann, *An die Korinther I/II.* Handbuch zum Neuen Testament 9 (Tübingen: 1969) on 2 Cor 1:22. On anointing with oil in Gnostic sects, see Schnackenburg, p. 152 notes 3 and 4. He speaks, p. 152 n. 2, of Reitzenstein's interpretation of χρῖσμα with reference to baptism, but Schnackenburg understands it as a symbol for doctrine.

the part of the believers. It is therefore an experience because it bestows knowledge, of whose possession the believers may be assured.

■ **21** Verse 21 simply confirms what has been said in v 20, in that the author assures the readers, in a negative and positive statement, that they know the truth,[13] and that they know that all lies (in this case, the false doctrine) do not arise from the truth. The "truth" acquires a fuller sense in the third ὅτι–clause than in the first: when the author says of the "lie," ἐκ τῆς ἀληθείας οὐκ ἔστιν ("it is not of the truth"), "truth" does not have the formal sense, but means (divine) reality.[14]

■ **22** In v 22 it is finally said what the heretical teaching is against which the congregation is warned. The question τίς ἐστιν ὁ ψεύστης εἰ μὴ κτλ. ("Who is the liar but . . .?") is not intended to define the "liar" (or does so only indirectly), but is rather designed to provide a basis for the historicization of the figure of the antichrist effected in v 18: who is to be called a liar other than the one who does not recognize Jesus as the Christ? And precisely he is the antichrist. The sacrilege of such a "denial" is characterized by the phrase, ὁ ἀρνούμενος τὸν πατέρα καὶ τὸν υἱόν ("the one denying the Father and the Son"), which stands in apposition to ὁ ἀντί-χριστος ("the antichrist").[15] The characterization is intelligible without further ado. As 1:2f already indicated, Father and Son belong together as a unity; and in 5:5 the content of the faith is embraced in the assertion, ὅτι Ἰησοῦς ἐστίν ὁ υἱὸς τοῦ θεοῦ ("Jesus is the Son of God"). Whoever then has a perverted view of Jesus, by that very fact also thinks wrongly of God. That, of course,

means: God is always to be perceived in his revelation in Jesus, just as, according to Jn 17:3, the knowledge of God and Jesus belong together.[16] There is, for the author, no such thing as faith in God apart from the historical revelation. The denial that Jesus is the Christ is thus nothing more or less than a denial of God.

The question now arises, in what sense do the heretical teachers deny that Jesus is the Christ? Since they belong, or claim to belong, to the Christian congregation, they must have believed in Christ in some sense, must have understood him as the revealer or bringer of salvation, indeed, even as the preexistent one (see below). In what sense they believed can only become clear when one perceives in what sense they denied his divine sonship.

According to 4:2f and 2 Jn 7 they dispute that Jesus Christ "came in the flesh," and when in 5:6 it is claimed, in opposition to them, that Jesus came δι᾽ ὕδατος καὶ αἵματος ("by water and blood"), then everything points to the fact that they deny that the Christ is identical with the earthly, historical Jesus. That can only be understood from the standpoint that the doctrine of the heretics is rooted in the dualism of Gnosticism, which asserts the exclusive antithesis between God and the sensible world. It is a secondary question whether we can determine more precisely the specific Gnostic tendency or sect that the author had in mind.[17] The decisive point is that Gnostic thought cannot comprehend the offense which the Christian idea of revelation offers, namely, the paradox that a historical event (or historical form) is the eschatological event (or form).

Since it is all but certain that the words of the author

13 Ὅτι is not to be understood causally, but as ὅτι–recitativum, as ἔγραψα requires; otherwise the verb would require ταῦτα as an object (as Schnackenburg correctly states, p. 154 n. 6). If the first two instances of ὅτι are dependent on ἔγραψα, the third is perhaps dependent on οἴδατε.

14 On εἶναι ἐκ, see p. 36 n. 6 on v 19; on ἀλήθεια, see above, pp. 18f, 22.

15 Schnackenburg, p. 157: "ὁ ἀρνούμενος picks up the ὁ ἀρνούμενος of v 22a and explains οὗτος."

16 Cf. further Jn 5:23: whoever honors the Son also honors the Father; 8:19; 14:7: whoever knows him also knows the Father; 15:23: whoever hates him also hates the Father; 16:3: whoever does not know him does not know the Father either; 14:9: whoever has seen him has also seen the Father; cf. further 12:44f. Cf. Bultmann, *passim*, e.g., pp. 607ff [469ff].

17 One is perhaps reminded of the disciples of Cerinthus, who indeed held Jesus to be a natural son of Joseph and Mary, but into whom, at his baptism,

(or his Source) regarding "fellowship" (1:6f), "keeping the commandments" (2:3f), and brotherly love (2:9–11), are aimed at the heretics, it must be concluded that they draw consequences from their doctrine that threaten or even destroy community life and Christian brotherhood. That does not mean that they organized themselves independently (as a sect), for they are evidently a danger to the believers within the congregation.[18] Even within the congregation they feel themselves sinless (1:8–10), and therefore despise the brothers who are not like–minded. It also does not follow from the indirect reproach that they do not keep the commandments (2:3f), that they disregard and overstep the moral commandments as libertines or pneumatics. The commandment they infringe is precisely brotherly love, which they lack.[19] It is not evident that they distinguish themselves, as do the gnosticizing Christians, by libertine spiritualism and ecstatic fanaticism. Their self–consciousness is apparently their consciousness that they have the right doctrine.[20] They are to be regarded as a group of "orthodox" people, who, within the congregation, hold themselves aloof from others and prompt others to take note of the fact— a type, therefore, that asserts itself again and again.

It can now only with difficulty be said whether or to what extent the author understands the incarnation of Jesus Christ mythologically, or whether he interprets the mythological assertion on the basis of the idea of

revelation, as does the Gospel of John (cf. Bultmann, pp. 60–66 [38–43]). In any case, he adheres to the identity of the historical event (the historical figure of Jesus) and the eschatological event (Jesus the "Christ," the "Son"). Cf. pp. 8ff on 1:1–3.

■ **23** In v 23 the author repeats the thought of v 22. In so doing he evidently takes a passage from the Source, for which the typical antithetical parallelism is characteristic:[21]

πᾶς ὁ ἀρνούμενος τὸν υἱόν
 οὐδὲ τὸν πατέρα ἔχει
ὁ ὁμολογῶν τὸν υἱόν
 καὶ τὸν πατέρα ἔχει.

No one denying the Son
 Has the Father
He who confesses the Son
 Has the Father also.

The relationship to the Father is here designated by ἔχειν ("have"), as in 2 Jn 9. This term does not differ materially from γινώσκειν ("know"), since the latter does not denote a theoretical knowledge, but that relationship in which the one knowing is determined existentially by the one who is the object of knowledge.[22]

■ **24** The author resumes in v 24 with his own formulation, and to the readers he addresses an admonition that flows out of the preceding: ὑμεῖς ὃ ἠκούσατε ἀπ' ἀρχῆς, ἐν ὑμῖν μενέτω ("Let what you heard from the

---

the "Christ" descended from the higher world (see Schnackenburg, p. 20). Or one may think of the "Docetics," who did not confess Jesus as the σαρκο-φόρος ("clothed in flesh," Ign. *Sm.* 5.2) and against whom Ignatius of Antioch contended (see Schnackenburg, pp. 20–22). In any case, it cannot be a matter of Jewish heretics ("Judaizers"). The "law" is nowhere the subject of debate. On the question of heretics, also cf. Braun, "Literar-Analyse," 287–92 [237–42].

18 See above, pp. 36f on 2:19.

19 See above, pp. 24ff on 2:3f.

20 Correctly Schnackenburg, pp. 17, 23.

21 Πᾶς ὁ with a participle is also characteristic; cf. v 29; 3:4, 6, 9, 10, 15; 4:7; 5:4; frequently imitated by the author, cf. 4:2f; 5:1.

22 See above, pp. 24ff on 2:3f. It is possible that the phrase ἔχειν θεόν derives from Gnosticism; see H. Hanse, "*Gott haben" in der Antike und im frühen Christentum: Eine religions- und begriffsgeschichtliche Untersuchung* (Berlin: Töpelmann, 1939). On ὁμολογεῖν, see p. 21 n. 28 on 1:9 and see 4:2f, 15; 2 Jn 7.

beginning abide in you"). It is an exhortation to faith-fulness.[23] In the context the meaning is self–evident, namely, that what they heard from the beginning is that Jesus is the Christ.[24] The exhortation is followed by the promise, which has the form of a conditional clause: ἐὰν ἐν ὑμῖν μείνῃ . . . καὶ ὑμεῖς . . . μενεῖτε ("If . . . abides in you, then you will abide . . .").[25] The corres-pondence of μένειν ἐν ὑμῖν ("abide in you") and μένειν ἐν τῷ υἱῷ καὶ τῷ πατρί ("abide in the Son and in the Father") is clear: the promise corresponds to the faith-fulness of the believers.

■ **25** The promise is expressly formulated in v 25: καὶ αὕτη ἐστὶν ἡ ἐπαγγελία κτλ. ("and this is the prom-ise. . .").[26] What is promised for faithfulness is ζωὴ αἰ-ώνιος ("eternal life"). Since "life" and "eternal life" are apparently used in the same sense,[27] it may be asked whether αἰώνιος ("eternal") has chronological meaning at all and is not simply a designation of quality. How-ever, both are presumably the case.

The corresponding question then arises whether ἐπαγ-γελία is the promise for the future, or whether it is the promise already fulfilled for the believers. There is certainly no question that, for the author, the present is still not fulfillment, and that it has not yet appeared "what we shall be" (3:2). In the same sentence, how-ever, it is affirmed that "we are God's children now," and the believers know that they "have passed out of

death into life" (3:14), insofar as they love the brethren; and the author gives the final assurance: "He who has the Son has life" (5:12). The promise is thus fulfilled, and yet again it is not; it points to the future just as surely as it is valid for the present.[28] Whether the pecu-liar double sense of "eternal life" and of "promise" is significant for the author, in contrast to Gnosticism, can scarcely be ascertained. The actual contrast to the Gnos-tic self–understanding, however, is clear. For the Gnostic, "life" is an assured possession, and he lacks the con-sciousness that he is a being 'on-the-way,' which is decisive for the Christian faith. This notion is also given expression in the hortatory passages of the epistle, which alternate with the didactic passages; the latter serve to strengthen the believers by bringing to consciousness that which has already been given to the present.

■ **26** Verses 26 and 27 introduce no new theme and no new thoughts, but are rather a somewhat extensive homiletical reinforcement and exhortation. The author introduces the section with ταῦτα ἔγραψα ὑμῖν ("I write these things to you"), looking back to what was said in vss 18–25:[29] περὶ τῶν πλανώντων ὑμᾶς ("about those who would deceive you"). The false teachers are designated as false leaders or seducers: in 3:7 the readers will be warned, μηδεὶς πλανάτω ὑμᾶς ("Let no one deceive you"), and in 4:6 the πνεῦμα τῆς πλάνης ("spirit of error") will be spoken of; in 2 John the false

23 On μένειν, see p. 26 n. 9 on 2:6. The ὑμεῖς added after οὖν in the Koine text is a pedantic correction (Schnackenburg).

24 On ἀπ' ἀρχῆς ("from the beginning"), as in 2:7, see p. 9 n. 10. Ὑμεῖς ("you") is a preceding suspended case; see Blass–Debrunner §466(1).

25 Καὶ ὑμεῖς ("and you") initiates the apodosis and so does not belong to the if–clause. Otherwise a μείνητε ("if you abide"), on the analogy of the preceding μείνῃ ("abides"), would have to be supplied, and that is very unlikely.

26 Αὕτη ("this") refers of course to what follows; cf. 1:5; 3:11; 5:11, 14. Ἐπαγγελία and ἐπαγγέλλε-σθαι ("promise") appear only here in 1 John; they

are also lacking in John. Αὐτός ("he") can only refer to Jesus Christ, not God. The reading ὑμῖν instead of ἡμῖν is probably caused by the ἐν ὑμῖν of v 24.

27 Ζωὴ αἰώνιος ("eternal life") occurs in 1:2; 3:15; 5:11, 13, 20, as often in John. It is not distinguished from ζωή ("life"), as the interchange in 1:2; 3:14f; 5:11f shows. Cf. Bultmann, p. 152 n. 2 [109 n. 2] on Jn 3:15. The accusative τὴν ζωὴν αἰώνιον, instead of an expected nominative, is caused by the pre-ceding relative clause, ἣν κτλ. (inverse attraction, Blass–Debrunner §295).

28 In John the emphasis is on the present possession of life; cf. 3:18, 36; 5:24; 11:25f (cf. Bultmann, passim, especially pp. 154f [111f], pp. 166f [121], pp. 257ff

teachers will be called πλάνοι ("deceivers"), and in each "deceiver" the "antichrist" is embodied.

■ **27** That the "deceivers" constitute a danger for the congregation and apparently propagandize is shown by v 27, in which the thought of vss 20f is repeated in order to buttress the self–consciousness of the believers: they have χρῖσμα ("anointing") from him (from Jesus Christ), and the author trusts that it will remain in them and that they therefore require no (further) instruction.[30] The indicative μένει includes the imperative μένετε ἐν αὐτῷ ("you abide in it").[31] The reader is to abide in what the χρῖσμα teaches,[32] corresponding (ὡς[33]) to the fact that it teaches περὶ πάντων ("about everything"), and that it is absolutely trustworthy.[34]

[193ff], pp. 402ff [307ff]). Nevertheless, the futuristic perspective is not lacking; 14:1ff; 17:24–26 (Bultmann, pp. 600ff [463ff], pp. 518ff [397ff]).

29 Ἔγραψα ("I write") refers, of course, to the present letter, as in 2:14f, 21; 5:13. Ταῦτα ("these things") refers to what precedes, as in 5:13.

30 Καὶ ὑμεῖς ("and you") is again a preceding suspended case, as in v 24. Τις ("any one") refers, of course, to the false teachers (Schnackenburg, p. 161, interprets differently). But it could also refer to the author, who would then be saying: I do not need to instruct you either.

31 The author again employs μένειν ἐν bilaterally, as in v 24. The ἐν αὐτῷ will here have to be referred to χρῖσμα, although μένετε ἐν αὐτῷ ("you abide in him") in v 27 can only refer to Jesus Christ.

32 There is no essential difference between διδάσκει and ἐδίδαξεν. On this subject, also see Conzelmann, " 'Was von Anfang war,' " 201, n. 22.

33 Ὡς is hardly to be omitted as in Codex B; the omission apparently only intends to alleviate the construction.

34 Ἀληθές ("true") corresponds to ἀλήθεια ("truth") in 2:21; analogously, ψεῦδος means lie, untruth, as also in v 21. Καὶ ἀληθές ἐστιν κτλ. ("and is true...") is hardly parenthetical; rather, it is the main clause going with ἀλλ' ὡς ... ("but as his anointing...")

2

Children of God and
Brotherly Love

28 And now, little children, abide in him, so that when he appears we may have confidence and not shrink from him in shame at his coming. 29 / If you know that he is righteous, you may be sure that every one who does right is born of him.

3

1 See what love the Father has given us, that we should be called children of God; and so we are. The reason why the world does not know us is that it did not know him. 2 / Beloved, we are God's children now; it does not yet appear what we shall be, but we know that when he appears we shall be like him, for we shall see him as he is. 3 / And every one who thus hopes in him purifies himself as he is pure.

4 Every one who commits sin is guilty of lawlessness; sin is lawlessness. 5 / You know that he appeared to take away sins, and in him there is no sin. 6 / No one who abides in him sins; no one who sins has either seen him or known him. 7 / Little children, let no one deceive you. He who does right is righteous, as he is righteous. 8 / He who commits sin is of the devil; for the devil has sinned from the beginning. The reason the Son of God appeared was to destroy the works of the devil. 9 / No one born of God commits sin; for God's seed abides in him, and he cannot sin because he is born of God. 10 / By this it may be seen who are the children of God, and who are the children of the devil: no one who does not do right is of God, nor any one who does not love his brother.

11 For this is the message which you have heard from the beginning, that we should love one another, 12 / and not be like Cain who was of the evil one and murdered his brother. And why did he murder him? Because his own deeds were evil and his brother's righteous. 13 / Do not wonder, brethren, that the world hates you. 14 / We know that we have passed out of death into life, because we love the brethren. He who does not love remains in death. 15 / Any one who hates his brother is a murderer, and you know that no murderer has eternal life abiding in him. 16 / By this

we know love, that he laid down his life for us; and we ought to lay down our lives for the brethren. 17 / But if any one has the world's goods and sees his brother in need, yet closes his heart against him, how does God's love abide in him? 18 / Little children, let us not love in word or speech but in deed and in truth.

19   By this we shall know that we are of the truth, and reassure our hearts before him 20 / whenever our hearts condemn us; for God is greater than our hearts, and he knows everything. 21 / Beloved, if our hearts do not condemn us, we have confidence before God; 22 / and we receive from him whatever we ask, because we keep his commandments and do what pleases him. 23 / And this is his commandment, that we should believe in the name of his Son Jesus Christ and love one another, just as he has commanded us. 24 / All who keep his commandments abide in him, and he in them. And by this we know that he abides in us, by the Spirit which he has given us.

[RSV modified]

The Epistle could have been concluded with 2:27 and originally probably was. The following sections contain no new ideas, but the same themes treated in 1:5–2:27 recur. There are occasional variations and new formulations, which are sometimes especially impressive. In 2:28 (2:29–3:34) is treated the correlation of a filial relation to God and brotherly love, a theme that was the point in 2:3–11 (knowledge of God and keeping the commandments), and one that was made indirectly in 1:5–10 (in the charge to have "fellowship with one another"). The Epistle could also be concluded with 3:24. However, there follows in 4:1–6 once again the warning against false teaching, which had been the theme of 2:18–27. This theme is combined with the motifs of ὁμολογεῖν ("confess"), taken from 2:23, and παρρησία ("confidence"), drawn from 2:28; 3:21. The new section

4:7–12 again treats brotherly love, which was the dominant motif in 2:28–3:24. The theme of brotherly love is taken up once more in 4:19–5:4, following the relatively brief reappearance of the motifs of "confession" and "confidence" in 4:13–18. Although the terminology is new, the content is not, being interlaced with the motifs of confession and faith (from 2:18–27) and of love. Finally, 5:4–12 returns to the theme of faith.

    Attempts to find a train of thought in 2:28–5:12 are futile. The whole section 2:28–5:12 is obviously not a coherent organic composition, but rather a compendium of various fragments collected as a supplement to 1:5–

2:27.[1] The entire section cannot be distinguished at all, with respect to theological content, from 1:5–2:27, and every one of its individual parts could have been written by the same author. One is tempted to conjecture that all these parts are sketches or meditations (indeed, one may be so bold as to inquire whether they are not reports from sessions of a seminar). It may be asked whether the author of 1:5–2:27 appended these sections himself, or whether his disciples added them, drawing upon the author's legacy.[2]

To be sure, the composition is not accidental and indiscriminate, but is guided by a sequence of thought, albeit quite loosely. When one considers that the theme of the filial relation to God, in 2:28–3:10a, is occasioned by the false teaching, namely by the Gnostic (or gnosticizing) notion of being begotten from God, then it becomes understandable that brotherly love appears as the express theme of 3:10b–24. For, deviant faith and the sin which consists of disregard of brotherly love hang

together, as 2:3–11 has already shown. This consideration leads to the independent treatment of the related themes of filial relation to God (2:29–3:9) and brotherly love (3:10–24), before the theme of false teaching is again taken up in 4:1. The addition of the subsequent passages was also guided by associations suggested by the preceding sections.

Although the whole Epistle is not a unified composition, but a compendium of various sections, it is nevertheless unified with regard to content. In this sense, the exegete should interpret the whole Epistle also as a unity. Accordingly, in what follows one may speak again simply of "the author."

■ **28** In 2:28 there is a formal transition to the theme, children of God, in that μένετε ἐν αὐτῷ ("you abide in him") is taken up from v 27.[3] It is doubtful, however, whether this transition stems from the author himself, or whether it was added by the ecclesiastical redactor.[4]

■ **29ff** Underlying the section 2:29–3:10 is probably a

---

1   This is not a question of source-analysis, either in the limited sense of editorial comments on and additions to a prior written source or of an extensive ecclesiastical redaction of the entire letter.

2   When dealing with the later compositions—if not the original versions—of many New Testament writings, one must, as a rule, take into account the possible existence of "schools" (although not in a formal sense). See Krister Stendahl, *The School of St. Matthew* (Philadelphia: Fortress Press, ²1968); Hans Conzelmann, "Paulus und die Weisheit," *NTS* 12 (1966): 231–44. That Schnackenburg also assumes a Johannine school is clear from the following remark on p. 41: "The scholar who retains, on balance, the view that the Apostle John, the son of Zebedee, is the author of the Fourth Gospel is not thereby prevented from also affirming that the author of I John is one of his students or at least one who shares his views."

3   Although μένετε ἐν αὐτῷ is an admonition to correct faith in v 27, in v 28 it seems to take on the larger sense of an admonition to correct conduct. The same form of address, τεκνία, is used here as in 2:1 (see above, p. 22 n. 34). Νῦν evidently has an inferential rather than a temporal sense: "now then"

(Schnackenburg).

4   I expressed the view in "Die kirchliche Redaktion," p. 196, that the editor merely reworked this verse. It is more likely, however, that the entire verse stems from his hand. On the basis of v 27 αὐτός ("him"), of whom it is said μένετε ἐν αὐτῷ ("abide in him"), can only refer to Jesus. Verse 28 speaks about his φανερωθῆναι ("appearance") and his παρουσία ("coming"). Therefore, v 28 (as well as 3:2; see below, pp. 48f) reflects the traditional eschatology, whereas the φανερωθῆναι ("manifestation") in 1:2; 3:5, 8, refers to the historical existence of Jesus. Moreover, παρουσία ("coming") occurs only here in 1 John (it does not occur at all in the Gospel of John). Likewise, the linking of μὴ αἰσχυνθῆναι (to be translated as a passive, "to be put to shame, to be disgraced," and not as a middle, "to feel ashamed") to παρρησίαν ἔχειν ("to have confidence") to form a hendiadys occurs only here in 1 John and not at all in the Gospel of John. The motif of παρρησία ("confidence") is also taken up in 3:21, but as παρρησία πρὸς τὸν θεόν ("confidence toward God"), whereas its meaning in 4:17 is doubtful and its occurrence in 5:14 owes to the editor. That the lan-

Source, which the author edited and expanded by means of glosses. With the reminder that caution is the better part of wisdom, the text of the Source may be reconstructed as in the accompanying versification:

2:29b πᾶς ὁ ποιῶν τὴν δικαιοσύνην ἐξ αὐτοῦ γεγέννηται,
3:4 πᾶς ὁ ποιῶν τὴν ἁμαρτίαν καὶ τὴν ἀνομίαν ποιεῖ.
3:6 πᾶς ὁ ἐν αὐτῷ μένων οὐχ ἁμαρτάνει.
πᾶς ὁ ἁμαρτάνων οὐχ ἑώρακεν οὐδὲ ἔγνωκεν αὐτόν.
3:7 ὁ ποιῶν τὴν δικαιοσύνην [? ἐκ τοῦ θεοῦ γεγέννηται],
3:8 ὁ ποιῶν τὴν ἁμαρτίαν ἐκ τοῦ διαβόλου ἐστίν.
3:9 πᾶς ὁ γεγεννημένος ἐκ τοῦ θεοῦ ἁμαρτίαν οὐ ποιεῖ,
ὅτι σπέρμα αὐτοῦ ἐν αὐτῷ μένει.
καὶ οὐ δύναται ἁμαρτάνειν
ὅτι ἐκ τοῦ θεοῦ γεγέννηται.

2:29b Every one who does right is born of him,
3:4 Every one who commits sin is guilty of lawlessness.
3:6 No one who abides in him sins.
No one who sins has either seen him or known him.
3:7 He who does right [? is born of God],
3:8 He who commits sin is of the devil.
3:9 No one born of God commits sin,
For his seed abides in him.
And he cannot sin
Because he is born of God. [5]

[RSV modified]

■ **29** Following the transition in v 28, the author intro-

duces the text of his Source in v 29a: ἐὰν εἰδῆτε ὅτι δίκαιός ἐστιν, γινώσκετε ὅτι ("If you know that he is righteous, you may be sure that . . ."). [6] On the basis of the sequel to v 29, it appears that the subject of "righteous" can only be Jesus, who is also characterized in 2:1; 3:7 as "righteous." However, Jesus cannot be intended, if it is immediately said of ποιῶν τὴν δικαιοσύνην ("the one who does right") that ἐξ αὐτοῦ γεγέννηται ("is born of him"). The notion of procreation from Jesus is not viable; the text can only mean born of God, as in 3:9; 4:7; 5:1, 4, which is further supported by the reference to children of God in the verse immediately following (3:1). It should therefore be clear that the second ὅτι–clause (v 29b: "[you may be sure] that every one who does right is born of him") stems from the Source and is clumsily appended by the author to the first ὅτι–clause (v 29a: "that he is righteous"). [7] The second ὅτι–clause (v 29b), taken from the Source, now presents the theme, "born of God," which dominates as far as 3:9. [8] Although the expression γεννηθῆναι ἐκ τοῦ θεοῦ ("born of God") is not attested in the same form in the mystery religions and Gnosticism, nevertheless there can be no doubt that this manner of speaking, i.e., the notion, born of God,

---

guage of v 28 differs from that of the author is also noticed by Schnackenburg (p. 165) when he comments on ". . . the proximity of the author's views, in spite of his own theology, to those of the community."

5 This reconstruction of the Source varies slightly from the one which I proposed earlier in "Analyse des ersten Johannesbriefes," pp. 157f. It is now doubtful to me whether 3:6 belongs to the Source. At least the phrase ὁ ἐν αὐτῷ μένων ("he who abides in him") must be credited to the author since he is very fond of the expression μένειν ἐν ("abide in") (see p. 26 n. 9 on 2:6). The original wording which has been replaced by this phrase probably was ὁ γεγεννημένος ἐκ τοῦ θεοῦ ("he who is born of God"). As I have already suggested in "Analyse des ersten Johannesbriefes," the author has also altered the Source in v 7. For the sentence ὁ ποιῶν τὴν δικαιοσύνην δίκαιός ἐστιν ("the one who does right is righteous") is not only trivial, but also contradicts

the antithetical style. Instead of δίκαιός ἐστιν ("is righteous"), the antithesis of v 7 requires either ἐκ τοῦ θεοῦ ἐστιν ("is of God") or ἐκ τοῦ θεοῦ γεγέννηται ("is born of God") corresponding to 2:29. It appears to me, however, that all of v 9 derives from the Source.

6 Like οἴδατε in 3:5, γινώσκετε is indicative, not imperative.

7 Schnackenburg (pp. 166f) also notices the contradiction between v 29a and 29b. He argues, however, that one should not explain away this "dilemma" by appealing to a Source; rather, one ". . . must assume that the author already has in mind what is to follow and thereby alters this verse accordingly." "V 29 cannot be explained without assuming that the author had already prepared certain concrete formulations as in 3:4ff."

8 See p. 39 n. 21, on 2:23 for a discussion of πᾶς joined to a participle. Whether the weakly attested καί

derives from this sphere.[9] If this formulation, as that in 3:9, comes from the Source, then the author speaks, 3:1f, 10, of being children of God instead of being born of God, although the phrases have the same sense, of course, as the entire sequence of thought shows. The formulation chosen by the author derives from old Jewish tradition.[10]

Schnackenburg does not reject the idea that this language comes from the realm of the mystery religions and Gnosticism, but he is of the opinion that only "terminological contact" is involved (p. 181). But that would be saying too little. The terminological relationship is also a material relationship, because in both spheres (in the Christian proclamation as in Gnosticism) the underlying consciousness is that the old, natural man cannot, without divine assistance, attain the salvation to which he aspires, but that he requires a renewal of his being. The Christian proclamation and Gnosticism are one in holding that this renewal does not spring from man's will and effort, but has its ground in an origin beyond the sphere of the human.

There is required, according to *Corp. Herm.* XIII.14, an οὐσιώδης γένεσις ("a true being"), which has left the old somatic being behind.[11] Παλιγγενεσία ("regeneration") is the theme of the entire tractate XIII of *Corpus Hermeticum*. That it is a gift is expressed by the notion that it depends on the θέλημα ("will") or ἔλεος ("mercy") of God (XIII.2, 3, 7f), with which one may still compare 1 Jn 3:1: ἴδετε ποταπὴν ἀγάπην δέδωκεν ἡμῖν ὁ πατὴρ κτλ. ("See what love the Father has given us, . . ."). And when, according to *Corp. Herm.* XIII.8,

---

should be retained before πᾶς remains an open question; if so, it stems from the author. The phrase ποιεῖν τὴν δικαιοσύνην ("to do right") is an Old Testament-Jewish expression and, furthermore, since δικαιοσύνη means correct moral behavior as in the phrase ἐργάζεσθαι δικαιοσύνην ("to do what is right") in Ps 14:2; Acts 10:35 and elsewhere (but not as, for example, in Gen 18:19; 2 Sam 8:15), it points to the righteousness of the Judge.

9   The dualistic understanding of world and man provides the background for this idea and its formulation. Illustrations can be found in Bultmann, p. 135, n. 4 [p. 96, n. 5 which begins on p. 95] on Jn 3:3; in Schnackenburg, pp. 180–82; and in the excursus to 1 Jn 3:9 in Windisch–Preisker. These same references also contain illustrations of the fact that Philo had already adopted the notion of divine procreation. On the basis of this dualistic conception, the phrase "born of God" signifies rebirth (παλιγγενεσία) in the mystery religions and Gnosticism (cf. especially *Corp. Herm.* XIII). Whereas the way of attaining this rebirth in the mystery religions was through the sacramental act, such is not the case in *Corp. Herm.* XIII or in 1 John. Schnackenburg (p. 176) is mistaken in his view that in 1 John baptism "is taken for granted as the place of divine procreation." Admittedly, Jn 3:5 does refer to baptism, but ἐξ ὕδατος καί ("of water and") must surely be an editorial addition here; cf. Bultmann p. 138, n. 3 [p. 98, n. 2] on Jn 3:5. The phrase λουτρὸν παλιγγενεσίας ("the washing of regeneration") occurs in Tit 3:5; otherwise, there are no further examples of the term παλιγγενεσία in the New Testament, with the exception of Matt 19:28 which exhibits a different meaning. The related phrase "to be born again" (ἀναγεννᾶν, especially ἀναγεννᾶσθαι) occurs only in 1 Petr 1:3, 23 and Jn 3:3, 7 (ἄνωθεν γεννηθῆναι). See Bultmann, p. 135, n. 1 [p. 95, n. 2] on Jn 3:3f.

10   Cf. Schnackenburg, pp. 178–80. An obvious example of this in the New Testament is Matt 5:9. This change in terminology shows that the widespread Gnostic idea of man's physical likeness to God (whether it be as one φύσει σωζόμενος ["redeemed by virtue of his nature"] or as one whose nature has been transformed through γνῶσις or the process of initiation) is clearly foreign. Moreover, the term φύσις ("nature") does not occur in 1 John or in the Gospel of John. (Luther quite naively remarks on this verse: Nasci ex deo est acquirere naturam dei [WA 20:692 R]. ["To be born of God is to acquire the nature of God."])

11   Cf. *Corp. Herm.* XIII, 3 where the mystic says: ἐμαυτὸν ἐξελήλυθα εἰς ἀθάνατον σῶμα, καί εἰμι νῦν οὐχ ὁ πρίν ("I have entered into an immortal body. I am not now the man I was." [Scott]).

the new being begins with: $\mathring{\eta}\lambda\theta\epsilon\nu\ \mathring{\eta}\mu\hat{\iota}\nu\ \gamma\nu\hat{\omega}\sigma\iota\varsigma\ \theta\epsilon o\hat{v}$ . . . $\mathring{\epsilon}\xi\eta\lambda\acute{\alpha}\theta\eta\ \mathring{\eta}\ \mathring{\alpha}\gamma\nu o\iota\alpha$ ("The knowledge of God has come to us . . . ignorance has been driven out"), then one is also reminded of the emphasis on $\gamma\iota\nu\acute{\omega}\sigma\kappa\epsilon\iota\nu\ \tau\grave{o}\nu\ \theta\epsilon\acute{o}\nu$ ("to know God") in 1 Jn 2:3ff etc.

The transcendent character of the new being is made very evident by the insistence that it is not visible to the natural eye and not objectively ascertainable (*Corp. Herm.* XIII.3, 6). With this 1 Jn 3:2 is to be compared: $o\mathring{v}\pi\omega\ \mathring{\epsilon}\phi\alpha\nu\epsilon\rho\acute{\omega}\theta\eta\ \tau\acute{\iota}\ \mathring{\epsilon}\sigma\acute{o}\mu\epsilon\theta\alpha$ ("it does not yet appear what we shall be"). The promise of a future eschatological vision of God that follows admittedly has no parallel in *Corp. Herm.* XIII, since the knowledge of God is present for the man whose nature has been made new. Nevertheless, this renewal could be designated as an eschatological event, because it is the transformation of the old man into a new. Yet one must doubtless take into consideration the fact that the filial relation to God, for 1 John, is not only future but also already present (3:1).

If the material kinship of the Christian proclamation and Gnostic religiosity is not to be overlooked, neither is the characteristic difference. The difference consists not only in the fact, already mentioned, that the hope of an eschatological future also belongs to Christian faith, but, above all, in the fact that the Christian faith asserts the paradox that the eschatological event (both as present and as future) is grounded in a historical event, in the fact that Jesus Christ has come (see pp. 8f on 1:1f). The gnosticizing false teachers deny precisely that Jesus has come in the flesh (4:1ff).[12] As a consequence, Gnosticism does indeed have a body of doctrine, but not a proclamation. It can only admonish: $\mathring{\epsilon}\pi\acute{\iota}\sigma\pi\alpha\sigma\alpha\iota\ \epsilon\mathring{\iota}\varsigma\ \mathring{\epsilon}\alpha\upsilon\tau\acute{o}\nu,\ \kappa\alpha\grave{\iota}\ \mathring{\epsilon}\lambda\epsilon\acute{\upsilon}\sigma\epsilon\tau\alpha\iota$ (*scil.* $\gamma\acute{\epsilon}\nu\epsilon\sigma\iota\varsigma\ \tau\hat{\eta}\varsigma\ \theta\epsilon\acute{o}\tau\eta\tau o\varsigma$) ("Draw it into you, and it will come [*scil.* 'birth of the divine nature']"; *Corp. Herm.* XIII.7). And if Gnosticism is also acquainted with the moral demand,[13] it is the condition and not, as in 1 John, the consequence of being children of God. $\mathrm{Ko\iota\nu\omega\nu\acute{\iota}\alpha}$ ("fellowship") does indeed belong to the virtues (as the opposite of $\pi\lambda\epsilon o\nu\epsilon\xi\acute{\iota}\alpha$, "greediness"), but there is no mention of brotherly love; the word $\mathring{\alpha}\gamma\acute{\alpha}\pi\eta$ ("love"), for example, does not appear in *Corp. Herm.* XIII.

■ **3:1** In 3:1–3 the author interprets the sentence taken from his Source in v 29, in the first instance (3:1), by making his readers aware of what it means to be begotten of God: it means being a child of God and thus the gift of God's love: $\mathring{\iota}\delta\epsilon\tau\epsilon\ \pi o\tau\alpha\pi\grave{\eta}\nu\ \mathring{\alpha}\gamma\acute{\alpha}\pi\eta\nu\ \delta\acute{\epsilon}\delta\omega\kappa\epsilon\nu\ \mathring{\eta}\mu\hat{\iota}\nu\ \mathring{o}\ \pi\alpha\tau\acute{\eta}\rho$ ("See what love the father has given us").[14] The gift consists of this: $\mathring{\iota}\nu\alpha\ \tau\acute{\epsilon}\kappa\nu\alpha\ \theta\epsilon o\hat{v}\ \kappa\lambda\eta\theta\hat{\omega}\mu\epsilon\nu$ ("that we should be called children of God").[15] The following $\kappa\alpha\grave{\iota}\ \mathring{\epsilon}\sigma\mu\acute{\epsilon}\nu$, which does not belong to the $\mathring{\iota}\nu\alpha$–clause but constitutes an independent sentence ("and so we are"), is not textually certain, but is appropriate to the meaning. It is also unnecessary to the extent that $\kappa\lambda\eta\theta\hat{\eta}\nu\alpha\iota$ ("be

---

12 To use some terminology which is controversial at the moment one could say: it is just at this point that the critical nature of the "that-ness" (the fleshly existence of Jesus) for the Christian proclamation becomes apparent. For, an understanding over the "what-ness" (the life and words of the historical Jesus) might possibly have been reached with the false teachers.

13 *Corp. Herm.* XIII, 7: $\kappa\acute{\alpha}\theta\alpha\rho\alpha\iota\ \sigma\epsilon\alpha\upsilon\tau\grave{o}\nu\ \mathring{\alpha}\pi\grave{o}\ \tau\hat{\omega}\nu$ $\mathring{\alpha}\lambda\acute{o}\gamma\omega\nu\ \tau\hat{\eta}\varsigma\ \mathring{v}\lambda\eta\varsigma\ \tau\iota\mu\omega\rho\iota\hat{\omega}\nu$ ("you must cleanse yourself from the irrational torments of matter." [Scott]; i.e., from the vices).

14 The absolute form $\mathring{o}\ \pi\alpha\tau\acute{\eta}\rho$ ("the father") as a designation for God is a specifically Johannine usage; its only other occurrences are in Matt 11:27 par. and Mk 13:32 par., never in Paul. In 4:10f, 19; Jn 3:16; 14:23 God's love is expressed by a form of the verb; otherwise the substantive is normally used as here, 2:5, etc. $\Pi o\tau\alpha\pi\acute{o}\varsigma$ ("what") is a later form of $\pi o\delta\alpha\pi\acute{o}\varsigma$ which replaces $\pi o\hat{\iota}o\varsigma$ in Hellenistic Greek (Blass–Debrunner § 298(3)). It is explained by the $\mathring{\iota}\nu\alpha$–clause, cf. 5:3.

15 The $\mathring{\iota}\nu\alpha$–clause is, of course, epexegetical (Blass–Debrunner §394). This explanation shows that being born of God (2:29) and being a child of God are synonymous for the author.

called") can have the meaning of εἶναι ("to be"), as in Matt 5:9.[16]

The next sentence, διὰ τοῦτο ὁ κόσμος οὐ γινώσκει ἡμᾶς ("for this reason the world does not know us"),[17] in the context, is not consolation for those persecuted by the κόσμος ("world"), but the foil for the statement about the filial relation to God: that the "world" does not recognize the children of God is precisely a proof that they really are God's children and that they no longer belong to the world. The failure of the world to recognize them is given this basis: ὅτι οὐκ ἔγνω αὐτόν ("because it did not know him"). By αὐτός ("him") one is first inclined to understand God, but according to v 2 it must be Christ who is intended, just as in v 28, since it is only his φανερωθῆναι ("manifestation") that is spoken of in v 2. The assertion, "did not know him," then corresponds to the statement in the Gospel of John that Jesus is not recognized by the unbelieving crowd (Jn 8:14; 16:3), that he is, as it were, an alien in the world,[18] just as the world does not know God either (Jn 5:37; 7:28; 16:3). "Knowing," whether it concerns God or Jesus, or even when it concerns the Christian community, is an acknowledgment. There is thus simply an Either/Or, so that not knowing, i.e., the refusal to acknowledge, can be designated as "hate," as it is immediately below in v 13 and in Jn 15:19.[19]

■ **2** In v 2 the address ἀγαπητοί ("beloved," as in 2:7, etc.) accentuates the meaning of the idea: being children of God is a present affair: νῦν τέκνα θεοῦ ἐσμεν ("we are God's children now"), but sonship finds its fulfillment in the future: καὶ οὔπω ἐφανερώθη τί ἐσόμεθα ("and it does not yet appear what we shall be").[20] The question must be left open whether ἐφανερώθη is to be understood as referring to the resurrection (so Schnackenburg), or is intended in the sense of Jn 14:1ff, viz., that the exalted one at any given time draws the individual believer to himself. In the first instance, the thought would be the same as that in Col 3:3f. In any case, it is an eschatological event that the author has in mind. That the hope is grounded in a promise is given expression in the following sentence: οἴδαμεν ὅτι ἐὰν φανερωθῇ ὅμοιοι αὐτῷ ἐσόμεθα ("we know that when he appears we shall be like him"). Οἴδαμεν ("we know") appeals to the Christian tradition, out of which the community lives, as does οἴδατε in v 5 and v 15.[21] This tradition contains the promise: "when he appears we shall be like him." In accordance with 2:28, this can certainly only refer to the parousia of Christ.[22] The following ὅτι-clause then also applies to Christ: ὅτι ὀψόμεθα αὐτὸν καθώς ἐστιν ("for we shall see him as he

---

16   Cf. Bauer, *s.v.* καλέω 1.a.δ.
17   Although the διὰ τοῦτο-clause is usually connected with the following ὅτι-clause, here it refers to what precedes: for the very reason that the believers are children of God, the "world" does not know them. One should probably read ἡμᾶς ("us") instead of the well-attested ὑμᾶς ("you"), since the believers are spoken of in the first person plural in v 2.
18   Cf. Bultmann, p. 280, n. 1 [p. 210, n. 6] on Jn 8:14; also, Bultmann, p. 143, n. 1 [p. 102, n. 1] on 3:8.
19   Cf. Bultmann, pp. 548f [p. 422] on Jn 15:19.
20   On τί as the predicate see Blass–Debrunner §299,2.
21   Schnackenburg refers also to the οἴδαμεν in 5:15. This is also an appeal to the tradition, but 5:14–21

belongs to the Christian redaction; see below, pp. 85ff. The δέ after οἴδαμεν is textually uncertain.
22   Schnackenburg, on the other hand, wants to understand God as the subject of φανερωθῆναι ("appear") and, therefore, as the referent of αὐτός ("him"), which is discussed in the second ὅτι-clause and v 3. Consequently, he is forced to translate ὅμοιοι as similarity, not as identity. One escapes the difficulty caused by passing from talk about Christ (2:28; 3:1b) to talk about God (2:29) if he assumes that ἐὰν φανερωθῇ is an editorial addition as I have done in "Die kirchliche Redaktion," pp. 197f. Schnackenburg, on the other hand, wants to take τί ἐσόμεθα as the subject of ἐὰν φανερωθῇ: "when

is").[23] The promised likeness with Christ will therefore be effected by the community of the believers seeing him,[24] and seeing him as he is. By καθὼς ἐστιν ("just as he is") the future eschatological φανερωθῆναι ("manifestation") is distinguished from the revelation occurring in history (1:2; 3:5, 8; 4:9).

It must doubtless be said, on the basis of Jn 17:1, 5, 24, that he who is to be seen in his future eschatological revelation is the glorified one, although δόξα ("glory") and δοξασθῆναι ("be glorified") are not mentioned in 1 John. The likeness of those beholding with the one beheld consists in the former participating in his glorification, or in their being glorified themselves. It is to be assumed that the idea is the same as that expressed in Rom 8:17–19; Phil 3:21; Col 3:4 (cf. also 1 Cor 15:43ff), since v 2 appeals to the tradition. In 2 Cor 3:18 it is said that the vision of the glorified one transfigures those beholding into glorified ones. In 2 Corinthians, to be sure, the vision and transfiguration are thought of as already commencing (as in Rom 12:2), but as being consummated in the future: μεταμορφούμεθα ἀπὸ δόξης εἰς δόξαν ("we are being changed from glory into glory," i.e., from one degree of glory into another).

■ 3 Although formulated in the indicative, v 3 is a parenetical expression, which connects with 2:28 and forms the transition to v 4. In v 3 the theme of 2:29, born of God, is taken up again. The parenetical expression is joined, with πᾶς ὁ ἔχων τὴν ἐλπίδα ταύτην ἐπ' αὐτῷ ("every one who thus hopes in him"), to v 2, in which the author speaks of hope, although the term ἐλπίς ("hope") is not used and does not appear elsewhere in

1 John and John (the verb ἐλπίζειν is found only in Jn 5:45, but in a different sense.) The pronoun αὐτός ("him"), i.e., he who is the object of hope, can only be Jesus, as in v 2 and as the following καθὼς ἐκεῖνος . . . ("just as he . . .") confirms. The parenetical point or exhortation is contained in ἀγνίζει ἑαυτόν ("purifies himself"). Verse 4 indicates that ἀγνίζει means to keep oneself free from sin. The term is not met elsewhere in 1 John,[25] and is here prompted by καθὼς ἐκεῖνος ἀγνός ἐστιν ("just as he [literally: that one] is pure"). Ἐκεῖνος of course refers to Jesus, who is designated as ἐκεῖνος here, in 2:6; 3:5, 7, 16; 4:17, and often in John. Ἀγνός ("pure") as a characteristic of Jesus appears only here in 1 John; it does not appear in John at all. Substantively ἀγνός does not mean anything different from δίκαιος ("righteous") in 2:29; 3:7. Similarly, the motivating clause, that the conduct of the believers must correspond to the nature of him in whom faith is vested, found also in 2:29; 3:7, 16, is expressed already in 2:6 (also cf. 4:17).

■ 4 In v 4 the author again takes up his Source, which he had worked into 2:29b, and thereby resumes the theme, begotten of God: πᾶς ὁ ποιῶν τὴν ἁμαρτίαν καὶ ἀνομίαν ποιεῖ ("every one who commits sin is guilty of lawlessness"). The point of this sentence, the interpretation of which is very much disputed, evidently is that the one who commits sin is guilty of ἀνομία ("lawlessness"). Now, since the false teachers assert, according to 1:8, that they are sinless, and since this assertion is called a delusion, it is brought home to them—who are in fact sinners—that they make themselves guilty of "lawlessness." The epistle and the false teachers evidently

---

it appears what we shall be."

23 The second ὅτι–clause of v 2, cannot, like the first one, be dependent on οἴδαμεν, but it gives the reason for the assertion ὅμοιοι αὐτῷ ἐσόμεθα ("we shall be like him").

24 As a result of the way Schnackenburg interprets αὐτός (see n. 22 above), it is a question for him of a vision of God. Regarding this matter (cf. Matt 5:8), see Schnackenburg, pp. 172f and Bultmann, pp.

79ff [pp. 54f] on Jn 1:18.

25 The term is used in Jn 11:55 to denote cultic purification, as well as in Acts 21:24, 26; 24:18; in Jas 4:8; 1 Petr 1:22 it appears in the sense of ethical purification.

presuppose a common conception of "lawlessness," viz., that "lawlessness" is a heinous sin. The difference between the epistle and the false teachers is that the epistle accuses the false teachers of making themselves guilty of "lawlessness," while the false teachers are of the opinion that they are not guilty because they imagine they are free from sin. To this the response is: No, for precisely that reason they make themselves guilty of "lawlessness."

What, then, does ἀνομία mean?[26] In any case, the term means "lawlessness, antinomianism." This usually implies the transgression of God's demand and therefore evil. Thus the ἄνομος is the evil one, the sinner.[27] Now there can be no doubt that for the false teachers ἀνομία as evil, heinous sin is understood in a radical sense, i.e., as service to Satan. It therefore follows, if the false teachers in fact commit sin, they are servants of the devil. This conclusion is immediately drawn in v 8: ὁ ποιῶν τὴν ἁμαρτίαν ἐκ τοῦ διαβόλου ἐστίν ("whoever commits sin is of the devil"). This corresponds to expressions found elsewhere. In 2 Thess 2:3 the antichrist (in 2:9 expressly characterized as σατανᾶς, "Satan") is called ὁ ἄνθρωπος τῆς ἀνομίας ("the man of lawlessness"), in 2:8 he is characterized as ὁ ἄνομος ("the lawless one"), and in 2:7 reference is made to μυστήριον τῆς ἀνομίας ("mystery of lawlessness"). In these passages Satan is thought of as an eschatological figure, and "lawlessness," therefore, as an eschatological phenomenon. In 1

John, as 2:18 shows, the figure of the eschatological antichrist has been historicized; correspondingly, "lawlessness" is also a contemporary phenomenon, with the result that the false teachers can also be accused of making themselves guilty of "lawlessness."[28]

The author expounds v 4a entirely correctly in v 4b: καὶ ἡ ἁμαρτία ἐστὶν ἡ ἀνομία ("and sin is lawlessness"). And that is just the accusation leveled against the false teachers: in the delusion that they are sinless, they have fallen prey to "lawlessness."

■ 5 Verse 5, which appeals to the Christian tradition with καὶ οἴδατε ("and we know"), as in v 2, also stems from the author. It might be asked whether the verse has been interpolated by the ecclesiastical redactor, as in the case of 1:7b (see p. 20); however, it is rather to be attributed to the author. For, ἐφανερώθη (which here again refers to the revelation that takes place in history) ἵνα τὰς ἁμαρτίας ἄρῃ ("he appeared to take away sins") evidently does not mean, as does 1:7b, the cleansing of past sins and does not mention the blood of Jesus, but asserts that the revealed one has brought the possibility of freedom from sinning.[29] Verse 8b confirms as much, for εἰς τοῦτο ἐφανερώθη . . . ἵνα λύσῃ τὰ ἔργα τοῦ διαβόλου ("for this reason he appeared . . . to destroy the works of the devil") evidently means the same thing. Ἁμαρτίαι ("sins") are nothing other than the works of the devil, since "sin" and "lawlessness" are equated

---

26 In traditional parlance no difference existed between ἁμαρτία ("sin") and ἀνομία ("lawlessness"). The fact that both terms mean "sin" as the transgression of God's commandments is seen in Paul's quotation of Ps 31:1 (LXX) in Rom 4:7 which places them in a pattern of *parallelismus membrorum*. A similar usage occurs in Ps 50:4 (LXX) and elsewhere, as well as in Heb 10:17 in the New Testament. Ἀνομία is also used to denote sin in the Old Testament expressions in Matt 7:23 (ἐργάζεσθαι τὴν ἀνομίαν ["to work lawlessness"]); 13:41 (ποιεῖν τὴν ἀνομίαν ["to do lawlessness"]); in addition, Matt 23:28; 24:12; Tit 2:14. It is joined antithetically to δικαιοσύνη ("righteousness") in Rom 6:19; 2 Cor 6:14;

Heb 1:9. Cf. 1 Tim 1:9; 2 Petr 2:8.

27 Ἄνομος, specifically the adverbial form ἀνόμως, is used quite differently in Rom 2:12; 1 Cor 9:21 where it does not mean opposition to the (Jewish) law, but living without any knowledge of it. Thus the Gentiles are designated as ἄνομοι ("lawless") in Acts 2:23.

28 Although my understanding of ἀνομία agrees with Schnackenburg's (see pp. 185f), I do not accept his view that v 4 is directed against those Christians who have not yet conquered ἁμαρτία ("sin"). Against Schnackenburg's view that the concept of eschatological ἀνομία is analogous to the concept of "malice" which is mentioned in the Qumran texts,

in v 4, and "sin" thereby characterized as the devil's work. Αἴρειν τὰς ἁμαρτίας ("take away sins") is therefore synonymous with λύειν τὰ ἔργα τοῦ διαβόλου ("destroy the works of the devil").

Καὶ ἁμαρτία ἐν αὐτῷ οὐκ ἔστιν ("and there is no sin in him") means the same thing as δίκαιός ἐστιν ("he is righteous," v 7 and earlier in 2:29) and ἁγνός ἐστιν ("he is pure," v 3). Perhaps the sentence is supposed to explain ". . . to take away sins": as one who is sinless, he can be the one to take away sins. However, it is probably better understood as preparation for v 6, which has the character of an admonition: because there is no sin "in him," those who are his are to be sinless: [30] πᾶς ὁ ἐν αὐτῷ μένων οὐχ ἁμαρτάνει ("every one who abides in him does not sin").

■ 6 This sentence appears at first to stand in contradiction to 1:8ff, where the readers are warned against the conceit that they are sinless, in contrast to the false teachers, who assert their sinlessness. There is, nevertheless, no real contradiction: v 6a states only the basic truth that every one who "abides in him," i.e., whoever remains faithfully bound to him,[31] does not sin. Thus "abiding in him" is the condition of "not sinning." In view of 1:8ff, however, the question becomes pressing: who can assert of himself that he always fulfills this condition? Verse 6a therefore indirectly contains the admonition to faithfulness, just as the sentences which speak of μένειν ("abide") are in part imperative (2:24, 27c, 28) and in part indicative though including an indirect imperative (2:27a; 3:24; 4:15f). Every one must and can know, consequently, whether and when "does not sin"

applies to him.

The admonition included in v 6a is made explicit by v 6b: πᾶς ὁ ἁμαρτάνων οὐχ ἑώρακεν αὐτὸν οὐδὲ ἔγνωκεν αὐτόν ("every one who sins has neither seen nor known him"). That applies to the one who does not "abide in him," and corresponds to what was said in 2:4: ὁ λέγων ὅτι ἔγνωκα αὐτὸν καὶ τὰς ἐντολὰς αὐτοῦ μὴ τηρῶν ψεύστης ἐστίν . . . ("whoever says that he knows him and does not keep his commandments is a liar . . ."). For, "does not keep his commandments" means the same thing as "sinning."[32] If, according to v 4, sinning can be designated as ἀνομία ("lawlessness"), as service to the devil, then that corresponds to the characterization of the one who does not keep the commandments as ψεύστης ("liar," 2:4), and likewise to the statement: ἐν τούτῳ ἡ ἀλήθεια οὐκ ἔστιν ("the truth is not in him"), i.e., he has no part in the reality of God, who is light (1:5), but is confined in darkness (2:9) and belongs to the sphere of the devil (3:8), who, according to Jn 8:44, is the "liar."

■ 7 The character of the admonition in vss 4–6 is once again expressed in v 7 and even more clearly by the new form of address τεκνία ("little children," as in 2:1): μηδεὶς πλανάτω ὑμᾶς ("let no one deceive you"). The warning against those who "deceive" in 2:26 refers to heterodox christology; v 7 warns against the wrong understanding of ἁμαρτία ("sin"), and that means against a false self-understanding, as v 8 makes evident. If v 8 derives from the Source, then there is some question with respect to v 7b. The phrase of v 7b ὁ ποιῶν τὴν δικαιοσύνην ("he who does right") appears to take up

see Braun, "Qumran und das Neue Testament," pp. 107f [296f]. Braun's remarks also turn against the attempt in Nauck, *Die Tradition und Charakter des ersten Johannesbriefes*, to explain 1 Jn 2:29–3:10 on the basis of the Qumran texts.

29 Αἴρειν means here, as in Jn 1:29, not "to take upon oneself," but "to get rid of"; see Bultmann, p. 96, n. 1 [p. 66, n. 5].

30 Although one would normally expect an inferential

ὥστε before v 6, this is not a stylistic trait of 1 John which, like 2 John and 3 John, omits ὥστε altogether. It occurs in John only in 3:16.

31 On μένειν ἐν see the discussion on 2:6, p. 26, n. 9.

32 See p. 25 on 2:4 and cf. 3 Jn 11: ὁ κακοποιῶν οὐχ ἑώρακεν τὸν θεόν ("whoever does evil has not seen God").

the sentence from 2:29 once again, since it forms antithetical parallelism with ὁ ποιῶν τὴν ἁμαρτίαν ("he who commits sin") in v 8; one is inclined, therefore, to assign it to the Source. The continuation δίκαιός ἐστιν ("he is righteous"), however, is remarkably weak. In accordance with 2:29 one expects: ἐκ τοῦ θεοῦ γεγέννηται ("is born of God"), and if v 7 really came from the Source, that might have been the original conclusion of the sentence, which the author altered to "he is righteous."[33] In any case, καθὼς ἐκεῖνος δίκαιός ἐστιν ("just as that one is righteous") stems from the author. It expresses the thought that the conduct of the believers must correspond to the nature of Jesus, which had also been said in 2:6, 29; 3:3.

■ 8   Verse 8a, however, is undoubtedly taken from the Source: ὁ ποιῶν τὴν ἁμαρτίαν ἐκ τοῦ διαβόλου ἐστίν ("he who commits sin is of the devil").[34] That corresponds in substance to v 4a, in which ἀνομία ("lawlessness") designated service to the devil. Formally, v 8a belongs together with v 9a in antithetical parallelism. The author first of all glossed the Source with a ὅτι–clause: ὅτι ἀπ' ἀρχῆς ὁ διάβολος ἁμαρτάνει ("for the devil sins from the beginning"), which is reminiscent of Jn 8:44;[35] and then with the following sentence: εἰς τοῦτο ἐφανερώθη ὁ υἱὸς τοῦ θεοῦ ἵνα λύσῃ τὰ ἔργα τοῦ διαβόλου ("the reason the Son of God appeared was to destroy the works of the devil"), which corresponds

to v 5, for "to destroy the works of the devil" is a variation on "to take away sins."

■ 9   With v 9 the author again takes up the Source: πᾶς ὁ γεγεννημένος ἐκ τοῦ θεοῦ ἁμαρτίαν οὐ ποιεῖ ("whoever is begotten of God does not sin"). That is a variation of what was said in v 6a, but in such a way that ὁ γεγεννημένος ἐκ τοῦ θεοῦ ("whoever is begotten of God") replaces ὁ μένων ἐν αὐτῷ ("whoever abides in him"). As in v 6, "not sinning" is certainly in principle to be understood as the realization of the possibility given to the believer.

The justification, however, is noteworthy: ὅτι σπέρμα αὐτοῦ ἐν αὐτῷ μένει ("for his seed abides in him"). Whereas v 6 speaks of the abiding (the "faithfulness") of the believers in Christ, in v 9 it is the abiding of the "seed" of God in those born of God.[36] Naturally the expression is to be understood figuratively, as is the case with "begotten of God." It designates the activity of God that forms the source and concomitantly sustains.[37] It is remarkable, however, that according to v 6 the "abiding" of the believers is the condition of freedom from sin, while in v 9 the "abiding" of the "seed" appears as the presupposition of freedom from sin, and both ὅτι–clauses describe this freedom as an abiding possession.

Do the two go together? They do indeed. To be sure, it appears that the assertion in v 9 contradicts 1:8f, where there is the warning against the delusion of holding

---

33   On ποιεῖν τὴν δικαιοσύνην see the preceding discussion on 2:29, pp. 45f, n. 8.

34   On εἶναι ἐκ see p. 34, n. 26 and p. 36, n. 6 on 2:16 and 19.

35   Bultmann, p. 320, n. 3 [p. 242, n. 4]. Ἀπ' ἀρχῆς ("from the beginning") can refer neither to the origin of the historical event of the proclamation as it does in 1:1, 2:13 (see p. 9, n. 10) nor to the Garden of Eden story in Genesis, but rather intends the primordial beginning since the nature of the devil is being characterized.

36   This terminology, as well as γεγεννημένος ἐκ τοῦ θεοῦ ("begotten of God") (see pp. 45f on 2:29), is taken from Gnosticism. In *Corp. Herm.* XIII, 2

ἀληθινὸν ἀγαθόν ("the true good") is designated as σπορά ("the seed") and to the question τίνος σπείραντος ("who is it that begets?") comes the answer τοῦ θελήματος τοῦ θεοῦ ("the will of God" [Scott]). The image of σπέρμα occurs also in Philo (see Windisch–Preisker on 3:9 for the references).

37   Whoever explains σπέρμα ("seed") on the basis of πνεῦμα ("spirit"), as Schnackenburg does, could adduce v 24 as support. Those who wish to take σπέρμα as a reference to the "Word" can appeal to the εἶναι ("to be") of the λόγος ἐν ἡμῖν ("word in us") in 1:10 or to 2:14 where the μένειν ("to abide") of the λόγος ἐν ὑμῖν ("word in you") is mentioned. The Zürich translation of this passage is not wrong

oneself to be sinless. Nevertheless, the contradiction is to be resolved in a way comparable to the one in v 6 (see p. 51), although ὁ μένων ἐν αὐτῷ (v 6) is lacking in v 9. The resolution of the contradiction lies in the fact that the μένειν ("abiding") of the σπορά ("seed") is understood as the gift of God's ἀγάπη ("love," 3:1), which remains for the believer a possibility not to be lost, so that he can always call upon that gift, even though he in fact sins.[38] Οὐ δύναται ἁμαρτάνειν ("he is not able to sin") is therefore to be understood as the possibility of not sinning, which the believer has received as the unforfeitable gift of God's love, a possibility that is always to be realized, as v 10 immediately indicates. The gift of a possibility always includes a demand, and thus the demand itself can be understood as a gift. Consequently, v 9 can speak one-sidedly of gift.

The two thus belong together: the "abiding" of the "seed" is freedom from sin, just as "abiding in him" (v 6) is the condition of this freedom. Gift and demand belong together in such a way that the one does not exist apart from the other, in such a way that the gift is prior, providing the ground of Christian existence.[39]

It is debatable whether the second ὅτι–clause of v 9:

ὅτι ἐκ τοῦ θεοῦ γεγέννηται ("because he is begotten of God") derives from the author. Substantively, it says nothing different from the first: ὅτι σπέρμα αὐτοῦ ἐν αὐτῷ μένει ("for his seed abides in him"). The clause is nevertheless to be attributed to the Source, because the expression, "begotten of God" belongs to the same gnosticizing language as the concept, "his seed." The author elsewhere avoids these expressions, and, just as he chooses the phrase "children of God" in 3:1, instead of the concept "begotten of God" (2:29), so does he show the same preference now in v 10.

■ 10 In any case, the section 3:10–24 goes back to the author. It is a homily in which the theme of brotherly love is again treated. The transition to this theme is not very smooth.[40] The author draws the antithesis of being children of God and children of the devil from the Source utilized in the preceding section, and elucidates ἐν τούτῳ φανερά ἐστιν τὰ τέκνα τοῦ θεοῦ καὶ τὰ τέκνα τοῦ διαβόλου ("by this it is evident who are the children of God and who are the children of the devil") by means of the sentence: πᾶς ὁ μὴ ποιῶν δικαιοσύνην οὐκ ἔστιν ἐκ τοῦ θεοῦ ("he who does not do righteousness is not of God").[41] While this formulation corresponds to what

---

in rendering σπέρμα as Lebenskeim ("the spark of life").

38 Cf. Luther on v 9: "Si ergo est natus [*scil.* ex deo], non facit peccatum, quia nasci ex deo purgat peccatum . . . . Nati estis ex semine . . . [per verbum dei!] Verbum dei manet, est aeternum semen . . . . Semen in nobis dei non patitur nobiscum ullum peccatum, quia Christus est purgator peccatorum." [WA 20: 705f R] ("If therefore he has been born [*scil.* of God], he does not commit sin, because being born of God purges sin . . . . You have been born of [this] seed . . . [by the word of God!] The word of God remains, it is the eternal seed . . . . The seed of God in us does not experience any sin with us, because Christ is the purger of sins.") [tr. by James Dunkly.]

39 Cf. Luther on v 10: "Fides et charitas sunt Christianismi partes. Fides est operculum vel propiciatorium, quod placat infinita peccata, quibus sumus rei coram deo" [WA 20:707 R] ("Faith and charity

are Christian attributes. Faith is a cover of propitiation, which reconciles an infinite number of sins, for which we are in fact before God.") [tr. by James Dunkly.]

40 As a result, it is uncertain whether the opening phrase of v 10, ἐν τούτῳ, refers to what precedes or what follows. The view that it points in both directions at once (Windisch–Preisker and Schnackenburg) is highly unlikely. Rather, it more plausibly refers to what follows, in which case it is explicated by the clause πᾶς ὁ μὴ ποιῶν δικαιοσύνην κτλ. ("he who does not do righteousness," etc.).

41 Instead of ὁ μὴ ποιῶν δικαιοσύνην the variant reading ὁ μὴ ὢν δίκαιος ("whoever is not righteous") is also well attested; see Schnackenburg, p. 192, n. 2.

was said in 2:29–3:9, the next sentence: καὶ ὁ μὴ ἀγα-πῶν τὸν ἀδελφὸν αὐτοῦ ("and he who does not love his brother") provides further elucidation and leads to a new theme. Καί has the sense of "that is, namely." Ἀδελ-φός ("brother") means "neighbor," as in 2:10 (see p. 28).

■ 11 Verse 11 provides the basis for the conclusion of v 10 by means of the sentence (ὅτι, "for") which states that mutual love is the content of the message heard from the beginning. The formulation αὕτη ἐστὶν ἡ ἀγγελία ἣν ἠκούσατε ἀπ᾽ ἀρχῆς ("this is the message which you heard from the beginning") is almost identical with that in 1:5.[42] That ἣν ἀκηκόαμεν ("which we have heard") is now replaced by ἣν ἠκούσατε ("which you heard") in the second person, makes no difference in it-self; however, the change is motivated by the fact that here ἀγγελία ("message") is explicated by a ἵνα–clause, unlike 1:5, where a ὅτι–clause is used.[43] The content of the "message" is now a matter of an ethical demand, while in 1:5 it is an article of faith. The "message" in this case is therefore an ἐντολή ("commandment"), just as, in v 23, the "commandment" is explicated by means of a ἵνα–clause, as also in 4:21; 2 Jn 5f.

The commandment runs: ἵνα ἀγαπῶμεν ἀλλήλους ("that we love one another"). It makes no difference that ἀλλήλους ("one another") is employed here rather than τὸν ἀδελφόν ("the brother"), as in v 10 (variant in v 15); 4:11f; nor is there any difference between these

and the plural τοὺς ἀδελφούς ("the brethren," v 14).[44] The meaning is everywhere the same: love of neighbor is demanded.

■ 12 Verse 12 delineates the antitype of love with refer-ence to the figure of Cain,[45] who "butchered" his brother and thereby demonstrated that he was ἐκ τοῦ πονηροῦ ("of the evil one"), i.e., of the devil, according to v 8.[46] It is curious that a question is raised concerning the motive of Cain's deed: χάριν τίνος ἔσφαξεν αὐτόν ("why did he slaughter him?"). Why is the answer not simply: because he hated him? In any case, that is certainly the motive, for he who hates is a murderer, as v 15 puts it. When the text reads instead: ὅτι τὰ ἔργα αὐτοῦ πονηρὰ ἦν, τὰ δὲ τοῦ ἀδελφοῦ αὐτοῦ δίκαια ("because his deeds were evil, and those of his brother righteous"), then the motive of the hate is thereby indicated.

■ 13 For v 13 shows that the contrast between evil and just deeds corresponds to the antithesis between the children of God and the "world." Whoever is conscious of being a child of God (and of the demand implied by that relationship), as is the believer, must be prepared for the enmity of the "world." For the "world" not only does not recognize the community of believers (v 1), but hates it as well. The community should not be amazed at this; the hate of the "world," which Cain represents, only confirms the fact that believers are children of God.[47]

---

42 Instead of ἀγγελία ("message") the variant read-ing ἐπαγγελία ("announcement") is likewise well attested; the two words are synonymous, however.

43 The use of a demonstrative with a following ἵνα–clause as also in vss 8b, 23 is a mark of the author's style. Cf. Bultmann, "Analyse des ersten Johannes-briefes," p. 142.

44 The variation ἀγαπᾶν ἀλλήλους ("love one an-other") also occurs in Jn 13:34; 15:12.

45 It is noteworthy that this is the only reference to an Old Testament story in 1 John. It is possible that the author has been induced to make this reference because a verse of his Source contained the term ἀνθρωποκτόνος ("murderer") which he wishes to

use in v 15. This verse can be roughly reconstructed as follows:
πᾶς ὁ μισῶν ἀνθρωποκτόνος ἐστίν
καὶ οὐκ ἔχει ζωὴν αἰώνιον.
Everyone who hates is a murderer
and does not have eternal life.

46 On εἶναι ἐκ, which designates the subject's origin and nature, see p. 34, n. 26 on 2:16.

47 When the hate of the world is mentioned, it can hardly be taken as a reference to a (bloody) perse-cution of the Christian community, as Schnacken-burg thinks. No mention is made of διώκειν ("to persecute," Jn 15:20; Matt 5:10ff) in 1 John, and v 17 shows that hate is the withholding of love.

■ **14** The consciousness that they are children of God (ἡμεῖς οἴδαμεν, "we know") is given strong—one may say arrogant—expression in v 14: ὅτι μεταβεβήκαμεν ἐκ τοῦ θανάτου εἰς τὴν ζωήν ("that we have passed from death to life"). The community is thereby saying that the promise of Jn 5:24 has been fulfilled in it: ὅτι ὁ τὸν λό-γον μου ἀκούων καὶ πιστεύων τῷ πέμψαντί με ἔχει ζωὴν αἰώνιον καὶ . . . μεταβέβηκεν ἐκ τοῦ θανάτου εἰς τὴν ζωήν ("he who hears my word and believes him who sent me has eternal life and . . . has passed from death to life"). Since the "we" obviously characterizes the congregation[48] as that of believers, it may be asked whether the basis, ὅτι ἀγαπῶμεν τοὺς ἀδελφούς ("be-cause we love the brethren"), may also be understood simply as a characteristic of the congregation as a com-munity of those who love. Apparently that is what it is supposed to be. And if ἀγαπᾶν ("love") in vss 10f (and v 23) is understood as demand, and therefore as a duty of the congregation, like πιστεύειν ("believe," v 23), the character of the congregation has been fundamentally articulated. The arrogant "we know" makes the congre-gation aware of its real character, against which each individual member is to measure himself. In this sense, therefore, v 14 is also an indirect admonition, as was the case with v 6a (see p. 51). The question is therefore posed for each individual, whether he belongs to the Christian congregation.

■ **15** The great Either/Or that dominates 2:29–3:9f, viz., children of God or children of the devil, comes to de-cision in the Either/Or of love and hate, and this decision determines the Either/Or of life and death, v 14: ὁ μὴ ἀγαπῶν μένει ἐν τῷ θανάτῳ ("he who does not love abides in death").[49] Whoever does not love has not only fallen prey to death, but even himself produces death: according to v 15 he is a murderer, πᾶς ὁ μισῶν τὸν ἀδελφὸν αὐτοῦ ἀνθρωποκτόνος ἐστιν ("every one who hates his brother is a murderer"). The believers know that such a person . . . οὐκ ἔχει ζωὴν αἰώνιον ἐν αὐτῷ μένουσαν ("does not have eternal life abiding in him").[50] The phrase ἐν αὐτῷ μένουσαν ("abiding in him") in-dicates that the believer, if he does not also practice love, can forfeit the gift of "eternal life."

■ **16** Verses 16ff indicate what genuine love is, or how it is to be tested. In v 16a Christ is named as the paradigm of love: ἐν τούτῳ ἐγνώκαμεν τὴν ἀγάπην, ὅτι ἐκεῖνος ὑπὲρ ἡμῶν τὴν ψυχὴν αὐτοῦ ἔθηκεν ("by this we know love, that that one laid down his life on our behalf").[51] The reference is thus to the passion of Christ, and since it is a historical event out of which this knowledge grows, the perfect (ἐγνώκαμεν) is employed rather than the present tense (γινώσκομεν), customary elsewhere for the most part. The phrase, ὑπὲρ ἡμῶν ("on our behalf"), contains the insight that active love is based on experi-enced love: from his love for us we learn what love is.

In v 16b the consequence is drawn: καὶ ἡμεῖς ὀφείλο-μεν ὑπὲρ τῶν ἀδελφῶν τὰς ψυχὰς θεῖναι ("and we ought to lay down our lives for the brethren"). That the author did not simply say, "we ought to love the breth-ren," implies that love must be prepared for the highest sacrifice, the giving of one's life.

■ **17** It is not thereby implied that this sacrifice is the single and necessary proof of love—a fact that is shown by v 17 in which an example of a simple act of compassion

---

48 See above, pp. 51 and 52f.
49 On μένειν ἐν see the discussion on 2:6, p. 26, n. 9.
50 This designation of ζωή ("life") as αἰώνιος ("eter-nal"), as also in 1:2; 2:25 and elsewhere, shows that it is an eschatological gift which is already present

for those who love (v 14). It is thereby distinguished from physical existence.
51 The name Jesus (or Christ) does not need to be men-tioned; every reader knows who ἐκεῖνος ("that one") is. See p. 26 on 2:6.

is characterized as proof of love.[52] It is absurd that the "love of God abides"[53] in one who is not compassionate. What does the genitive τοῦ θεοῦ mean here? It could be a qualitative genitive and thus designate the "divine kind of love."[54] But the genitive can also be understood as a genitive of the author, in which case it means the love of God given to us. Since the love of God given to us is the presupposition of brotherly love (4:10, 19), this understanding may best fit the context, which is concerned with brotherly love.

■ **18** Verse 18, which contains a new vocative (τεκνία, "little children," as in 2:1, etc.), puts the consequence in imperative form: we ought therefore to love. The seriousness of the command to love is deepened by the construction μὴ . . . ἀλλά . . . ("not . . . but . . ."). Genuine love is evidenced not by empty words (λόγῳ . . . τῇ γλώσσῃ, "in word . . . in speech," hendiadys), but by actual deeds (ἐν ἔργῳ καὶ ἀληθείᾳ, "in deed and truth," also hendiadys).[55]

■ **19, 20** Verses 19 and 20 are so closely related that they can only be understood together. However, the exposition is uncertain and controversial, and one can hardly avoid the assumption that the text is corrupt.

In any case, ἐν τούτῳ γνωσόμεθα ("by this we shall know") is explicated by the ὅτι–clause:[56] "by this we shall know that we are of the truth," namely by just this, that we fulfill the command to love "in deed and truth."[57] The next sentence, καὶ ἔμπροσθεν αὐτοῦ πείσομεν τὴν καρδίαν ἡμῶν, taken by itself, is readily understood: "and before him we shall reassure (or: set at ease) our hearts."[58] According to v 20, it is a question of the self–condemning heart. In that case, ἔμπροσθεν αὐτοῦ ("before him") must mean, before God as judge; a glance at God precipitates the self–condemnation of the heart.[59]

How is the sentence to be understood, however, in the structure of vss 19f? It is very improbable that καὶ . . . πείσομεν . . . ("and . . . we shall reassure . . .") belongs to the first ὅτι–clause so that like the verb ἐσμέν ("we are") it serves as the object of γνωσόμεθα (thus: "By this we shall know that we are of the truth and [that] we shall reassure our hearts"); for πείσομεν cannot be referred back to ἐν τούτῳ ("by this"), as can ἐσμέν. It is more likely that καὶ . . . πείσομεν . . . continues γνωσόμεθα (thus: "By this we shall know that we are of the truth and [so] we shall reassure our hearts")—note that καὶ is understood as "and so" (Schnackenburg). This

---

52 Schnackenburg points to the importance which Judaism assigned to "almsgiving," but it was significant for the Mandaeans as well. See Schnackenburg, p. 199, n. 4, on the Old Testament expression σπλάγχνα ("bowels").

53 On μένειν ἐν see p. 26, n. 9, on 2:6.

54 Thus Schnackenburg.

55 Ἔργον ("work," "deed") does not refer to ἔργον νόμου ("a work of the law"), but simply to "deed" or "act." Ἀλήθεια ("truth") does not here denote genuine reality, the reality of God, as it does in 1:8; 2:4, but is used in the formal sense of objective reality. While it is possible that the author's warning against empty, affected language is yet another attempt "to strike a blow" against the Gnosticizers (Schnackenburg), it is highly unlikely in this context.

56 On this formula see p. 24, n. 1 on 2:3. The future tense occurs only here.

57 Contrary to v 18, ἀλήθεια ("truth") here denotes the reality of God, the essential reality; see pp. 18f on 1:7a, b. On εἶναι ἐκ, which designates the essence of something by referring to its origin, see p. 36, n. 6 on 2:19.

58 On πείθειν as "to reassure," "to set at ease," see Bauer s.v.

59 Schnackenburg wishes to understand ἔμπροσθεν ("before [God]") in a nonforensic sense because "the heart's present verdict of condemnation should be silenced through a glance at the greater God of grace." Is not this precisely the point, however; viz., that the heart which knows it is placed before God as judge also knows it can be certain of his grace?

is the view most commentators take. All these translations are unable satisfactorily to explain the two ὅτι–clauses in v 20. Schnackenburg overcomes the difficulty by resolving the ὅτι of the first ὅτι–clause into ὅ τι (ἐάν): "about everything regarding which our hearts might condemn us."[60] He must then understand the second ὅτι causally ("for"). Most interpreters take both instances of ὅτι as "that," in which the second resumes the first, and ἐὰν καταγινώσκῃ ἡμῶν ἡ καρδία ("if our hearts condemn us") is therefore understood as a parenthesis. That the second ὅτι is then basically superfluous, indeed even disruptive, becomes evident in many translations by the simple omission of the second ὅτι.[61] It would be convenient to strike it, were it not so well attested textually. If it is retained, there is the possibility of understanding it causally: "for God is greater . . . ."[62] It is possible to take "and before him we shall reassure . . ." as a new, independent sentence and then understand the first ὅτι as causal ("for"), but at the price of having to strike the second in the face of good evidence. It is simply the case that the problem cannot be resolved without assuming some textual corruption. It would be simplest to assume that an οἴδαμεν ("we know") has dropped out

before ὅτι μείζων ἐστὶν ὁ θεός ("that God is greater").[63] In that case, if one takes "and before him we shall . . ." as an independent sentence, the first ὅτι would be understood as causal, the second as explicative: "And before him we shall reassure our hearts (i.e., in the knowledge that we are of the truth). For when our heart accuses us, we know that God is greater than our heart."[64]

However the sentence is to be understood, μείζων ἐστὶν ὁ θεός . . . καὶ γινώσκει πάντα ("God is greater . . . and knows all things") means, in any case, that God's standards are different from those of the human heart, that God is, so to speak, more magnanimous, and that, consequently, human self–condemnation can be silent before him. That God's magnanimity consists of his knowledge of all things can only mean, in this context, that he knows we are basically lovers of the brethren (v 14) and as such, are "of the truth" (v 19).[65]

■ 21 The author begins anew in v 21 with ἀγαπητοί ("beloved"),[66] in a way comparable to his use of τεκνία ("little children") in v 18. While v 18 introduces an imperative, v 21 introduces a homiletical commentary on vss 19f, which leads again directly to parenetical exposition.

---

60 Although this division of ὅτι into ὅ τι is surely possible in Koine Greek, it would be unique in 1 John and is hardly confirmed by ὅ τι ἄν in Jn 2:5; 14:13; 15:16.

61 E.g., Carl von Weizsäcker's translation and also the Vulgate.

62 Thus J. D. Michaelis' translation, Schnackenburg and the RSV. One can adduce 3:14; 4:13 in support of the double occurrence of ὅτι in one sentence, the first of which is explicative and the second causal.

63 For the sequence ἐὰν γινώσκῃ . . . οἴδαμεν ὅτι one may compare 2:29, ἐὰν εἰδῆτε . . . γινώσκετε ὅτι.

64 In "Analyse des ersten Johannesbriefes," pp. 150f, I suggested that the difficulty with vss 19f is occasioned by the fact that the author has reworked a section of his Source, which might have read as follows:

ἔμπροσθεν αὐτοῦ πείσομεν τὴν καρδίαν ἡμῶν,
ἐὰν καταγινώσκῃ ἡμῶν ἡ καρδία.
Before him we shall reassure our hearts,
if our hearts condemn us.
This conjecture has been accepted by H. W. Beyer in his review of the *Festgabe für Adolf Jülicher* in *ThLZ* 54 (1929): 611f, and carried forward by Herbert Preisker in Windisch–Preisker. While I still believe that this conjecture is worthy of consideration, I must agree with Schnackenburg that the reconstruction is problematical.

65 In this connection one may refer to Jn 21:17 where Peter answers the question of Jesus as follows: κύριε, πάντα σὺ οἶδας, σὺ γινώσκεις ὅτι φιλῶ σε ("Lord, you know everything; you know that I love you.").

66 Ἀγαπητοί as in 2:7, etc.; see p. 26, n. 13.

Ἐὰν ἡ καρδία μὴ καταγινώσκῃ ("If our hearts do not condemn us")[67] can surely only mean: when all self–condemnation is laid to rest through God's magnanimity,[68] when our heart therefore no longer convicts us, then it can be said, παρρησίαν ἔχομεν πρὸς τὸν θεόν ("we have confidence before God"). This "confidence," which in 2:28 is promised to the one who "abides in him" for the situation of the parousia of Christ, is now granted as a present possibility to him whose heart is freed from self–condemnation.[69] As v 22 shows, it is especially the ingenuousness of prayer.[70]

■ **22** For that is what v 22 says: καὶ ὃ ἐὰν αἰτῶμεν λαμβάνομεν ἀπ' αὐτοῦ ("and whatever we ask we receive from him"). This certainty has its basis, to be sure, in: ὅτι τὰς ἐντολὰς αὐτοῦ τηροῦμεν ("because we keep the commandments").[71] If in vss 18f the fulfillment of the command to love was the condition of the promise given in vss 19b, 20, here the condition of "confidence" is the keeping of the commandments.[72] It may come as a surprise that the text does not read: ὅτι ἀγαπῶμεν ("because we love"). However, it makes no substantive difference, for the knowledge of God which, according to vss 20f, is the presupposition of "confidence," is

also presupposed in v 22. Καὶ τὰ ἀρεστὰ ἐνώπιον αὐτοῦ ποιοῦμεν ("and we do what pleases him") (which naturally includes the love commandment) is connected to τὰς ἐντολὰς αὐτοῦ τηροῦμεν ("we keep his commandments") as hendiadys.[73]

■ **23** The indirect imperative of v 22 becomes a direct imperative in v 23, insofar as v 23 offers an explanation of v 22: καὶ αὕτη ἐστὶν ἡ ἐντολὴ αὐτοῦ, ἵνα . . . ("And this is his commandment, that . . .").[74] It may be noted that the plural of v 22 ("the commandments") is now replaced in the definition by the singular, especially since the definition also contains two commandments: ἵνα πιστεύσωμεν . . . καὶ ἀγαπῶμεν . . . ("that we should believe . . . and love . . ."). But the following καθὼς ἔδωκεν ἐντολὴν ἡμῖν ("just as he commanded us")[75] shows how faith and love constitute a unity for the author, which corresponds to the whole sequence of thought

---

67 The occurrences of ἡμῶν after καρδία and καταγινώσκῃ appear to be obvious expansions, and the shorter text is preferable. Thus Schnackenburg as well, p. 204, n. 1.

68 Or through the knowledge of God's magnanimity, in case one may add an οἴδαμεν ("we know") in v 20b (see above).

69 This is materially related to Rom 5:1: δικαιωθέντες οὖν . . . εἰρήνην ἔχομεν πρὸς τὸν θεόν ("Being, therefore, justified . . . we have peace with God.").

70 Cf. Erik Peterson, "Zur Bedeutungsgeschichte von παρρησία," Reinhold–Seeberg–Festschrift, ed. Wilhelm Koepp (Leipzig: Deichert, 1929) I: 293.

71 On τὰς ἐντολὰς τηρεῖν ("to keep the commandments") see pp. 24f on 2:3. The ὅτι is, of course, causal.

72 If τὰς ἐντολὰς τηρεῖν ("to keep the commandments") is a condition of the promise, it is not a reversion to legalistic piety (Windisch in Windisch–

Preisker; Schnackenburg is correct in rejecting Windisch's view). Rather, 3:19–24 displays the connection between the indicative and the imperative. In v 22 an imperative is contained in the indicative (in agreement with Schnackenburg).

73 Τὰ ἀρεστὰ ποιεῖν ("to do what is pleasing"—as in Jn 8:29) is a common Jewish–Christian expression (see Bauer, s.v.). Cf. also Heb 13:21: ποιεῖν τὸ εὐάρεστον ("to do what is well pleasing"). Εὐάρεστον also replaces ἀρεστόν elsewhere in the New Testament.

74 On the epexegetical ἵνα after the demonstrative see p. 15, n. 1 on 1:5.

75 Καθώς is used in a causal sense: "corresponding to the fact that." The statement καθὼς ἔδωκεν is a reference by the author to Jn 13:24; 15:12, 17, although the ἐντολή ("commandment") of God is intended here rather than the ἐντολή of Jesus as in the John passages.

from 2:28 to 3:24.[76] The fact that "believe"[77] is mentioned before "love" indicates a priority in the correlation of the two, or, better, indicates that love has its basis in faith, as is also expressed in v 16 (see p. 55).

Πιστεύειν ("believe") is met here for the first time in 1 John; it appears subsequently at 4:1, 16; 5:1, 5, 10, 13 (πίστις, "faith," appears only at 5:4). It is not contrasted, as in Paul, with ἐργάζεσθαι ("to achieve," Rom 4:4f), but has "dogmatic" character, not only, to be sure, in the simple sense of "believe," i.e., "hold to be true," but in the sense of acknowledge.[78] Πιστεύειν is therefore always connected with an object.[79] Here ὄνομα τοῦ υἱοῦ αὐτοῦ Ἰησοῦ Χριστοῦ ("the name of his son Jesus Christ") is given as the object of faith, just as ὄνομα τοῦ υἱοῦ τοῦ θεοῦ ("the name of the Son of God") is the object in 5:13.[80] More simply but with essentially the same meaning, 5:10 has πιστεύειν εἰς τὸν υἱὸν τοῦ θεοῦ ("believe in the Son of God"). Ὄνομα, of course, means the person.

■ 24 In v 24, he who keeps the commandments is promised that he ἐν αὐτῷ μένει καὶ αὐτὸς ἐν αὐτῷ ("abides in him and he in him"). In view of v 23, αὐτός ("he") can only be God. Μένειν ἐν ("abide in") designates the abiding relationship.[81] It is here characterized as a mutual (or reciprocal) relationship, as in 4:13 and 4:15.[82]

If v 24a is a promise, albeit a conditional one, then in v 24b the certainty of this promise is emphasized:

ἐν τούτῳ γινώσκομεν ὅτι μένει ἐν ἡμῖν . . . ("by this we know that he abides in us . . .").[83] In view of v 18 and v 23, it may come as a surprise that the basis for μένει ἐν ἡμῖν ("he abides in us") is not given as ὅτι (or ἐάν) ἀγαπῶμεν (ἀλλήλους) ("because [or 'if'] we love [one another]"), instead of ἐκ τοῦ πνεύματος . . . ("by the spirit . . ."); 4:13 is almost identical. There, however, the basis of knowledge is precisely love for another, as the result of v 13 following upon vss 11f. From that it follows that the gift of the spirit consists in loving one another.

What follows, however, for the understanding of πνεῦμα ("spirit")? Precisely this: love is not a general human possibility, but a gift. More exactly, the possibility of love is given as a gift which must be repeatedly realized by the believer. For the "we" referred to in v 24 is the same "we" mentioned in v 14 (see p. 55). It is true that they have received the gift of the spirit. That the spirit is not a permanent possession is shown by the admonition to love following upon v 14, and by the warning against false πνεύματα ("spirits") in 4:1ff. If, then, the "spirit" effects love and thereby "abiding in God," so it must be the power of divine activity, but in such a way, however, that this power does not act magically, but grants the possibility of a new understanding of existence—naturally not a theoretical understanding, but a knowledge of being open to the future, with its

---

76 See p. 43. Cf. also the interchange of ἐντολαί ("commandments," plural) in 2:3f. and ἐντολή (singular) in 2:7.

77 When faith is called an ἐντολή ("commandment"), it is not thereby understood to be an ἔργον ("work") in the sense of the Pauline antithesis to πίστις ("faith"). Paradoxically, faith is designated as an ἔργον in Jn 6:29.

78 Schnackenburg is thus correct. It is, therefore, barely distinguishable from ὁμολογεῖν ("to confess") in 2:23; 4:2f, 15.

79 In the dative as here, in the accusative in 4:16, with εἰς in 5:10, 13 or with a ὅτι–clause in 5:1, 5. The dative τῷ ὀνόματι ("the name") is synonymous

with the construction with εἰς.

80 Πιστεύειν εἰς τὸ ὄνομα ("to believe in the name") also occurs in Jn 1:12; 2:23; 3:18 (see Bultmann, p. 59, n. 2 [p. 37, n. 4]). In 5:1, 5 ὄνομα ("name") is explicated by the clause ὅτι Ἰησοῦς ἐστιν ὁ Χριστός or ὁ υἱὸς τοῦ θεοῦ ("that Jesus is the Christ" or "the Son of God"). On the title υἱὸς τοῦ θεοῦ ("Son of God") see p. 13, n. 25 on 1:3.

81 See p. 26, n. 9 on 2:6.

82 On the reciprocal εἶναι ἐν ("to be in") see p. 20, n. 21 on 1:7.

83 On this formula see p. 24, n. 1 on 2:3. Ἐν τούτῳ γινώσκομεν refers here to what follows and is explicated first by the ὅτι–clause and then by the phrase

promise as well as its demand.[84] When it can be said of the spirit: οὗ ἡμῖν ἔδωκεν (*scil.* ὁ θεός) ("which God has given us"), the consciousness of the congregation that it has already received the expected gift of the spirit as eschatological gift is thereby expressed.[85] The receiving of the spirit is therefore likewise historicized, just as are the conception of the antichrist[86] and the receiving of χρῖσμα ("anointing").[87]

In referring here, surprisingly for the first time, to the spirit as the effective power of God, the author has created the transition to 4:1ff, which indicates, however, that the effect of the spirit consists not only in the keeping of the commandments and in mutual love, and therefore not only in a new self–understanding, but also in faith in the revelation in Jesus Christ, which serves as their basis; the effect of the spirit thus also consists in right confession, just as "anointing," according to 2:20, 27, also bestows right knowledge.

ἐκ τοῦ πνεύματος ("by the spirit") (on γινώσκειν ἐκ as "to know by," see Matt 12:33; Lk 6:44).

84 Cf. the discussion on Jn 3:5 in Bultmann, p. 139, n. 1 [pp. 99f (n. 3 which begins on p. 98)]. In an instructive excursus entitled "Zur Vorstellung vom Geist in 1 Joh," Schnackenburg (pp. 209–15) proposes that the reception of the spirit is probably understood sacramentally. Even if this understanding was originally grasped in terms of the visible effects of the spirit, the emphasis quickly "shifted to the inner experiences of salvation." The gift of the spirit is hardly thought of as an endowment with spirit which is tendered with the sacrament. This is so, not only because sacramental thinking is foreign to 1 John (as also to the Gospel of John), but also because, if it were so construed, the community would not need to be warned against false πνεύματα ("spirits") which are at work through the false teachers (4:1ff). For the false teachers are also baptized, as one must conclude from 2:19. Moreover, what could Schnackenburg's reference to "inner experiences of salvation" mean, if not a new self-understanding?

85 The Greek understanding of spirit as νοῦς ("mind") is not, of course, in view.

86 See pp. 35ff on 2:18f.

87 See pp. 37f and 41 on 2:20 and 27 respectively.

4   Warning against False Teaching

1   Beloved, do not believe every spirit, but test the spirits to see whether they are of God; for many false prophets have gone out into the world. 2/ By this you know the Spirit of God: every spirit which confesses Jesus Christ as having come in the flesh is of God, 3/ and every spirit which annuls Jesus is not of God. And this, moreover, is the spirit of antichrist, which you heard is coming, and now is in the world. 4/ Little children, you are of God, and have overcome them; for he who is in you is greater than he who is in the world. 5/ They are of the world, therefore what they say is of the world, and the world listens to them. 6/ We are of God. Whoever knows God listens to us, and he who is not of God does not listen to us. By this we know the spirit of truth and the spirit of error.

[RSV modified]

■1   With 4:1, the theme of false teaching is once again taken up. The author introduces the section with a fresh vocative, ἀγαπητοί ("beloved"), as in 2:7; 3:21. To the warning against false teaching in 2:18–27 now corresponds the admonition: μὴ παντὶ πνεύματι πιστεύετε ("do not believe every spirit"). The warning is scarcely to be understood as an "admonition of prudence" (Schnackenburg): "Do not trust every spirit." Rather, πιστεύειν ("believe") is to be understood just as in 3:23, and thus as faith in the sense of acknowledgment: "do not come into the power of every spirit." For, the notion of πνεῦμα ("spirit") in the warning is surely to be taken, analogous to its use in 3:24, as an operative power, which promises results and is therefore seductive. As a consequence, the readers must be warned: δοκιμάζετε τὰ πνεύματα ("test the spirits"). There are thus several of these seductive powers, and it is necessary to test them to see εἰ ἐκ τοῦ θεοῦ ἐστιν ("whether they are of God").[1] Does that perhaps mean that there are also "spirits" among those to be tested in which one could place his faith? In support of an affirmative answer, one could appeal to 1 Thess 5:21, but hardly correctly. According to 1 John, there is only one πνεῦμα τοῦ θεοῦ ("spirit of God"), which in v 6 is called the πνεῦμα τῆς ἀληθείας ("the spirit of truth"), and whose opposite is the πνεῦμα τῆς πλάνης ("the spirit of error") or the antichrist. It is important to recognize this, and when the warning refers to "spirits" in the plural, it is undoubtedly for the reason that the "spirit of error" is operative in a plurality of seducers. Accordingly, the admonition is

---

1   On εἶναι ἐκ, which designates the origin and thereby the essence, see p. 36, n. 6 on 2:19. Schnackenburg, p. 224, is correct in stressing the following: "One's basic nature may be inferred from his practical behavior . . ., but not the reverse: there is no basis for determining in advance whether one will decide for faith or unfaith."

provided with a ὅτι–clause as its premise: ὅτι πολλοὶ ψευδοπροφῆται ἐξεληλύθασιν εἰς τὸν κόσμον ("for many false prophets have gone out into the world").

The ψευδοπροφῆται ("false prophets") are undoubtedly the false teachers, and it is probable that the author has in mind the false prophets prophesied for the endtime (Mk 13:22; Matt 24:11, 24). He therefore historicizes the prophesied eschatological phenomenon in the same way as the prophecy of the antichrist in 2:18 and immediately below in v 3. It is a matter of indifference whether the false prophets lead the believers astray by means of σημεῖα καὶ τέρατα ("signs and wonders," Mk 13:22).[2] It is decisive that they are false teachers,[3] that is, that they do not confess Jesus Christ come in the flesh, as v 2 immediately shows. Although they are many, nevertheless only the one "spirit," that of the antichrist, is at work in them.

■ 2 The criterion by means of which δοκιμάζειν ("testing") is to be carried out is given in v 2: ἐν τούτῳ γινώσκετε τὸ πνεῦμα τοῦ θεοῦ ("by this you know the spirit of God").[4] Γινώσκετε ("you know") can be understood as an imperative, but probably better as an indicative, just as in 3:20 the readers are reminded of the knowledge which they possess.[5] It is the knowledge that πᾶν πνεῦμα ὃ ὁμολογεῖ Ἰησοῦν Χριστὸν ἐν σαρκὶ ἐληλυθότα ἐκ τοῦ θεοῦ ἐστιν ("every spirit which confesses Jesus Christ as having come in the flesh is of God").[6] That is just

what the false teachers dispute, according to 2:22, when they deny ὅτι Ἰησοῦς . . . ἔστιν ὁ Χριστός ("that Jesus is . . . the Christ"),[7] that is, they deny that the Christ, whom they also revere as the bringer of salvation, has appeared in the historical Jesus. It involves nothing other than that he has come ἐν σαρκί ("in the flesh"). It therefore appears to be a question of Docetism in the case of the heretical doctrine.[8] Of the one who makes the right confession it can be said: ἐκ τοῦ θεοῦ ἐστιν ("he is of God").[9] This confession therefore asserts the paradoxical identity of the historical and the eschatological figure of Jesus Christ.

■ 3 Verse 3a completes the criterion of δοκιμάζειν ("testing"), in that the false confession is set over against the right one: καὶ πᾶν πνεῦμα, ὃ λύει τὸν Ἰησοῦν ἐκ τοῦ θεοῦ οὐκ ἔστιν ("and every spirit which annuls Jesus is not of God") [Trans.]. Whereas ἀρνεῖσθαι ("deny") is used of the antithesis to right confession in 2:22f, here it is λύειν, i.e., annul, abolish—in the event this reading, attested early, is correct.[10] In any case, λύει does not differ substantively in meaning from μὴ ὁμολογεῖ ("does not confess"), attested by most witnesses. The latter, however, was a correction very probably occasioned by v 2. The use of λύειν in this sense is admittedly exceptional and striking; but the meaning cannot be in doubt: to deny Jesus Christ as having come in the flesh.

Verse 3b serves to strengthen ". . . is not of God"

---

2   The fact that false prophets have come into the world means only that they appear everywhere publicly (thus Schnackenburg is correct).

3   Cf. 2 Petr 2:1 where the ψευδοπροφῆται ("false prophets") are characterized as ψευδοδιδάσκαλοι ("false teachers").

4   Ἐν τούτῳ refers to what follows. On this formula see p. 24 n. 1 on 2:3.

5   The other apparently secondary readings have also understood it as indicative: γινώσκεται ("he is known") and γινώσκομεν ("we know").

6   The translation of this phrase is "Jesus Christ as having come in the flesh." The accusative Χριστόν ("Christ"), therefore, is to be understood as a predi-

cate accusative (as Schnackenburg correctly interprets it). Moreover, the combination Ἰησοῦς Χριστός ("Jesus Christ") is common (cf. 1:3; 2:1), especially in formulaic sentences such as 3:23; 5:6.

7   Likewise, 2 Jn 7.

8   See pp. 38f on 2:22.

9   Ὁμολογεῖν has the same meaning, "confession," in vss 2f as it does in 2:23; 4:17; 2 Jn 7; Rom 10:9f, etc. (see p. 21 n. 28 on 1:9).

10   On the manuscript evidence cf. esp. Schnackenburg, p. 222. The other reading, ὃ μὴ ὁμολογεῖ ("which does not confess"), is indeed well attested; nevertheless, it apparently is a correction which is made on the basis of v 2. The negative μή ("not") in the

by means of καὶ τοῦτό ἐστιν τὸ τοῦ ἀντιχρίστου ("and this, moreover, is the [spirit] of antichrist").[11] Whether one understands the sentence to mean, "just this, i.e., the annulling of Jesus, is the essence of the antichrist," or whether one supplies πνεῦμα after τό ("this is the [spirit]"), the content remains the same. For, in any case, the false teaching is traced back to the antichrist, who, as already stated in 2:18, is at work in the heretical teachers. The mythological figure of the antichrist is thereby demythologized and historicized. When it is said of the spirit ὃ ἀκηκόατε ὅτι ἔρχεται ("which you heard is coming") [Trans.], the author alludes to the prophecy of mythological apocalyptic, as in 2:18; this prophecy is demythologized in the sentence, καὶ νῦν ἐν τῷ κόσμῳ ἐστίν ("and now it is in the world"), the νῦν ("now") of which corresponds to the νῦν of 2:18.[12] According to v 1, it is clear that the prophecy has been fulfilled in the appearance of the false prophets.[13] The κόσμος ("world") is thus here simply the perceptible world in which the congregation lives and the false teachers appear.

■ 4 Just as 3:14 gave expression to the triumphal self-consciousness of the congregation, so does v 4a: ὑμεῖς ἐκ τοῦ θεοῦ ἐστε, τεκνία, καὶ νενικήκατε αὐτούς ("Little children, you are of God, and have overcome them"). As 3:14 is in the first person, "we," so here the person is second plural "you," since the readers are addressed as "little children" here as in 2:1. As the "we" in 3:14 referred to the congregation in its real nature, so the "you" here. In this is also contained an indirect admonition, following the direct warning in v 1. The consciousness of victory distinguishes the congregation, just as

in 2:13f the νεανίσκοι ("young men") were brought to the consciousness that νενικήκατε τὸν πονηρόν ("you have overcome the evil one").[14]

The certainty of victory has its basis in the knowledge, ὅτι μείζων ἐστὶν ὁ ἐν ὑμῖν ἢ ὁ ἐν τῷ κόσμῳ ("for he who is in you is greater than he who is in the world," v 4b). That "he who is in you" refers to God is self-evident; but who is "he who is in the world"? It is striking that the antithesis to "in you" is not "in them," although it was just said, "you have overcome them." But the author cannot speak in this way. For, the αὐτοί ("them"), over whom the congregation has been victorious, are the false teachers, and if the antichrist is at work in them, it nevertheless cannot be said of him that he is in them. For the figure of the antichrist has been historicized: he is not *in* them, but they themselves *are* antichrists (2:18). The opponent of God (as v 5 confirms) is Satan, the "evil one" (πονηρός) of 2:13f. When he is characterized as ὁ ἐν τῷ κόσμῳ ("the one in the world"), one is inclined to understand κόσμος ("world") in the same sense as in v 3, i.e. as the openness of the perceptible world.

■ 5 But when there immediately follows in v 5: αὐτοὶ ἐκ τοῦ κόσμου εἰσίν κτλ. ("they are of the world . . ."), then it is clear that "world" is meant as the "world" which is hostile to God, as in 2:15ff. It does not therefore designate the space in which the false teachers (as all men) find themselves, but its nature, as that comes to expression in their language: διὰ τοῦτο ἐκ τοῦ κόσμου λαλοῦσιν ("therefore what they say is of the world"). The further explication, καὶ ὁ κόσμος αὐτῶν ἀκούει

---

relative clause is also remarkable, since it is very seldom so used. As such, its meaning must be iterative; see Blass–Debrunner §428(4).

11 Καί means "and, moreover" in this clause.

12 This sentence is independent; i.e., it is not related to the previous ὅτι ("that").

13 Schnackenburg, therefore, is correct in emphasizing that the antichrist "is not pictured as a concrete figure." This follows from the fact that the relative

clause does not begin with ὅν ("whom") but reads ὃ ἀκηκόατε ("which you heard") and, therefore, refers to τὸ τοῦ ἀντιχρίστου (" the [spirit] of antichrist").

14 Victory does not mean that the false teachers have been condemned and expelled from the community (as Windisch argues). On the contrary, this is the victory of faith which has no reference to a historical situation; cf. 5:4f; Jn 16:33.

("and the world listens to them"), thereby likewise indicates that they belong to a "world" alien to God, indeed, hostile to God.

■ **6** In contrast to these, it can be said of the community of the believers (v 6): ἡμεῖς ἐκ τοῦ θεοῦ ἐσμεν· ὁ γινώσκων τὸν θεὸν ἀκούει ἡμῶν ("We are of God; whoever knows God listens to us").[15] The following clause, ὃς οὐκ ἔστιν ἐκ τοῦ θεοῦ οὐκ ἀκούει ἡμῶν ("he who is not of God does not listen to us"), corresponds to what was said in 3:1: ὁ κόσμος οὐ γινώσκει ἡμᾶς ("the world does not know us"). It was said in 3:13 that this fact can be pointedly designated as the hate of the world. What is said of Jesus in Jn 8:47; 18:37 can therefore also be applied to the congregation.

In vss 2f the confession of Jesus Christ was given as the criterion of δοκιμάζειν ("testing"); now in v 6b a new criterion is advanced: ἐκ τούτου γινώσκομεν τὸ πνεῦμα τῆς ἀληθείας καὶ τὸ πνεῦμα τῆς πλάνης (By this we know the spirit of truth and the spirit of error").

The difference between the spirit of truth and the spirit of deception becomes discernible in whether the proclaimed word is heard or not.[16] Πνεῦμα τῆς ἀληθείας ("spirit of truth") naturally means the same thing as πνεῦμα τοῦ θεοῦ ("spirit of God") in v 2.[17] The "spirit of error" is the satanic power at work in the false teachers. These are they of whom it is said in 2:26 that "they would deceive you," and against whom 3:7 warns: "let no one deceive you."[18] The entire section 4:1–6 sets in bold relief the decisive contrast between God and "world," truth and delusion, and thus true faith and false teaching.[19]

---

15 The substitution of ἡμεῖς ("us") for the ὑμεῖς ("you") of v 4 does not indicate a material difference; in both cases the reference is to the community of faith. Cf. the interchange of "we" and "you" in 2:19f, 24f, 28; 3:13f; 5:13f.

16 Ἐκ τούτου ("by this") refers here to what precedes.

17 Ἀλήθεια ("truth") is the genuine, divine reality; see pp. 18f on 1:6. The formula πνεῦμα τῆς ἀληθείας ("spirit of truth") occurs only here in 1 John, but is found in Jn 14:17; 15:26; 16:13. Cf. also 1 Jn 5:6.

18 The meaning remains the same whether one translates as "error," "delusion," or in an active sense as "deceiving." The meaning of πνεῦμα τῆς πλάνης ("spirit of error") is the same as that of ἐνέργεια

πλάνης ("influence of error") in 2 Thess 2:11.

19 The antithesis between the two spirits occurs elsewhere, especially in the Testament of the XII Patriarchs and in the Qumran texts. See Schnackenburg, pp. 226f and Excursus 9, pp. 209–15. The relationship of 1 Jn 4:1–6 to Qumran is treated in detail by Braun, "Qumran und das Neue Testament," pp. 108–11 [297–300].

4

**Brotherly Love as Response
to the Love of God**

7 Beloved, let us love one another; for love is
of God, and he who loves is born of
God and knows God. 8 / He who does
not love does not know God; for God is
love. 9 / In this the love of God was made
manifest among us, that God sent his
only Son into the world, so that we
might live through him. 10 / In this is
love, not that we loved God but that he
loved us and sent his Son to be the
expiation for our sins. 11 / Beloved, if
God so loved us, we also ought to love
one another. 12 / No man has ever
seen God; if we love one another, God
abides in us and his love is perfected
in us.

The section on false teaching, 4:1–6, is followed by a
section on the theme of love of neighbor, 4:7–12, which
had already been treated in 2:28–3:24. It is once again a
discussion with the false teachers, and insofar as 4:7–12
follows upon 4:1–6, there is a relation between the
two sections. While in 2:28–3:24 the controlling idea
was brotherly love as a sign of birth out of God, a motif
that is again taken up in v 7, the theme is now the knowledge of God, which was already denied the false teachers
in 2:3.

■ **7** The section is initiated afresh in v 7 with the address,
ἀγαπητοί ("beloved"), as in v 1; 2:7. The admonition
ἀγαπῶμεν ἀλλήλους ("let us love one another")
repeats, in direct imperative form, the admonition of
3:11–23; it is again repeated by vss 11f immediately
following. As an admonition to love the brother or the
brethren, it extends from 2:10 through the whole writing.
The imperative ἀγαπῶμεν ("let us love") is used in
3:18; 4:19 without an object, but of course in an identical

sense. [1]

The admonition in v 7a is given a premise by means of
a ὅτι–clause, which the author has presumably taken
from his Source, and which prompted him to make the
relation of love to knowledge of God the dominant
theme. In the Source, v 7b formed antithetical parallelism with v 8a:

πᾶς ὁ ἀγαπῶν ἐκ τοῦ θεοῦ γεγέννηται
ὁ μὴ ἀγαπῶν οὐκ ἔγνω τὸν θεόν
"He who loves is born of God;
    He who does not love does not know God"
The author probably expanded these lines by adding καὶ
γινώσκει τὸν θεόν ("and knows God") to the first line,
prompted by οὐκ ἔγνω τὸν θεόν ("does not know God")
in the second line,[2] and provided a basis for v 8a by the
addition of v 8b: ὅτι ὁ θεὸς ἀγάπη ἐστίν ("for God
is love").

The initial imperative, "let us love one another,"
leaves no doubt that πᾶς ὁ ἀγαπῶν ("he who loves")

---

1 Codex Alexandrinus (A) inserts τὸν θεόν ("God")
as the direct object after πᾶς ὁ ἀγαπῶν ("He who
loves") in v 7b.

2 Instead of ἔγνω (aorist tense), a few MSS read
γινώσκει (present tense) which is, no doubt, an

assimilation to the γινώσκει of v 7b. The aorist tense
(as in 3:1 and the perfect tense in 3:6) "indicates
that such a man has not yet come to a knowledge of
God." (Schnackenburg, p. 229 n. 1).

means the love of neighbor, even though no object is appended. Schnackenburg contests that brotherly love is the theme of 4:7–5:4 (especially of 4:7). According to him, the real theme is the nature of love in general ("love in and of itself," p. 229). He is right in holding that the theme is the nature of love, but is wrong in opposing the nature of love and brotherly love.[3] The love of God is certainly not simply to be equated with love of brother; however, the former not only is the basis of the latter, but includes it. There is certainly no love without a vis-à-vis. The vis-à-vis of God is the world, as indicated in Jn 3:16: (οὕτως γὰρ ἠγάπησεν ὁ θεὸς τὸν κόσμον (ὥστε κτλ.) ("[For] God [so] loved the world [that . . .]").[4] To the world also belong ἡμεῖς ("we"), whom God loved (v 11; cf. v 9), and on whom he bestowed his love (3:1).[5] If the love of God has as its object the world and thereby "we," the object of those loved by God is accordingly the neighbors. It is therefore appropriate to say, "let us love one another," v 7; and, as v 11 shows, the gift of God's love includes the demand for mutual love

■ **8**   The sentence, ὁ θεὸς ἀγάπη ἐστίν ("God is love," v 8b), is not intended to describe the nature of love as such, but indicates the basis of the demand to love. One can doubtless say that the nature of God is thereby also depicted, but the assertion is not a definition, any more than "God is light" (1:5) and "God is spirit"

(Jn 4:24[6]) are. Rather, God's work is described, i.e., his acts in their significance for man, which becomes the subject matter in what immediately follows (vss 9f). Moreover, the sentence cannot be reversed to read, "love is God." In that case, "love" would be presupposed as a universal human possibility, from which a knowledge of the nature of God could be derived.[7] The theme of 4:7–5:4 is therefore the love of brother which has its basis in God's love, and this theme is so important to the author, moreover, because love characterizes the nature of Christian faith in contrast to the false teaching. The claim of the false teachers that they know God, even behold him, is refuted by the fact that they lack brotherly love.[8]

In other respects, vss 7 and 8 do not require detailed comment, since in them the concepts and expressions already used recur. When it is said of "love" that ἐκ τοῦ θεοῦ ἐστιν ("it is of God"), then εἶναι ἐκ ("to be of") characterizes the origin and thus the nature of love, as elsewhere (see p. 36 n. 6 on 2:19); it is the "way of God" (to use a phrase of Schnackenburg). That it can be said of one loving that ἐκ τοῦ θεοῦ γεγέννηται ("he is born of God") corresponds to expressions in 2:29 and 3:9 (see pp. 45ff, 52f), and in such a way that love is emphasized as the mark of having been born of God. Again, καὶ γινώσκει τὸν θεόν ("and knows God") corresponds to expressions in 2:3f, and if in the earlier

---

3   Schnackenburg is also correct in his assertion that the nature of Christian love differs from a possible "love" of the "world" and that the love intended in 1 John is the "way of God" (p. 228).

4   In this context the world refers, of course, to humanity, not to the "world" of v 5, etc.

5   Although the revelation of God's love manifested itself as God ἐν ἡμῖν ("among us," v 9) and although "we" are the object of this love according to v 11, one may not conclude that "the universality of the divine activity of love" is thereby restricted. This interpretation of Schnackenburg, p. 233, is correct and not that of Herbert Preisker, *Die urchristliche Botschaft von der Liebe Gottes im Lichte der vergleichenden Religions-*

geschichte (Giessen: 1930), pp. 47, 58f. "We" refers here, as in v 6, etc., to the Christian community which confesses that the revelation of the ἀγάπη τοῦ θεοῦ ("love of God") has come to it as a gift. As a result, no one is excluded except the one who chooses to exclude himself by refusing to believe.

6   See above pp. 16f on 1:5 and Bultmann, pp. 191f [141] on Jn 4:24.

7   I am in general accord with Schnackenburg's comments in his instructive excursus entitled "Die Liebe als Wesen Gottes" ("Love as the nature of God"), pp. 231–39.

8   See pp. 24f on 2:3ff and p. 44 on 2:28ff.

passage keeping the commandments serves as the mark of knowledge of God, here it is "love," which, according to v 21; 2:10 (and 3:23), together with "belief," is the content of the commandments (or commandment).

■ **9** "God is love" (v 8) is explicated in v 9 in such a way that ἀγάπη is depicted as God's fact of love: ἐν τούτῳ ἐφανερώθη ἡ ἀγάπη τοῦ θεοῦ ἐν ἡμῖν, ὅτι κτλ. ("In this the love of God was made manifest among us, that . . .").[9] It is uncertain how ἐν ἡμῖν is to be understood and what its reference is. If it is referred to ἐφανερώθη ("made manifest"), then it can mean "among us." In that case, the "we" would be either the Christian congregation or the world as the place where the revelation appeared; ἀπέσταλκεν . . . εἰς τὸν κόσμον ("sent . . . into the world") here and in v 14 could be taken to support this reading. Ἐφανερώθη ἐν ἡμῖν ("made manifest among us") would have the same sense as the absolute ἡ ζωὴ ἐφανερώθη ("the life was made manifest") in 1:2a. Or, ἐν ἡμῖν could mean "to us."[10] "We" would then likewise mean either the congregation or the world. If one assumes a "faded" meaning, as does Schnackenburg (p. 229 n. 2), the meaning would be the same as ἡ ζωὴ ἐφανερώθη . . . ἡμῖν ("the life was made manifest . . . to us," 1:2); "we" would then refer to the congregation. But it is also possible to refer ἐν ἡμῖν to ἡ ἀγάπη τοῦ θεοῦ ("the love of God"). Verse 16 speaks for this interpretation: . . . τὴν ἀγάπην ἣν ἔχει

ὁ θεὸς ἐν ἡμῖν ("the love which God has for us"), but so does v 10, insofar as God's act of love "for us" is being underscored. In that case, too, "we" could be the congregation or the world.

In any case, ἐφανερώθη ("made manifest") means the revelation in the historical event of Jesus' appearance, as the ὅτι–clause shows: ὅτι τὸν υἱὸν αὐτοῦ τὸν μονογενῆ ἀπέσταλκεν ὁ θεὸς εἰς τὸν κόσμον ("that God sent his only Son into the world"). The formulation that God has sent his Son is common in Christian discourse and occurs especially often in John (cf. Jn 3:17 in particular[11]). Although ἔδωκεν ("gave") appears instead of ἀπέστειλεν ("sent") in Jn 3:16, the meaning is of course identical. Verse 9 is therefore also identical in meaning to Jn 3:16, since υἱός ("Son") is designated as μονογενής ("only") in both instances (the term appears elsewhere only in Jn 1:14, 18; 3:18).[12] Μονογενής, which means "only," is both a predicate of value and designates the unique one as beloved at the same time.[13] The historical event can and must also be understood as the eschatological event, insofar as the question of life and death is decided by one's disposition to it.[14] That is made clear by the clause, ἵνα ζήσωμεν δι' αὐτοῦ ("so that we might live through him"). It is indeed the event by means of which sin is taken away (3:5) and the work of the devil nullified (3:8). The paradox that the eschatological event is being consummated in the present

---

9   Ἐν τούτῳ ("In this") is explicated by the ὅτι–clause (see p. 24 n. 1 on 2:3).

10   On this cf. Jn 9:3: ἵνα φανερωθῇ τὰ ἔργα τοῦ θεοῦ ἐν αὐτῷ ("that the works of God might be manifested to him"). Φανερωθῇ ἐν would then be used like ποιεῖν τι ἔν τινι ("to do something to/for someone") or γίνεσθαι ἐν ("to appear to"); see Blass–Debrunner §220 (1).

11   See pp. 8f on 1:2.

12   The interchange between the aorist tense ἀπέστειλεν (as in v 10 and usually in John) and the perfect tense ἀπέσταλκεν which occurs here is not an indication of any material difference. Cf. also Schnackenburg, p. 230 n. 3.

13   Just like the Hebrew יָחִיד ("only son"), which is also translated in the LXX with ἀγαπητός ("beloved"). This adjective, moreover, is used in Matt 12:18; Mk 1:11; 9:7 to describe the υἱός ("son"). Cf. Bultmann, p. 71 n. 2 [47 n. 2]; Schnackenburg, p. 230 n. 1.

14   See pp. 8f on 1:2. This φανερωθῆναι ("appearance"), which is both an historical and an eschatological event, must, of course, be distinguished from the φανερωθῆναι which is still outstanding in the future in 2:28; 3:2; see pp. 44f n. 4 and pp. 48f.

was expressed in 3:14 by μεταβεβήκαμεν ἐκ τοῦ θανάτου εἰς τὴν ζωήν ("we have passed out of death into life").

■ **10** Verse 10 explicates δι' αὐτοῦ ("through him") in v 9: ἐν τούτῳ ἐστὶν ἡ ἀγάπη, οὐχ ὅτι... ἀλλ' ὅτι... ("In this is love, not that . . . but that . . .").[15] When the question is posed whether the ὅτι–clauses describe the nature of love in and of itself (Schnackenburg), or intend our love, which is directed to God, the answer must be: the latter. For the first ὅτι–clause: οὐχ ὅτι ἡμεῖς ἠγαπήκαμεν τὸν θεόν ("not that we loved God") is evidently directed against the opinion that God is directly available as an object of love for the natural man. This is the opinion of the false teachers, who also do not understand the revelation as historical event. The clause, ἀλλ' ὅτι αὐτὸς ἠγάπησεν ἡμᾶς ("but that he loved us"), functions to contradict this opinion. Love which has God as its object can only be a response to God's love for us, which, in its φανερωθῆναι ("manifestation"), is addressed to us, so to speak, as a question.

The fact that the further elaboration in v 10b: καὶ ἀπέστειλεν τὸν υἱὸν αὐτοῦ ἱλασμὸν περὶ τῶν ἁμαρτιῶν ἡμῶν ("and he sent his Son to be the expiation for our sins") follows upon v 9 is striking and so disturbs the rhythm that it must be attributed to the ecclesiastical redactor, as was the identical attribute of Jesus in 2:2 (see p. 23).[16]

■ **11** The thought of v 10a was suggested already in 3:16a (see p. 55), and there the consequence was drawn in 3:16b: καὶ ἡμεῖς ὀφείλομεν κτλ. ("and we ought . . ."); the sequence is entirely comparable in v 11:

ἀγαπητοί, εἰ οὕτως ὁ θεὸς ἠγάπησεν ἡμᾶς, καὶ ἡμεῖς ὀφείλομεν ἀλλήλους ἀγαπᾶν ("Beloved, if God so loved us, we also ought to love one another"). The demand of v 7 is thus repeated, after being given its basis in vss 8–10a.

■ **12** Verse 12, however, expands that basis still further by adding θεὸν οὐδεὶς πώποτε τεθέαται ("No man has ever seen God"), which, like v 10a, is aimed at the idea, apparently characteristic of the gnosticizing false teachers, that God himself can be a direct object of love arising from man—a thought so important to the author that he repeats it in v 20.[17] It is likewise expressed in Jn 1:18. There is no direct relationship to God, only an indirect one, which consists of men loving each other: ἐὰν ἀγαπῶμεν ἀλλήλους, ὁ θεὸς ἐν ἡμῖν μένει ("if we love one another, God abides in us").[18] That mutual love is the way to love of God is confirmed by the following sentence: καὶ ἡ ἀγάπη αὐτοῦ τετελειωμένη ἐν ἡμῖν ἐστιν ("and his love is perfected in us").[19] Αὐτοῦ ("his") can only be a subjective genitive; for, the demand for brotherly love, placed at the beginning and constantly repeated (vss 11f, 19–21), is expressly grounded by the reference to the love with which God loved us (vss 9, 10a, 11, 19–21).[20] Τετελειωμένη . . . ἐστιν ("is perfected") then means: the love of God conferred upon us reaches its goal in brotherly love.[21]

In Jn 1:18 the thought that no one has seen God is expressed in order to emphasize that God is accessible only through his revelation (ἐκεῖνος ἐξηγήσατο, "that one has made him known"). Here in v 12 the thought serves to say that a relation to God is realized only in

---

15 Ἐν τούτῳ ("in this") is again explicated by the following ὅτι–clauses.

16 See Bultmann, "Die kirchliche Redaktion," 201.

17 Schnackenburg (pp. 240f) thinks that v 12 is directed against the Gnostics, "for whom the soul's (ecstatic) 'journey to heaven' was a form of 'divine knowledge' or 'divine wisdom.' " It is not clear to me, however, whether actual Gnostics or only false teachers of a gnosticizing Christian type are under attack.

18 On μένειν ἐν ("to abide in") see p. 26 n. 9 on 2:6.

19 In "Analyse des ersten Johannesbriefes," 152, I conjectured that v 12 contains a reworked section of the Source which reads roughly as follows:
    ἐὰν ἀγαπῶμεν ἀλλήλους, ὁ θεὸς ἐν ἡμῖν μένει
    καὶ ἡ ἀγάπη αὐτοῦ τετελειωμένη ἐν ἡμῖν ἐστιν,
    If we love one another, God abides in us
    and his love is perfected in us,
    I must admit, however, that Schnackenburg's misgivings about this hypothesis are justified.

20 According to Schnackenburg, the theme of 4:7–10

mutual love. That the two belong together, that faith in God's revelation in Jesus Christ and brotherly love therefore form a unity, is expressed not only by the fact that the revelation is expressly characterized, in vss 7–12, as the basis of brotherly love, but also by the fact that the revelation becomes the dominant theme in the verses that immediately follow (vss 13–16). The theme of the revelation of course involves ὁμολογεῖν ("confession") and πιστεύειν ("believing"). The conclusion of v 16 speaks of God "abiding" (μένειν) in us, as v 12 had done. Brotherly love does not actually again become the theme in v 17. That occurs only in 4:19–5:4. But even with the new theme of vss 17f, viz., the theme of παρρησία ("confidence"), there is a certain connection which expresses itself in the fact that the τετελειωμένη ("is

perfected") of v 12 is again taken up in a somewhat modified form.

It cannot be denied that in 4:7–5:12 there is no unified sequence of thought. Although there is no lack of connective ideas, vss 13–16 and vss 17f are nevertheless felt to be interruptions in the flow of thought,[22] and one is inclined to conjecture that passages originally conceived in isolation are being combined in 4:7–5:12. One is inclined to the view that we have to do here with the work of a school. One could almost say that in 4:7–5:12 there is reflected something like the discussion of a theological "seminar" of the Johannine "school."

---

is not brotherly love, but the nature of love in general. Consequently, he does not wish to understand αὐτοῦ ("his") as a subjective genitive, nor, on the other hand, as an objective genitive, but as a "qualitative" genitive which conveys the meaning of "the divine love, the love which belongs to God alone." Against this see above pp. 55f.

21 On τελειοῦσθαι see p. 14 n. 30 on 1:4.

22 Schnackenburg also senses the lack of connection

between 4:12 and 4:13ff, as well as the internal disunity in the latter section (pp. 241f). He terms vss 14f a digression, following which the author returns to the theme of love in v 16.

4

**Confession and Faith
in God's Act of Salvation**

13 By this we know that we abide in him and
he in us, because he has given us of his
own Spirit. 14/ And we have seen
and testify that the Father has sent his
Son as the Savior of the world. 15/ Whoever confesses that Jesus is the Son of
God, God abides in him, and he in God.
16/ So we know and believe the love
God has for us. God is love, and he who
abides in love abides in God, and God
abides in him.

■ **13** The knowledge that God μένει ἐν ἡμῖν ("abides in us"), in 3:24b, is stated first by means of a ὅτι–clause and then given a premise by means of a prepositional phrase, ἐκ τοῦ πνεύματος ("by the spirit") (see pp. 59f). In 4:13, similarly, there are two ὅτι–clauses, the first of which is explicative, the second causal. The second corresponds not only formally to the ἐκ τοῦ πνεύματος of 3:24b, but is virtually identical verbally: ἐν τούτῳ γινώσκομεν, . . . ὅτι ἐκ τοῦ πνεύματος αὐτοῦ δέδωκεν ἡμῖν ("By this we know . . . because he has given us of his own spirit").[1] It is also the basis, moreover, of the same knowledge, viz., the knowledge that God abides in us. In contrast to 3:24b, the μένειν ("abiding") is now characterized as reciprocal (ὅτι ἐν αὐτῷ μένομεν καὶ αὐτὸς ἐν ἡμῖν, "that we abide in him and he in us"); this corresponds to what is said of reciprocal abiding in 3:24a.[2] In the earlier passage, of course, the reciprocal abiding consists in our keeping his commandments; here in the fact that God has given us of his spirit. Since now the commandments (or commandment) are concentrated in brotherly love, on the one hand, and since, on the other, v 13 follows the admonition to brotherly love, the proof for the reception of the spirit must be seen precisely in the fact that it grants us the possibility of brotherly love.[3] According to v 14, however, the spirit grants us the knowledge of and witness to God's love in the sending of his Son, from which ὁμολογεῖν ("confession") and πιστεύειν ("belief," vss 15f) then follows as a consequence. For the author, however, there is evidently no difference. For in 3:23 also the ἐντολή ("commandment") is double: faith and love. Ὅτι ἐκ τοῦ πνεύματος αὐτοῦ δέδωκεν ("because he has given us of his own spirit") therefore has a twofold sense, the first of which points backward (to the command to love one another, which is grounded in God's love), the second of which looks forward to confession and faith.

■ **14** It is precisely this which appears as the theme in vss 14f: καὶ ἡμεῖς τεθεάμεθα καὶ μαρτυροῦμεν ὅτι κτλ. ("And we have seen and testify that . . .). Τεθεάμεθα points back to v 12 and emphasizes that there is a θεᾶσθαι ("seeing") of God, in spite of the fact that "no man has ever seen God." However, the seeing is precisely not direct—which is contested, indeed, in v 11—but indirect. If this seeing in v 12 was the relationship to God fulfilled in love for one another, then according to v 14 the relationship to God has its basis in God's act of salva-

---

1 On διδόναι ἐκ see Blass–Debrunner §169.
2 On the reciprocity of the relationship, see p. 20 n. 21 on 1:7.
3 On the concept πνεῦμα ("spirit"), see above pp. 59f on 3:24. Schnackenburg doubts (p. 241) "that the spirit strengthens the conviction in Christians to love the brethren. The parenetical emphasis, which in v 12 falls on ἀγαπῶμεν ("we love"), would thereby be weakened."

tion in sending his Son. The seeing of faith[4] evinces its certainty in the fact that it carries its testimony with it: καὶ μαρτυροῦμεν ("and testify").[5] What faith sees and testifies to is stated in almost the same words as in v 9: ὅτι ὁ πατὴρ ἀπέσταλκεν τὸν υἱὸν σωτῆρα τοῦ κόσμου ("that the Father has sent his Son as savior of the world").[6] In place of the attributive μονογενής ("only") of v 9, we now find: σωτῆρα τοῦ κόσμου ("savior of the world"), which means the same thing as "so that we might live through him" (v 9).[7]

■ **15** Verse 15 interprets, as it were, how "the savior of the world" is made effective: ὃς ἐὰν ὁμολογήσῃ ὅτι . . . ὁ θεὸς ἐν αὐτῷ μένει καὶ αὐτὸς μένει ἐν τῷ θεῷ ("Whoever confesses that . . . God abides in him, and he in God"), in that the relationship described by the reciprocal abiding, which is spoken of previously in v 13, is naturally identical with the meaning of Jesus as "savior." The presupposition for this is stressed in the relative clause: ὃς ἐὰν ὁμολογήσῃ κτλ. ("Whoever

confesses that . . .").[8] The content of the confession, ὅτι Ἰησοῦς ἐστιν ὁ υἱὸς τοῦ θεοῦ ("that Jesus is the Son of God"), is used like that in vss 2f, only more briefly formulated, and like the phrase in 3:8; 5:5, 10, 13, and is similar to 4:3.

■ **16** That this presupposition has been fulfilled in the congregation is claimed in v 16a: καὶ ἡμεῖς ἐγνώκαμεν καὶ πεπιστεύκαμεν τὴν ἀγάπην ἣν ἔχει ὁ θεὸς ἐν ἡμῖν ("So we know and believe the love God has for you"). For the acknowledgment of and faith in God's love is identical to the content of the confession that Jesus is the Son of God. The love of God consists in the sending of his Son, as was already said in vss 9f.[9] Verse 16b repeats the sentence from v 8b (see pp. 66ff), and adds a description of the reciprocity of the love relationship between God and the believers, in a way similar to that in vss 12 and 13 (see the comment on v 13, and p. 59 on 3:24).

---

4   It goes without saying that θεᾶσθαι ("to see") is a seeing of faith, as πεπιστεύκαμεν ("we believe") in v 16 indeed shows; see Bultmann, pp. 67ff [44f] on Jn 1:14. Although τεθεάμεθα ("we have seen") appears here without an object, the object is doubtless to be supplied from the ὅτι–clause, as Schnackenburg (p. 242) rightly suggests.

5   On the term μαρτυρέω ("testify"), see Bultmann, 50f n. 5 [30 n. 5] on Jn 1:7.

6   Although πατήρ ("father") appears here in place of ὁ θεός ("God") as in v 9, this does not, of course, signify a difference. On πατήρ as a designation of God, see p. 9 n. 9 on 1:2.

7   The title σωτήρ τοῦ κόσμου ("savior of the world") appears only here in 1 John, in addition to Jn 4:42. Simple σωτήρ ("savior") otherwise occurs frequently in the New Testament, as do σῴζειν ("to save"; this term occurs in John also) and σωτηρία

("salvation"). See Bultmann, p. 154 n. 1 [111 n. 1] on Jn 3:17; p. 201 n. 4 [149 n. 2] on Jn 4:22; also see Schnackenburg, p. 243.

8   On ὃς ἐάν see Blass–Debrunner §§107, 377. On ὁμολογεῖν ("confess") see p. 21 n. 28.

9   On the expression ἔχει ἐν ἡμῖν ("have for us"), see above on v 9, p. 67; also Schnackenburg, p. 244 n. 2. It is self–evident that γινώσκειν ("know") is not theoretical knowledge, but rather a knowing that includes acknowledgment; see 2:3–5 and pp. 24ff. Πιστεύειν ("believe") also incorporates acknowledgment; see 3:23; 4:1, and p. 59. The perfect characterizes the knowledge of God as an abiding and firm knowledge (Schnackenburg, p. 244).

4

Confidence as the Fruit of Love

17 In this is love perfected with us, that we
may have confidence for the day of judgment, because as that one is so are we
in this world. 18/ There is no fear in
love, but perfect love casts out fear. For
fear has its own agony, and he who
fears is not perfected in love.

[RSV modified]

■ **17** The motif of ἀγάπη ("love") does indeed appear
in vss 17f, but the real theme is not love but παρρησία
("confidence"). Verse 17a asserts at the outset that
confidence is a fruit of love, in that the introductory ἐν
τούτῳ ("In this") is explicated by the ἵνα–clause:[1]
τετελείωται ἡ ἀγάπη μεθ᾿ ἡμῶν, ἵνα παρρησίαν
ἔχωμεν . . . (". . . is love perfected with us, that we may
have confidence . . ."). Τετελείωται means: love has
reached its goal, corresponding to the τετελειωμένη . . .
ἐστιν ("is perfected") of v 12.[2] Ἡ ἀγάπη μεθ᾿ ἡμῶν
("love . . . with us") can only have the same meaning
as (εἰ οὕτως) ὁ θεὸς ἠγάπησεν ἡμᾶς ("[if] God [so]
loved us," v 11) and τὴν ἀγάπην ἣν ἔχει ὁ θεὸς ἐν ἡμῖν
("the love God has for us," v 16). The "love" is therefore God's love.[3]

God's love has fulfilled its aim in granting us "confidence." In the transmitted text, "confidence" is qualified
by ἐν τῇ ἡμέρᾳ τῆς κρίσεως ("for the day of judgment"). Since "day of judgment" can only be the future
eschatological judgment, this qualification appears to
correspond to what was said in 2:28. In 2:28, however,
the reference is to παρρησία ("confidence") in view
of the παρουσία ("coming") of Jesus, while here it can

only be a matter of God's judgment, just as in 3:21
παρρησία πρὸς τὸν θεόν ("confidence before God") is
spoken of, and the latter alone can be intended in 5:14.[4]
However, ἐν τῇ ἡμέρᾳ τῆς κρίσεως ("for the day of
judgment") comes under suspicion as an addition by the
ecclesiastical redactor since the following ὅτι–clause
does not make sense: ὅτι καθὼς ἐκεῖνός ἐστιν καὶ ἡμεῖς
ἐσμεν ἐν τῷ κόσμῳ τούτῳ ("because as that one is so
are we in this world").[5] Ἐκεῖνος ("that one") can only
refer to Jesus, as it always does elsewhere, and if παρρησία ("confidence") is intended as the "confidence"
before him on the day of judgment, then the clause
καθὼς . . . ἐστιν ("as that one is") does not make sense.
The text would then have to read ἦν ("was") instead
of ἐστιν ("is"), which, in fact, is read by some manuscripts. For, the ἐν τῷ κόσμῳ τούτῳ ("in this world"),
which goes with ἡμεῖς ἐσμεν ("we are"), cannot be
brought into relation to καθὼς . . . ἐστιν ("as that one
is"). But what is it supposed to mean to say that he is in
the world?[6] It would be natural if one were permitted
to add to καθὼς ἐκεῖνός ἐστιν ("as that one is"): ἐν τῇ
ἀγάπῃ (τοῦ πατρός) ("in the love [of the Father]"),
which would correspond to the statement in Jn 15:10.

---

1   Ἐν τούτῳ refers to what follows (see p. 23 n. 1 on
    2:3); on the explication of a demonstrative by means
    of a ἵνα–clause, see p. 15 n. 1 on 1:5.
2   On v 12 see pp. 68f; on τελειοῦν see p. 26 n. 6 on
    2:5.
3   Schnackenburg contests this because "love" in v 18
    means love in human behavior. See further below on
    v 18.
4   On παρρησία see pp. 44f n. 4 on 2:28.
5   The textual variants show that the traditional text

does not make unambiguous sense.
6   Schnackenburg attempts to make do with ἐστίν by
    explaining: "he 'is' ever, even morally, what he
    was on earth, and therefore an example for those
    bound to him who are still 'in this world' " (p. 247).
    He must then assert that ἐν τῷ κόσμῳ τούτῳ ("in
    this world") goes only with ἐσμέν ("we are"). How-
    ever, this interpretation of καθὼς ἐκεῖνός ἐστιν ("as
    that one is") does not appear to me to be possible.

A further emendation then suggests itself: read ἐν τῇ ἀγάπῃ ("in love") after ἐσμέν ("we are") instead of ἐν τῷ κόσμῳ τούτῳ ("in this world"), and φόβος οὐκ ἔστιν ἐν τῇ ἀγάπῃ ("There is no fear in love") would also follow very well. On the other hand, "in this world" fits better after παρρησίαν ἔχωμεν ("we have confidence"), where the redactor may have replaced it with "in the day of judgment," which does not suit the context. The aim of the love of God to give us confidence in the world is reminiscent of the prayer of Jesus in Jn 17:15: "I do not pray that thou shouldst take them out of the world, but that thou shouldst keep them from the evil one."[7]

It seems to me to be beyond doubt that the traditional text is not in order. It would be only a hypothetical attempt, of course, were one to conjecture as the original text:

ἐν τούτῳ τετελείωται ἡ ἀγάπη μεθ' ἡμῶν,
ἵνα παρρησίαν ἔχωμεν ἐν τῷ κόσμῳ τούτῳ,
ὅτι καθὼς ἐκεῖνός ἐστιν (ἐν τῇ ἀγάπῃ τοῦ πατρός
καὶ ἡμεῖς ἐσμεν ἐν τῇ ἀγάπῃ).[8]

"In this is love perfected with us,
That we may have confidence in this world,
Because as that one is in the love of the father,
So are we in love." [Trans.]

Φόβος οὐκ ἔστιν ἐν τῇ ἀγάπῃ ("there is no fear in love") would fit in any case. This sentence sounds like an aphorism, and is intended, in the context, to serve as justification for the fact that the believers are permitted to have "confidence." "Confidence" is the freedom from "fear."[9] It is indeed tempting, in view of the contrast φόβος–ἀγάπη ("fear–love"), to understand ἀγάπη as the love of man for God. But ἀγάπη cannot be understood other than as God's "love with us," and must therefore be the love of God given to us.[10] Precisely of this love can it be said, however, that it is without fear, for fear can only be fear before God. But there can be no fear for those who know themselves to be endowed with God's love.

■ 18 Verse 18 corresponds to what has just been said: ἀλλ' ἡ τελεία ἀγάπη ἔξω βάλλει τὸν φόβον ("but perfect love casts out fear"). For τελεία ἀγάπη ("perfect love") means τετελείωται ἡ ἀγάπη μεθ' ἡμῶν ("love is perfected with us"), and in this sense it can then be said: ὁ δὲ φοβούμενος οὐ τετελείωται ἐν τῇ ἀγάπῃ ("he who fears is not perfected in love"):[11] Whoever still fears before God has still not reached the goal opened up to him by the gift of God's love; for him God's love has not yet become ἐν ἀληθείᾳ ("reality") (cf. 2 Jn 3; 3 Jn 1). That "perfect love" drives out "fear" is given a basis by the ὅτι–clause: ὅτι ὁ φόβος κόλασιν ἔχει. This sentence again has an aphoristic ring. In Matt 25:46 and elsewhere, κόλασις indeed means the punishment associated with eschatological judgment, and it may

---

7 One cannot appeal to 5:14, however, since 5:14–21 is added by the ecclesiastical redactor.

8 One might also consider whether ἔμπροσθεν αὐτοῦ ("before him") originally followed "that we may have confidence." In that case, ὅτι καθὼς ἐκεῖνός ἐστιν ("because as that one is") would connect up well. Ἐν τῷ κόσμῳ τούτῳ ("in this world") would then have to be deleted as an inferior addition. But how did it get into the text?

9 Φόβος ("fear") in this sense only here in 1 John (it means something different in Jn 7:13; 19:38; 20:19, viz., fear of the Jews). Rom 8:15 is materially related: οὐ γὰρ ἐλάβετε πνεῦμα δουλείας πάλιν εἰς φόβον, ἀλλὰ ἐλάβετε πνεῦμα υἱοθεσίας ("For you did not receive the spirit of slavery to fall back into fear, but you have received the spirit of sonship.").

10 Schnackenburg is of the opinion, on the contrary, that it is love with respect to human behavior.

11 Schnackenburg is right in holding that this sentence is not the continuation of the ὅτι–clause, but an antithesis to v 18a.

be understood accordingly: "Because fear has to do with punishment" (Weizsäcker) or "Because fear has punishment (in view)" (Windisch). However, Luther's understanding suits the context better: "For fear has its own agony" (so also the Zürich translation). That would mean: fear contains its own punishment. In that case, the concept of the eschatological κόλασις ("punishment") is historicized like the concept κρίσις ("judgment") in Jn 3:19; 5:24, which corresponds to the statement in 3:14 that those who love have already passed out of death into life.[12]

12 Schnackenburg interprets differently, but rightly sees that the problem of the relation of fear and love, with which Judaism is concerned (p. 247 n. 4), is not posed, and that the reflection "that love is to be valued more highly than fear in the posture of piety," is accordingly absent (p. 248). But he believes that 4:18 shows that "Christians have not yet achieved the fruits of fellowship with God in practice" and exhibit "too little trust in the power that comes from God." One can of course say that 4:17f contains an indirect admonition. But first and foremost these verses extol the possibility of the gift of παρρησία ("confidence").

4
Brotherly Love as Commandment or as the Essence of the Commandments

5

19 We love, because he first loved us. 20 / If any one says, "I love God," and hates his brother, he is a liar; for he who does not love his brother whom he has seen, cannot love God whom he has not seen. 21 / And this commandment we have from him, that he who loves God should love his brother also. 5:1 / Every one who believes that Jesus is the Christ is a child of God, and every one who loves the parent loves the child. 2 / By this we know that we love the children of God, when we love God and obey his commandments. 3 / For this is the love of God, that we keep his commandments. And his commandments are not burdensome. 4 / For whatever is born of God overcomes the world; and this is the victory that overcomes the world, our faith.

[RSV modified]

The theme of brotherly love, which dominated in vss 7–12, is resumed with 4:19, following the intervening sections, vss 13–16 and vss 17f. (See p. 43). If the caption brotherly love is suitable for 4:19–5:4a, the section is nevertheless not characterized by a closely articulated sequence of thought, and is not given a firmer connection with the following section, 5:4b–12, than the transitional v 4b provides.[1] With respect to 4:7–12, 4:19–5:4a does not contain any new and developing thoughts, but repeats, with slight variations, what had already been said. The impression is confirmed that what we have here is not an original, coherent composition, but rather a combination of individual meditations or discussions of the Johannine "school" (see pp. 43f).

■ **19** There is a difficulty at the outset: it is uncertain whether ἡμεῖς ἀγαπῶμεν ("we love") is to be understood as indicative or as imperative. With 4:7 in view, one is inclined to take it as indicative, in view of 4:8–12 as imperative, and so also as imperative in the case of 4:20–5:2.[2] A second difficulty goes together with the first, viz., which object is to be supplied with ἀγαπῶμεν ("we love"): θεόν ("God"), or ἀλλήλους ("one another") or τοὺς ἀδελφούς ("the brethren")? If 4:11f favors "one another," the causal clause: ὅτι αὐτὸς πρῶτος ἠγάπησεν ἡμᾶς ("because he first loved us")[3] supports the view that "God" is to be supplied.[4] But vss 20f above all support the latter; these verses are evidently directed against the gnosticizing notion that human love can be aimed directly at God, and endeavor to say that love intended for God can only be demon-

---

1 See above, pp. 43f.
2 Of course, there is no emphasis on ἡμεῖς ("we"). Otherwise a particle like οὖν (some manuscripts) or, better still, δέ would be expected.
3 Πρῶτος of course has comparative force (Blass–Debrunner §62), thus not "in the first place, to begin with," but "earlier than."
4 Some MSS read τὸν θεόν ("God"); although others supply αὐτόν ("him"), the meaning is of course identical.

strated in love for the brother. The leading question is therefore the question of the love which has God as its object. The thought thus repeats the content of 4:10a: Our love is the response to the love of God granted to us.

Since 4:20–5:2 makes the point that our love of God is realized only in love of brother, v 19 can be designated the transition to the theme of brotherly love (with Schnackenburg).

■ **20** And it is just this thought, that love of God becomes actual only in love of brother, which v 20 expresses. This verse varies the motif of 3:17, and in such a way, moreover, that conduct devoid of compassion is designated as hate;[5] the one who claims to love God in spite of such behavior is a liar ($\psi\epsilon\acute{v}\sigma\tau\eta s$). "Liar" thus has a double sense: the liar does not speak the truth, and he thereby divorces himself from the reality of God.[6] That he is therefore a sinner is expressed by the assertion that he has not seen God, as in 3:6; 3 Jn 11. It is again unmistakable that the author's remarks are aimed at the gnosticizing false teachers, who boast of an immediate vision of God.

■ **21** Verse 21 does not present a fresh thought, but now formulates the exhortation to brotherly love, corresponding to the love of God, as a "commandment" ($\dot{\epsilon}\nu\tau o\lambda\acute{\eta}$);[7] this admonition is pervasive in 4:7ff, was expressed similarly in 2:7ff; 3:23, and reappears again in 5:2f.

■ **5:1** The requirements of faith and brotherly love were already combined in 3:23. In 5:1–4 they are again connected, and in 5:1 in the special sense that faith appears as the presupposition of brotherly love.[8] The content of faith is formulated as in 2:22: $\ddot{o}\tau\iota$ 'I$\eta\sigma o\hat{v}s$ $\dot{\epsilon}\sigma\tau\iota\nu$ $\dot{o}$

$X\rho\iota\sigma\tau\acute{o}s$ ("that Jesus is the Christ"), which is identical in meaning with the formulation in 3:23 and 5:5. It is said of the believer: $\dot{\epsilon}\kappa$ $\tauo\hat{v}$ $\theta\epsilon o\hat{v}$ $\gamma\epsilon\gamma\acute{\epsilon}\nu\nu\eta\tau\alpha\iota$ ("[he] is born of God" [Trans.]), as in the corresponding sentences in 2:29; 3:9; 4:7.[9] The fact that the author produces this sentence as the presupposition for the demand for brotherly love, vss 1b, 2, is surprising, and one is inclined to conjecture that the author is prompted to do so by a text of his Source, which he wishes to make use of here. This text could originally have formed a parallelism with v 4a. It may be reconstructed as follows:

$$\pi\hat{a}s\ \dot{o}\ \dot{a}\gamma\alpha\pi\hat{\omega}\nu\ \tau\dot{o}\nu\ \dot{a}\delta\epsilon\lambda\phi\acute{o}\nu\ \alpha\dot{v}\tau o\hat{v}$$
$$\dot{\epsilon}\kappa\ \tauo\hat{v}\ \theta\epsilon o\hat{v}\ \gamma\epsilon\gamma\acute{\epsilon}\nu\nu\eta\tau\alpha\iota$$
$$\kappa\alpha\grave{\iota}\ \pi\hat{a}\nu\ \tau\dot{o}\ \gamma\epsilon\gamma\epsilon\nu\nu\eta\mu\acute{\epsilon}\nu o\nu\ \dot{\epsilon}\kappa\ \tauo\hat{v}\ \theta\epsilon o\hat{v}$$
$$\nu\iota\kappa\hat{a}\ \tau\dot{o}\nu\ \kappa\acute{o}\sigma\mu o\nu.^{10}$$

"Every one who loves his brother
  is born of God
And whatever is born of God
  overcomes the world."

The author may thus have made use of the idea, "born of God," in order to emphasize once again the notion of brotherly love: $\kappa\alpha\grave{\iota}\ \pi\hat{a}s\ \dot{o}\ \dot{a}\gamma\alpha\pi\hat{\omega}\nu\ \tau\dot{o}\nu\ \gamma\epsilon\nu\nu\acute{\eta}\sigma\alpha\nu\tau\alpha$ $\dot{a}\gamma\alpha\pi\hat{a}\ \tau\dot{o}\nu\ \gamma\epsilon\gamma\epsilon\nu\nu\eta\mu\acute{\epsilon}\nu o\nu\ \dot{\epsilon}\xi\ \alpha\dot{v}\tau o\hat{v}$ ("and every one who loves the parent loves the child," literally "every one who loves the one begetting loves what is begotten of him"). This sentence again has the character of an aphorism: Whoever loves his father also loves his son, his brother. In the context, however, it of course means: whoever loves God also loves his brother. Whether the reference here is specifically to the Christian brother or to the "neighbor" is a moot question,[11] although v 2 sup-

---

5   Cf. 2:9, 11; 3:15.
6   See above, pp. 18f on 1:6, and cf. 2:4, 22.
7   On $\tau\alpha\acute{v}\tau\eta\nu$ . . . $\ddot{\iota}\nu\alpha$, see p. 13 n. 27 on 1:4.
8   See p. 59 (3:23) on $\pi\iota\sigma\tau\epsilon\acute{v}\epsilon\iota\nu$, which occurs here again following its appearance in 3:23; 4:1, 16. For $\pi\hat{a}s$ combined with a participle, see p. 39 n. 21 on 2:23.
9   See pp. 45ff on 2:29 for a discussion of $\gamma\epsilon\gamma\acute{\epsilon}\nu\nu\eta\tau\alpha\iota$ $\dot{\epsilon}\kappa$ $\tauo\hat{v}$ $\theta\epsilon o\hat{v}$.
10   See Bultmann, "Analyse des ersten Johannesbriefes," 154.
11   On the double meaning of "brother," see pp. 28f (2:9) on $\dot{a}\delta\epsilon\lambda\phi\acute{o}s$.

ports the former, if it is here a question of love for the τέκνα τοῦ θεοῦ ("children of God"). With the concept "children of God" the author has again taken up the concept of γεγέννηται ἐξ αὐτοῦ (*scil. τοῦ θεοῦ*) ("born of him," i.e., "of God") from 3:1.

■ **2** Verse 2 is most difficult, indeed almost incomprehensible. To be sure, ἐν τούτῳ γινώσκομεν ("By this we know") clearly refers to what follows,[12] and the content of γινώσκομεν is given by the ὅτι–clause: ὅτι ἀγαπῶμεν τὰ τέκνα τοῦ θεοῦ ("that we love the children of God"). It is also clear that the basis of such knowledge is given by the ὅταν–clause: ὅταν τὸν θεὸν ἀγαπῶμεν κτλ. ("when we love God . . ."). But it is strange that here love directed to God serves as the basis of the knowledge that one loves the brother, while elsewhere it is the reverse (vss 1b; 4:7f, 20f). Is the paradox actually being ventured that because brotherly love is proof of love of God, so also love of God is proof of brotherly love? In that case, a circle would be formed, so to speak, which, from the perspective of a mere spectator, is not comprehensible, but is comprehensible only from the viewpoint of someone standing within the circle, as both the agent and recipient of love. Or may the continuation of the ὅταν–clause: καὶ τὰς ἐντολὰς αὐτοῦ ποιῶμεν ("and obey his commandments"), be taken so closely with "when we love God" that the two parts of the clause form hendiadys, with the result that love of God is understood as "keeping his commandments"?

■ **3** Verse 3 could be taken as support for this interpretation, since ἐντολαί ("commandments") are defined as: αὕτη γάρ ἐστιν ἡ ἀγάπη τοῦ θεοῦ, ἵνα τὰς ἐντολὰς αὐτοῦ τηρῶμεν ("For this is the love of God, that we keep his commandments").[13] In homiletical style the author adds: καὶ αἱ ἐντολαὶ αὐτοῦ βαρεῖαι οὐκ εἰσίν ("And his commandments are not burdensome").[14]

■ **4** The explication that follows in v 4a shows that it is not a matter of ethical idealism or optimism, but that the sentence is conceived on the presupposition of faith: ὅτι πᾶν τὸ γεγεννημένον ἐκ τοῦ θεοῦ νικᾷ τὸν κόσμον ("For whatever is born of God overcomes the world").[15] Since this sentence again has the form of an aphorism,[16] v 4b follows with an explanation:[16] καὶ αὕτη ἐστὶν ἡ νίκη ἡ νικήσασα τὸν κόσμον, ἡ πίστις ἡμῶν ("and this is the victory that overcomes the world, our faith"). It is once again a proud confession on the part of the Christian congregation, such as those found in 3:14 (see p. 55) and 4:4 (see p. 63). It is the consciousness of the superiority of the congregation over the κόσμος, which is here designated "world," as in 2:15f. The confessional character of the sentence is shown by the fact that the aorist (ἡ νικήσασα) now replaces the present tense of v 4a (νικᾷ). The victory is already won. That "world" here means the world not only divorced from God but also hostile to him at the same time, is shown by the talk about a victory over it, which of course pre-

---

12   Schnackenburg takes it to refer to what precedes: "On the basis of this principle . . . we know," namely on the basis of v 1b. But he then runs into difficulties with the ὅταν–clause, and must conclude that in this clause the sequence is reversed and the sentence actually means: "We always (then) love the children of God, when we really love God (our and their procreator)." However, this reversal appears to be arbitrary. Holtzmann rightly opposed such transpositions proposed earlier.

13   On the interchange of the plural and singular of ἐντολή see pp. 26f on 2:7. On the demonstrative with ἵνα following, as in 4:21, etc., see p. 15 n. 1. On τηρεῖν τὰς ἐντολάς see pp. 24f on 2:3.

14   There are parallels in Philo and the Shepherd of Hermas, to which Windisch refers.

15   For the possibility that v 4a originally stood in parallelism with v 1, see above p. 76. On τὸ γεγεννημένον ἐκ τοῦ θεοῦ (as in v 1), see pp. 45ff on 2:29.

16   In the typical form of a demonstrative clause (see

supposes a war between God and world.[17] The πίστις ("faith") of the congregation is designated as the subject of the victory; the substantive is used only here in 1 John (and in John), while the verb πιστεύειν appears in 5:1; 3:23; 4:1, 16. Πίστις (like πιστεύειν) is not used in the specifically Pauline sense, in contrast to "works," but means acknowledgment, and πιστεύειν is virtually synonymous with ὁμολογεῖν ("confess") as used in 2:23; 4:2f, 15.

We are brought with 5:4 to the transition to the new theme taken up in 5:5–13.

---

p. 15 n. 1), which here provides the explication by means of a noun in the nominative.

17 Although the victory in 2:13f is called a victory over the πονηρός ("the evil one"), the meaning is nevertheless synonymous, since κόσμος ("world") substitutes for πονηρός in 2:2, 15. Schnackenburg points out (p. 254 n. 3) that the Qumran community is also filled with "the spirit of battle and confidence of victory," but that there is a decisive difference between Qumran and 1 John, in that at Qumran the eschatological victory is expected soon but is still outstanding, while in 1 John the victory over the world has already been achieved by Christ and is continuing in his congregation.

5

**Faith in the Son of God
and Witness for Him**

5   Who is it that overcomes the world but he
who believes that Jesus is the Son of
God? 6/ This is he who came by water
and blood, Jesus Christ, not with the
water only but with the water and the
blood. 7/ And the Spirit is the witness,
because the Spirit is the truth. 8/ There
are three witnesses, the Spirit, the
water, and the blood; and these three
agree. 9/ If we receive the testimony of
men, the testimony of God is greater;
for this is the testimony of God that he
has borne witness to his Son. 10/ He
who believes in the Son of God has the
testimony in himself. He who does
not believe God, has made him a liar,
because he has not believed in the
testimony that God has borne to his
Son. 11/ And this is the testimony, that
God gave us eternal life, and this life
is in his Son. 12/ He who has the Son has
life; he who has not the Son of God
has not life. 13/ I write this to you who
believe in the name of the Son of God,
that you may know that you have
eternal life.

[RSV modified]

■ **5** The faith that is certain of victory over the world (v 4), is the faith ὅτι Ἰησοῦς ἐστιν ὁ υἱὸς τοῦ θεοῦ ("that Jesus is the Son of God"), according to v 5. This definition of faith is substantively identical to that found in 2:22f, and verbally the same as in 4:15, where the content of the confession is formulated: ὃς ἐὰν ὁμολογήσῃ ὅτι Ἰησοῦς ἐστιν ὁ υἱὸς τοῦ θεοῦ ("Whoever confesses that Jesus is the Son of God"). It was clear already from 2:22f that such formulations are aimed at the christology of the gnosticizing false teachers, who of course see Jesus Christ as the bringer of salvation, but who deny that the Christ is to be identified with the historical Jesus (see pp. 38f). This was made especially evident in 4:2, where the confession was characterized as a confession of Jesus Christ, the one who has come in the flesh (see pp. 62f).

■ **6** The same point is scored in a new form in v 6a: οὗτός ἐστιν ὁ ἐλθὼν δι' ὕδατος καὶ αἵματος ("This is he who came by water and blood").[1] For this sentence affirms: the Son of God is the historical Jesus, who was baptized and crucified. The addition of v 6b makes the opposition to the false teachers plainly evident: οὐκ

---

1   On the form of predication οὗτός ἐστιν, cf. Eduard Norden, *Agnostos Theos. Untersuchungen zur Formengeschichte religiöser Rede* (Leipzig–Berlin, 1913; reprint 1956), pp. 187f. See Blass–Debrunner §223(3) on ἔρχεσθαι διά to denote manner of coming. Ἐν can be used in a synonymous way (as in what immediately follows) to denote manner, see Blass–Debrunner §198(4).

ἐν τῷ ὕδατι μόνον, ἀλλ' ἐν τῷ ὕδατι καὶ ἐν τῷ αἵματι ("not with the water only but with the water and the blood").[2] This obviously contradicts the gnosticizing view that the heavenly Christ descended into Jesus at his baptism, and then abandoned Jesus again before his death.[3] In support of the truth of true faith, which confesses the paradoxical identity of the Son of God and the historical Jesus, the author calls upon the witness of the spirit (v 6c): καὶ τὸ πνεῦμά ἐστιν τὸ μαρτυροῦν ("And the spirit is the witness"). That evidently corresponds to what was said of the χρῖσμα ("anointing") in 2:20, 27, viz., that it imparts the right knowledge and instruction (see pp. 57f, 41); it also corresponds to what was said of πνεῦμα ("spirit") in 4:2, viz., that the right confession has its basis in the spirit. But in what sense does the spirit attest the faith as characterized in v 6a–b? Where else does the spirit give its testimony than in the faith, knowledge, and confession of the congregation itself? Faith, knowledge, and confession are, after all, gifts imparted by "anointing" or by the "spirit," according to 2:20, 27; 4:2. Of course one may also say: the witness of the spirit occurs in the word which is proclaimed and believed in the congregation, in the ἀγγελία ("message," 1:5), in the λόγος, which the congregation has heard (2:7, 14).[4] The witness of the spirit is thus not a datum which could be used to establish the correctness of the assertion of faith on a neutral basis. Faith as faith in the proclaimed word is certain of itself.[5]

The witness of the spirit is nevertheless valid: ὅτι τὸ πνεῦμά ἐστιν ἡ ἀλήθεια ("because the spirit is the truth").[6] The ἀλήθεια ("truth," with article) is the reality of God, which discloses itself (see pp. 18f), reveals itself. The matter can therefore be formulated: the revelation bears witness for itself.

■ **7f** The appropriate continuation of this line of thought comes in v 10: ὁ πιστεύων . . . ἔχει τὴν μαρτυρίαν ἐν αὑτῷ ("He who believes . . . has the testimony in himself"). But vss 7–9 come between. Verses 7 and 8 can only be a redactorial gloss. In v 6 "spirit" is designated as "witness." Now τρεῖς μαρτυροῦντες ("three witnesses") are mentioned, and if it is mildly surprising that the "spirit" which testifies is conceived as a unity with the testimony of the "water" and the "blood,"[7] it is startling that "water" and "blood" are called witnesses. In v 6 they mean baptism and crucifixion, and thus the beginning and end of the activity of the historical Jesus, and the witness of the spirit was precisely that the historical Jesus is the Son of God. In vss 7f the facts attested by the spirit now themselves appear as witnesses. "Water" and "blood" therefore must have a different meaning than in v 6. What they now mean can scarcely be in doubt: they are now the sacraments of baptism and the Lord's supper, which bear testimony for Jesus

---

2   The addition of καὶ πνεύματι ("and the spirit") in ℵ A al. is evidently supplied on the basis of what follows, but it is spurious since the point is the characterization of the historical reality of the Son of God having come in the flesh. See Schnackenburg (p. 260 n. 3) also for discussion of the various textual variants.

3   On the question of which heterodox teachers are meant, see pp. 38ff. The view of Windisch, that the sentence is aimed at the Jews and disciples of John, who were acquainted only with purification and baptism by water, is erroneous.

4   Also cf. Jn 6:63: τὰ ῥήματα ἃ ἐγὼ λελάληκα ὑμῖν πνεῦμά ἐστιν καὶ ζωή ἐστιν ("The words that I have spoken to you are spirit and life").

5   There is no reference, of course, to experiences of inspiration or to a *lumen internum* ("inner light"). Nevertheless, one may well point to the remarks regarding the paraclete in Jn 14–16 as material parallels (so Schnackenburg).

6   The reading Χριστός ("Christ") in place of τὸ πνεῦμα ("the spirit") is nonsensical; it probably arose only from the reminiscence of Jn 14:6. One might have expected a δέ instead of the ὅτι. However, it is apparently an intermediate (but unexpressed) step in the reasoning that is to be given a basis: the testimony of the spirit is credible (, for . . .).

7   It is difficult to believe (with Schnackenburg) that

Christ as God's Son, since they mediate the salvation of the community imparted through him. [8] This may also serve to explain why the "spirit" as witness is combined into a unity with the two other witnesses. If this combination was initially prompted by the fact that the "spirit" was called "witness" in v 6, it nevertheless has a special meaning for the redactor: the two sacraments, baptism and Lord's supper, "are witnesses out of the power of the spirit." [9]

The so-called *Comma Johanneum* (vss 7f) is found in Latin manuscripts dating before A.D. 400, the text of which (it varies in details in individual manuscripts) was also taken up into the Sixto-Clementine edition of the Vulgate in the following form: "Quoniam tres sunt, qui testimonium dant in coelo Pater, Verbum et Spiritus Sanctus, et hi tres unum sunt. Et tres sunt, qui testimonium dant in terra Spiritus et aqua et sanguis, et hi tres unum sunt." ("For there are three who bear witness in heaven, the Father, the Word, and the Holy Spirit, and these three are one. And there are three who bear witness on earth, the Spirit and the water and the blood, and these three are one.") Although the decree of the Holy Office in 1897 decided in favor of the authenticity of the *Comma Johanneum*, today its spuriousness is also recognized by Catholic scholars. The passage is unknown to the entire Greek textual tradition. According to W. Thiele ("Beobachtungen zum Comma Iohanneum (I Joh 5:7f)," *ZNW* 50 [1959]:

61–73), it is possible that Cyprian already found the text as a part of his bible. "In that case, the home of the famous interpolation is to be sought in North Africa"—so Schnackenburg, who provides an excursus on the *Comma Johanneum*, pp. 44–46. Also cf. Windisch, with further bibliographical references.

■ **9** Since vss 7 and 8 are to be ascribed to the ecclesiastical redactor, the question arises whether v 9 is not also to be ascribed to him. [10] This verse would indeed connect up well with v 6 to the extent that it, like the conclusion of v 6, expresses the validity of the testimony in new form: it is God's testimony. However, it is precisely this way of putting it that sounds strange. Why, now, is the testimony of God contrasted with the testimony of men? On the basis of v 6, one anticipates that it would have to be the testimony of the spirit. Even were one to resolve the difficulty by considering that the testimony of the spirit also stands for the testimony of God, especially since in v 10 the testimony of God is referred to, the difficulty remains, nevertheless, that v 9 (like vss 7f) severely ruptures the context. The appropriate continuation of v 6 is v 10. It is therefore necessary to ascribe v 9 to the redactor as well.

■ **10** Verse 10 provides the suitable continuation of

the reference here is to Jewish jurisprudence, which required the agreement of at least two witnesses.
8 This is similar to Jn 19:34b, 35 (see Bultmann, pp. 677f [525]), to which Schnackenburg also calls attention. As is the case with earlier exegetes, he also holds fast to the sacramental interpretation of the water and blood in vss 7f; however, he does not feel the contradiction between v 6 and vss 7f, but thinks he can maintain the unity by speaking of "the ambiguity and double reference of the concepts water and blood." Nauck, *Die Tradition und der Charakter des ersten Johannesbriefes*, pp. 147–82, treats "spirit, water and blood" in detail.
9 So Holtzmann. Schnackenburg, p. 261, says sub-

stantially the same thing: "The spirit is the principle of life from which these sacraments acquire their supernatural power." The interpretation of Nauck (*ibid.*) is peculiar. He also proposes to take $\pi\nu\epsilon\hat{\upsilon}\mu\alpha$ in this combination as a sacramental rite, namely as the sacrament of anointing, by means of which the spirit is imparted. Although the reception of the spirit followed baptism almost everywhere in the primitive church, the sequence: reception of the spirit, baptism, eucharist, is said to be found nevertheless in the Syrian Church.
10 Ὅτι μεμαρτύρηκεν ("that he has borne witness . . .") is to be read, not ἣν μεμαρτύρηκεν ("which he has witnessed"), which is read by some

v 6.[11] When v 6 asserts that the "spirit" testifies that the historical Jesus is the Son of God, and that testimony was nothing other than the event of faith, it may now be said accordingly: ὁ πιστεύων εἰς τὸν υἱὸν τοῦ θεοῦ ἔχει τὴν μαρτυρίαν ἐν αὐτῷ ("He who believes in the Son of God has the testimony in himself").[12] The believer therefore requires no testimony other than his own demonstrable witness. When the text continues: ὁ μὴ πιστεύων τῷ θεῷ ψεύστην πεποίηκεν αὐτόν ("He who does not believe God, has made him a liar"),[13] then the self–evident presupposition is that faith in the Son of God is at once faith directed to God, as 2:23 indicates: "He who confesses the Son has the Father also." Jn 3:33 says the same thing: "he who receives his [Jesus'] testimony sets his seal to this, that God is true." To Jn 3:33 corresponds this sentence from 1 John: "He who does not believe God, has made him a liar." The reason the faithless man makes God a liar is explicitly stated: ὅτι οὐ πεπίστευκεν εἰς τὴν μαρτυρίαν, ἣν μεμαρτύρηκεν ὁ θεὸς περὶ τοῦ υἱοῦ αὐτοῦ ("because he has not believed in the testimony that God has borne to his Son").[14] Just as faith in the Son of God and faith in God are identical, so also is the testimony given by God the same thing as the witness of the spirit which demands faith. Since according to v 6, the "spirit" is the "truth," he who does not grant faith to God's witness also declares God a liar.[15]

Schnackenburg rightly says, "If we ask when and how God bore witness to his Son, we get no information from this passage" (p. 264). He points to the Gospel of John where one may find the information—he is correct in that too, but in what sense? Reference must again be made to Jn 3:33, cited above, where the text says that nothing other than the event of faith can be referred to as the witness (see also Bultmann, p. 163 [118]). And that is what is said in v 6, where the witness of the spirit is pointed to (see above, pp. 79f), and it is put baldly in v 10 with the words: ὁ πιστεύων . . . ἔχει τὴν μαρτυρίαν ἐν αὐτῷ ("He who believes . . . has the testimony in himself"). So Schnackenburg (p. 265) comes to the same point: "The witness of God in v 10a is not an 'inner' witness, not one speaking out of the depths, but rather the 'internalized' witness, the testimony that has become the possession of faith. . . ." But that only means: the event of faith is the witness.

■ 11 This is confirmed by the remarkable definition of μαρτυρία ("testimony") given in v 11: καὶ αὕτη ἐστὶν ἡ μαρτυρία ὅτι ζωὴν αἰώνιον ἔδωκεν ὁ θεὸς ἡμῖν ("And this is the testimony, that God gave us eternal life").[16] This testimony can no more be exhibited as something at hand than can the testimony of the spirit.

MSS. Αὕτη ἐστίν ("this is") points ahead and is explicated by the ὅτι-clause (see p. 15 n. 1 on 1:5).

11 It is tempting to assume that the first two antithetical sentences were taken over from the Source and glossed by the author by means of the ὅτι-clause; this was the view set forth in "Analyse des ersten Johannesbriefes," p. 156. But it is necessary to ascribe them to the author, who wrote v 6. He imitated the style of the Source (antithetical parallelism).

12 Πιστεύειν εἰς ("believe in") appears in 1 John only at v 10 (twice) and 5:13, while it is very frequent in John. Elsewhere πιστεύειν ("believe") appears in 1 John with the dative or a ὅτι-clause (both occur also in John). There is no difference between them,

as the occurrence of πιστεύειν with the dative immediately following demonstrates. The insertion of τοῦ θεοῦ ("of God") after τὴν μαρτυρίαν ("the testimony") in some MSS is certainly secondary; it was of course prompted by the following clause. The strongly attested reading ἑαυτῷ for αὐτῷ is likewise an easily understood correction.

13 The reading τῷ υἱῷ ("his Son") or Iesu Christo for τῷ θεῷ ("God") is certainly a correction, as the following ὅτι-clause shows.

14 The variant οὐκ ἐπίστευσεν for οὐ πεπίστευκεν (aorist for perfect) is understandable but secondary.

15 See p. 22 on 1:10.

16 The demonstrative, as in v 9, points ahead and is

Ζωὴ αἰώνιος ("eternal life")[17] belongs to the eschatological time of salvation, but is already present for
faith; for God has given it to us as a gift, and according to
3:14 we know "that we have passed out of death into
life." It can thus only be testimony in the sense that this
knowledge is inherent in faith. One can only add, in
accordance with 3:14, that faith is certain of this knowledge because it loves the brother. The "we" who speak
thus are the community of believers.[18] The basis of
this knowledge is given by: καὶ αὕτη ἡ ζωὴ ἐν τῷ υἱῷ
αὐτοῦ ἐστιν ("and this life is in his Son"). That the
"life" can be the "testimony" lies in the fact that life is
there in the Son of God for the believer, indeed in the
historical Jesus, in whom the life was made manifest, according to 1:1–3. On the basis of v 6, it is specifically
to this historical Jesus that the spirit bears witness: the
testimony given by the spirit and the testimony of God to
the life bestowed upon us as a gift are one and the same,
because life is given in the Son. One would not be sur-
prised were the text to read: ἡ ζωὴ ὁ υἱός ἐστιν ("The
life is the Son"). But, certain as it is that the revelation of
the life is given in the historical Jesus, the author does
not risk the direct equation of "life" and "Son" (as is
done in Jn 11:25; 14:6), but chooses to say that "life" is
given "in the Son," a formulation that appears also in
Jn 3:15 (similarly Jn 16:33; 20:31).

■ **12** In v 12, the Either/Or with which man is con-

fronted is expressed in a pair of sentences, which stand in
antithetical parallelism and were probably taken from
the Source:

ὁ ἔχων τὸν υἱὸν ἔχει τὴν ζωήν·
ὁ μὴ ἔχων τὸν υἱὸν τοῦ θεοῦ τὴν ζωὴν οὐκ ἔχει.[19]
"He who has the Son has life;
He who has not the Son of God has not life."

This demand for the decision of faith, in substance, is an
exact parallel to 2:23. In 2:23 the relationship to the
Father is expressed by ἔχειν ("have"); here the same
verb expresses the relationship to the Son. That the two
are materially identical is obvious, and one can cite
2 Jn 9 as confirmation: there ἔχειν describes the relation
to both Father and Son.

With this call to decision the whole Epistle, which
encompasses 1:1–2:27 and the following sections, is
effectively concluded. There follows in v 13 a postscript,[20]
which states the purpose of the Epistle. To it the ecclesiastical redactor has added an appendix in 5:14–21.[21]

■ **13** Ταῦτα ἔγραψα ("I write these things") naturally
refers back to the whole Epistle, and, as in 1:4 and often
elsewhere, it is explicated by means of a ἵνα–clause.[22]
The subject of the verb ("I write") is the author as
authoritative representative of the tradition, as in 2:14,
21 and elsewhere.[23] Those addressed are the readers
as believers, not the congregation as such; the latter was
referred to in v 11 with ἡμῖν ("to us"). Accordingly,

---

explicated by the ὅτι–clause. Schnackenburg points
rightly to the fact that in the ὅτι–clause the accusative object precedes the subject and is thereby given
strong emphasis. At the end of the clause he prefers
the reading ἡμεῖς ὁ θεός (a matter of word order).

17 Ζωὴ αἰώνιος ("life eternal") and ζωή ("life") are
used in the same sense, as v 11 shows and 1:2 had
already demonstrated.

18 On the "we" in 1 John, see pp. 9ff on 1:1ff, and
p. 55 on 3:14.

19 It is of course possible that the τοῦ θεοῦ ("of God")
in the second line is an addition of the author.

20 Cf. my discussion in "Die kirchliche Redaktion,"
pp. 189f.

21 See below, and "Die kirchliche Redaktion," pp.
191–96. Schnackenburg (pp. 14, 273) interprets
differently; he attributes the lack of a coherent sequence of thought to the author's "way of proceed-
ing by association."

22 See p. 15 n. 1 on 1:5.

23 See pp. 11f.

the indirect imperative contained in the ἵνα–clause is distinguished from the indicative of v 11: ἵνα εἰδῆτε ὅτι κτλ. ("that you may know . . .").[24] The readers certainly know, on the basis of 2:27, that they require no instruction; but their knowledge becomes a certainty if they are believers, and with such confidence (thus also stipulating the condition)[25] the author writes

ὑμῖν . . . τοῖς πιστεύουσιν ("to you . . . who believe").[26] The object of faith is given by εἰς τὸ ὄνομα τοῦ υἱοῦ τοῦ θεοῦ ("in the name of the Son of God"), as in 3:23, and in accordance with the admonition or warning against heretical doctrine that pervades the whole Epistle.

---

24 The conclusion of John (20:31) is quite similar.

25 It cannot therefore be said that the author writes to "mature and determined Christians" (Holtzmann). It is even less correct to say: "The author has not observed any deficiencies in the religious condition of the readers which he had to remedy, but rather merely recognized an available possession" (Windisch). Schnackenburg (p. 273) rightly opposes these views: The author "intends to strengthen the sound Christian self–consciousness . . . ." And on p. 274 he adds: "The experience of God bestowed upon those who believe in Christ should become a life . . . grasped with keen watchfulness."

26 Τοῖς πιστεύσουσιν κτλ. is almost exactly as in Jn 1:12, where it may be an addition to the Source (Bultmann, p. 59 n. 2 [37 n. 4]). Here in v 13 it is appropriate in the context of the author's conclusion. The reading οἱ πιστεύοντες (A al.) smoothes. Other MSS place τοῖς πιστεύσουσιν κτλ. before the ἵνα–clause. Εἰς τὸ ὄνομα ("in the name") is completely synonymous with τῷ ὀνόματι in 3:23.

5   Appendix

14   And this is the confidence which we have in him, that if we ask anything according to his will he hears us. 15 / And if we know that he hears us in whatever we ask, we know that we have obtained the requests made of him. 16 / If any one sees his brother committing what is not a mortal sin, he will ask, and will give him life, for those whose sin is not mortal. There is sin which is mortal; I do not say that one is to pray for that. 17 / All wrongdoing is sin, but there is sin which is not mortal.

18   We know that any one born of God does not sin, but He who was born of God keeps him, and the evil one does not touch him. 19 / We know that we are of God, and the whole world is in the power of the evil one. 20 / And we know that the Son of God has come and has given us understanding, to know him who is true; and we are in him who is true, insofar as we are in his Son Jesus Christ. This is the true God and eternal life. 21 / Little children, keep yourselves from idols.

[RSV modified]

The appendix falls into two parts, vss 14–17 and vss 18–21. The theme of the first part is the prayer of Christians, that of the second, Christian knowledge.

■ **14f** Verse 14 is couched entirely in the style of the author: αὕτη ἐστὶν . . . ὅτι ("this is . . . that").[1] With ἡ παρρησία ἣν ἔχομεν πρὸς αὐτόν ("the confidence which we have in him") the redactor takes up a motif that was treated in 3:21f and 4:17. In 3:21 it was the παρρησία πρὸς τὸν θεόν ("confidence before God"). In 5:14 it is πρὸς αὐτόν ("before him"), and in sequence with v 13 it is not clear whether God or the Son of God is meant. The explication of the "confidence," ὅτι ἐάν τι αἰτώμεθα . . . ἀκούει ἡμῶν[2] ("if we ask anything . . . he hears us"), corresponds to 3:22, except that in 3:22

---

1   See p. 15 n. 1 on the demonstrative that is explicated by means of a ὅτι–clause.

2   There is, of course, no material difference between αἰτεῖν ("ask") in 3:22 and αἰτεῖσθαι in 5:14; there is an interchange of forms also in Jas 4:2f. Nor are αἰτεῖν and ἐρωτᾶν distinguished. Αἰτεῖν and αἰτεῖσθαι are also used for prayer in Jn 16:23f, 26, in verses in which the departing Jesus promises the disciples that prayers addressed to the Father in his name will be answered. The concept παρρησία ("confidence, boldness") in the sense of the freedom of prayer is not found in John.

there is a causal clause: ὅτι τὰς ἐντολὰς αὐτοῦ τηροῦμεν καὶ τὰ ἀρεστὰ ἐνώπιον αὐτοῦ ποιοῦμεν ("because we keep his commandments and do what pleases
him"), while here there is no causal clause; instead,
the condition for a prayer certain to be heard is given as
κατὰ τὸ θέλημα αὐτοῦ ("according to his will"). That
παρρησία ("confidence") in 3:21, as in 4:17, is confidence in prayer addressed to God as judge does not play
a role in 5:14. But above all, it is not evident why παρρησία is taken as the theme at all; it is not, in any case,
motivated by what precedes. Yet, there can be no doubt
that the prayer theme is what genuinely interests the
redactor, and that vss 14f are intended only to prepare for
the new thing to be said in vss 16f. It is precisely for this
reason that the redactor used the motif of 3:21f, and
further emphasized (in relation to 3:22) the assurance of
the certainty of answered prayer in v 15, although not
exactly in a logical form. For, the apodosis, οἴδαμεν
ὅτι κτλ. ("we know that . . ."), says exactly the same
thing as the if–clause, ἐὰν οἴδαμεν ὅτι κτλ. ("if we
know that . . ."):[3] if prayer is sustained by the knowledge
of its being heard, then it follows that the one praying
is certain of being heard.[4] Οἴδαμεν ὅτι ἔχομεν τὰ αἰτή-
ματα κτλ. ("we know that we have obtained the
requests . . .") can only mean this.[5]

■ 16f With vss 16f the redactor comes to his particular
concern. After strongly emphasizing, in vss 14f, the
certainty of answered prayer, it now comes as a complete
surprise that prayer has a peculiar limit. It is likewise
surprising that the subject is now intercessory prayer;
there is no mention of this mode of prayer in vss 14f (nor
anywhere in 1 John).[6] The subject, indeed, is not intercessory prayer in general, but intercession on behalf of a
sinful brother, and even here a distinction is made:
one is certainly to pray for a sinful brother, but only when
his sin is not ἁμαρτία πρὸς θάνατον ("a mortal sin").[7]

The problem of the sin of Christians is thus formulated
as the question of which sins can be forgiven and which
not.[8] It is a question which had already provoked reflection in the Old Testament and in Judaism, where the
unforgivable sin could also be designated as "sin unto
death."[9] The question arose early in the development of
Christianity, as Heb 10:26; Herm. Sim. VI.2 show.[10]
The appearance of this theme in 1 Jn 5:16 clearly demonstrates the character of the appendix, i.e., that it is the
work of an ecclesiastical redactor. For, this distinction

---

3   On the indicative οἴδαμεν incorrectly used after
    ἐάν, see Blass–Debrunner §372(1a): ἐάν is a vulgar-
    ism for ἐπεί. Ὁ ἐάν = ὅ (τί) ἄν, see Blass–Debrunner
    §107.
4   In this οἴδαμεν, the οἴδαμεν of 3:2, 14 (cf. οἴδατε in
    2:20f; 3:5, 15) is being imitated. The "we" here is
    not the congregation as such, as in the other pas-
    sages, but those who pray from time to time.
5   Αἴτημα means "request, demand" in Phil 4:6; Lk
    23:24 (see Bauer s.v.). Here the sense is "what is
    obtained by prayer." On ἔχειν "possess," see v 12
    and 2:23.
6   Nor is intercessory prayer discussed in Jn 16:23f, 26,
    where the promise of answered prayer is made
    (moreover, without the concept παρρησία, "con-
    fidence").
7   The usage ἁμαρτάνει ἁμαρτίαν, "he sins a sin"
    (instead of ποιεῖν τὴν ἁμαρτίαν, as in 3:4, 8f) ap-
    pears only here.

8   On vss 16f, cf. the excursus "Christ und Sünde," in
    Schnackenburg, pp. 281–88.
9   The phrase עָוֹן מִיתָה "sin unto death," Sota 48a is
    found in Strack-Billerbeck III:779. According to
    Lev 4:2ff; 5:1ff; Num 15:22ff, the deliberate sin is
    considered unforgivable; it is punishable by death,
    or God will punish by death. For later Judaism, see
    Schnackenburg, p. 276 n. 5; Otto Michel, Der Brief
    an die Hebräer, KEK 13 (Göttingen: [11]1960), p. 350
    n. 1; especially for Qumran see Braun, "Qumran
    und das Neue Testament," 113–15 [I:302–04].
10   The expression ἑκουσίως ἁμαρτάνειν ("sin delib-
    erately") also appears in Heb 10:26; cf. Michel, Der
    Brief an die Hebräer, pp. 351f.

between kinds of sin[11] stands in contradiction to 1:5–2:2, as well as to 3:4–10. In 1:5–2:2, Christian existence is understood as being constantly under forgiveness. The sinlessness of the believer is not understood as something earned, but as a gift which becomes present in forgiveness, and as gift makes the believer conscious, at the same time, of the constant demand of love. This dialectical understanding of Christian existence is abandoned in 5:16f.[12] In 3:4–10, Christian existence is presented as exempt from sin, with the consequence that the problem of sins actually committed is never given thematic consideration. Rather, it is intended that the readers be made aware of the fact that Christian existence constantly hangs in the balance. The emphasis on the fact that whoever sins shows that he is not "born of God" is a call to decision, and serves as the motivation of the admonition to "do right," to brotherly love.[13] The distinction between forgivable and unforgivable sins would completely destroy this Either/Or. The statement in 3:4 that every ἁμαρτία ("sin") has the character of ἀνομία ("lawlessness") also prohibits the distinction.[14] In contradiction to this statement, it is said in 5:17 that every ἀδικία ("wrongdoing") is to be considered as ἁμαρτία ("sin"), but not every "sin" is, as such, πρὸς θάνατον ("mortal").

What does the redactor understand by ἁμαρτία πρὸς θάνατον ("mortal sin")?[15] Death is of course to be understood in contrast to life, which the one praying gives to the one not sinning πρὸς θάνατον ("unto death").[16] Since ζωή ("life") can hardly be the corporeal life, but must refer (vss 11–13) to the ζωὴ (αἰώνιος) ("life [eternal]") given by God, so is death to be understood here not as physical death, but as eternal death, and thus as the nothingness into which the unbeliever has fallen, according to 3:15. What will happen to such a futile life after physical death (as, for example, torment in hell), is reflected upon in neither 1 John nor in John.

What is the "sin" which leads to such a "death"? If the redactor is thinking of the bent of the entire Epistle, then one thinks first of the apostasy from the true faith, and thus of the heretical doctrine (cf. especially 2:22; 4:3; 5:12). And that is supported by v 21 (see below). But if the Appendix presupposes reflection on sin in an already advanced stage (see above, pp. 86f on vss 16f), it is also possible that the redactor is thinking in general of a wanton transgression of the divine commandments, like the ἑκουσίως ἁμαρτάνειν ("to sin deliberately") in Heb 10:26, or even more concretely of grievous sins, such as adultery and murder, which were subsequently looked upon as unforgivable. A decision can scarcely be taken, as the diverse efforts of exegetes indicate.[17]

What the redactor wants to say, however, is clear: intercession on behalf of the sinner has its limitation in this: an intercessory prayer certain of being answered may

---

11   Nauck thinks that the distinction is not between two kinds of sin, but two kinds of sinners. Rightly opposed to this view are Schnackenburg, p. 277; and Braun, "Qumran und das Neue Testament," p. 114 [I:303].

12   See p. 51 on 3:6.

13   See pp. 52ff on 3:9f.

14   See pp. 49f on 3:4.

15   Πρὸς θάνατον means: leading to death (as the necessary consequence); cf. Jn (4:35); 11:4a; see Bauer s.v. πρός III. 3b.

16   The subject of δώσει ("will give") is very likely not God (so Schnackenburg), but the one praying, for a change of subject between αἰτήσει ("will ask") and δώσει and the ἐρωτήσῃ ("pray") following is improbable. Otherwise a τις would be required before (ἵνα) ἐρωτήσῃ in v 16d, which is added in some MSS. In all probability, no importance is to be attached to the absence of the article before ζωήν ("life") (thus Schnackenburg, p. 276); it is missing in the corresponding phrase (πρὸς) θάνατον ("unto death").

17   In any case, one is not to think of Mk 3:28f par., since the sins of those having Christian faith are not under discussion. On the question cf. Schnackenburg, pp. 276f.

be made only on behalf of one who has not sinned "unto death." The thought is expressed very diffusely and clumsily, and one is at loss, consequently, to know which text to follow in the concluding sentence in v 17. The best attested text is: καὶ ἔστιν ἁμαρτία οὐ πρὸς θάνατον ("but there is sin which is not mortal"). That would sound comforting, so to speak, to those who may be anxiously on guard against praying for a sinner, because it does not seem certain to them whether or not they are interceding for a mortal sinner. In that case, one wonders why this statement was not placed in v 16 before ἔστιν ἁμαρτία πρὸς θάνατον ("there is sin which is mortal").[18] Some witnesses omit the οὐ ("not").[19] In this case, the sentence would only be a repetition of v 16c.

The second part of the appendix (5:18–21) is not related conceptually to the first, and also is not itself bound together by a closely knit train of thought. Verses 18–20 consist of sentences strung together, which repeat, with variation, thoughts of the whole epistle and end in v 21 with an imperative. The repetition of earlier motifs in vss 18–20 apparently seemed to the redactor an appropriate conclusion to a writing edited by him. These motifs are introduced by οἴδαμεν ("we know"), already employed in v 15.[20]

■ **18** Verse 18a is a variation of 3:9, expanded by the addition of ἀλλ' ὁ γεννηθεὶς ἐκ τοῦ θεοῦ τηρεῖ αὐτόν κτλ. ("but He who was born of God keeps him"). It is dubious whether ὁ γεννηθείς ("the one born," aorist passive) resumes ὁ γεγεννημένος (perfect passive) from the preceding clause; that would be an odd change of expression. Also, the designation of the believer as γεννηθεὶς ἐκ τοῦ θεοῦ ("born of God") would be singular.[21] Then, too, one would expect ἑαυτόν ("himself") rather than αὐτόν ("him"), which some witnesses indeed read. But against this view is the fact that ἑαυτόν would require a predicate noun, such as ἄσπιλον ("spotless," Jas 1:27) or ἁγνόν ("pure"), as in 1 Tim 5:22.[22] It therefore seems that Jesus Christ is to be understood by γεννηθεὶς ἐκ τοῦ θεοῦ ("who was born of God"), although this designation is also singular and surprising.[23] If one prefers to stick to the identification of the subjects of the two clauses (ὁ γεννηθεὶς ἐκ τοῦ θεοῦ and ὁ γεγεννημένος ἐκ τοῦ θεοῦ) and also keep the reading αὐτόν ("him"), there is no other possibility than to understand ὁ γεννηθείς as a conditional participle and translate: "He who (or: if any one) is born of God, that one he keeps (viz., God)."[24] The expression τηρεῖ αὐτόν ("keep him"), used of God, would con-

---

18 The transposition considered by Windisch is a make-shift solution.

19 According to Harnack and others, this omission may be original. Also cf. Schnackenburg, p. 278, who supports the retention of οὐ.

20 On οἴδαμεν see p. 86 n. 4. The "we" of οἴδαμεν ("we know") now embraces the entire Christisn congregation, however.

21 The poorly attested reading ἡ γέννησις is preferred by Harnack; on this point see Schnackenburg, pp. 280 n. 2 and 281.

22 Τηρεῖν ("keep") occurs elsewhere in 1 John (as in John) with the object τὰς ἐντολάς ("the command-ments") or τὸν λόγον ("the word") (see pp. 24f

on 2:3), thus in the sense of "observe, fulfill," while here it means "keep" in the sense of "guard, protect."

23 Schnackenburg rightly asks: "Why not ὁ υἱὸς τοῦ θεοῦ?" ("the Son of God"). That is suggested by v 20.

24 Thus K. Beyer, *Semitische Syntax im Neuen Testament*, Studien zur Umwelt des Neuen Testaments 1 (Göt-tingen, 1962), I/1: 216f. Schnackenburg, p. 280, now agrees with him, whereas in the first edition he had understood ". . . whoever is (once) born of God holds fast to him"; in his earlier view he perceived the difficulty, to be sure, that τηρεῖν τὸν θεόν ("hold fast to God") is an extraordinary expression.

form to Jn 17:11, 12, 15 and Rev 3:10.[25] It is difficult to understand why this could not also be said of Jesus Christ.[26] In any case, v 18c is understandable, whichever possibility one elects: καὶ ὁ πονηρὸς οὐχ ἅπτεται αὐτοῦ ("and the evil one does not touch him"). There can be no doubt that πονηρός ("evil one") refers to Satan, to the devil;[27] likewise there is no doubt that οὐχ ἅπτεται αὐτοῦ means: "he is not able to do him harm, cannot become his lord."[28]

■ **19** The first part of v 19 is a repetition of 3:9. The second part, which indirectly expresses the victory of faith over the world (5:4), contains its confirmation, so to speak, in the assertion: καὶ ὁ κόσμος ὅλος ἐν τῷ πονηρῷ κεῖται ("and the whole world is in the power of the evil one"). The assertion draws the consequence, as it were, from 2:15–17. It may remain an open question whether κόσμος ("world") is understood with respect to its nothingness or its hostility to God.[29] It is also dubious whether ἐν πονηρῷ κεῖται means that the world lies in power of Satan,[30] and thus whether πονηρῷ is masculine as in v 18, or whether it is to be taken as neuter, so that it would mean that the world is in a desperate state.

■ **20** Motifs drawn from earlier parts of the letter are also taken up in v 20. The (third) οἴδαμεν ("we know") introduces what in substance is a repetition of what was said in 1:2; 3:5, 8, although formally it is noteworthy

that ἥκει ("has come") now replaces ἐφανερώθη ("was made manifest"). However, ἥκει is very likely synonymous with ἐφανερώθη and can only mean "he has come"; it thus refers to the appearance of God's Son in history.[31] The continuation, καὶ δέδωκεν ἡμῖν διάνοιαν κτλ. ("and has given us understanding"), is formally unique,[32] but corresponds in substance to the assertion that χρῖσμα ("anointing"), which bestows true knowledge (2:20f, 27), is given to the believer. The content of the διάνοια ("understanding") is given by the subordinate clause: ἵνα γινώσκομεν τὸν ἀληθινόν ("that we might know the true . . .").[33] Ἀληθινός ("true"), in accordance with common usage, can only refer to God, as in Jn 17:3; 1 Thess 1:9, and in accordance with Old Testament and Jewish terminology; but it also corresponds to the motif of the knowledge of God often repeated in 1 John (2:3f, 13f; 3:1; 4:6, 7f).[34] God is also intended in the independent (i.e., no longer dependent upon the subordinator ἵνα) continuation: καὶ ἐσμὲν ἐν τῷ ἀληθινῷ ("and we are in him who is true"),[35] in substance not distinguishable from ἐκ τοῦ θεοῦ ἐσμεν ("we are of God"), v 19. The following phrase, ἐν τῷ υἱῷ αὐτοῦ Ἰησοῦ Χριστῷ ("in his Son Jesus Christ"), is striking; it cannot stand in simple opposition to ἐν τῷ ἀληθινῷ ("in the true one"), for then the Son would be identical with "the true one." It can only be a prepositional attributive (explanatory) going with ἐσμέν ("we

---

25 See Bultmann, p. 502 n. 2 [384 n. 2] on Jn 17:11.
26 As φυλάττειν ("guard") is used of κύριος ("Lord") in 2 Thess 3:3 (v.l., θεός, "God").
27 See p. 32 on 2:13f.
28 Ἅπτεσθαι ("touch, take hold of") in this sense occurs only here in the New Testament, but it appears with this meaning in the LXX and elsewhere; Bauer s.v.
29 See pp. 32f on 2:15.
30 The formulation is unique; κεῖσθαι in this sense also occurs in the LXX and in Greek literature; see Bauer s.v. 2b and Schnackenburg, pp. 288f.
31 See pp. 8f on 1:2. Ἥκει is thus used like (ἐκ τοῦ θεοῦ ἐξῆλθον καὶ) ἥκω ("[from God I proceeded

and] came forth") in Jn 8:42. See Bauer s.v. 1d: ἥκω as a religious term = the coming of deity.
32 Διάνοια ("understanding") occurs only here in 1 John (and John), but cf. Col 1:21; Eph 4:18, etc.
33 The ἵνα–clause is not dependent on δέδωκεν ("has given"), but explains διάνοιαν ("understanding").
34 The variant readings τὸν ἀληθινὸν θεόν ("the true God") and τὸ ἀληθινόν ("the true thing") are corrections.
35 On "being in God," see p. 20 n. 21 and 2:5.

are") and is therefore to be translated: "by virtue of the fact that (or: insofar as) we are in his Son Jesus Christ."[36] One might happily accept the conjecture of Harnack that an ὄντες ("being") has dropped out after ἐν . . . Ἰησοῦ Χριστῷ; however, one is also tempted to inquire with Bousset[37] whether the phrase, "in his Son Jesus Christ," is not a gloss through which the affirmation of the full divinity of Christ first came into the text. For this is expressly asserted in the following sentence: οὗτός ἐστιν κτλ. ("this is . . ."). However, οὗτος ("this one"), in its position after the phrase "in his Son Jesus Christ," cannot refer to God, but only to Jesus Christ, although the preceding ἐν τῷ ἀληθινῷ ("in the true one") can refer only to God. But if the sentence is original, it is designed to provide a rationale for the claim that we are in God, in the "true one," because (insofar as) we are in his Son, by designating the Son himself as ἀληθινὸς θεός ("true God"). The attribution would be superfluous as a characteristic of the Father.[38] Furthermore, it would be strange to say not only, οὗτός ἐστιν ὁ ἀληθινός ("this is the true one"), but ὁ ἀληθινὸς θεός ("the true God"). In addition, καὶ ζωὴ αἰώνιος ("and eternal life") as a characteristic of Jesus Christ agrees with v 11: αὕτη ἡ ζωὴ (scil. αἰώνιος) ἐν τῷ υἱῷ αὐτοῦ ἐστιν ("this life [eternal] is in his Son"), and with Jn 11:25; 14:6.[39]

■ **21** The last sentence of v 20, which is similar to a confessional formula, is followed by an imperative in v 21 as a conclusion. The imperative is introduced by the customary address τεκνία ("little children"), which contrasts strongly with the threefold οἴδαμεν ("we know") of vss 18–20. It is understandable that the redactor concludes with an imperative, and it may be assumed that in his sense the admonition in v 21 is a suitable conclusion for the whole writing. In that case, however, φυλάξατε ἑαυτὰ ἀπὸ τῶν εἰδώλων ("keep yourselves from idols")[40] must have the meaning of an admonition not to fall prey to false teaching, since this warning runs through the whole letter. The formulation is indeed striking. The phrase itself is odd, since it is not found elsewhere in the epistle.[41] Most striking, however, is the phrase ἀπὸ τῶν εἰδώλων ("from idols"). It is improbable that "idols," i.e., "images," are meant by εἴδωλα;[42] for then the sense of the admonition would have to be not to participate in pagan cults. Since, however, in accordance with the warning that persists throughout 1 John and corresponding to the characteristic of faith given in v 20, it can only be an admonition to guard oneself from false doctrine—εἴδωλα is to be understood in the sense of "false gods."[43] The redactor has therefore evidently understood the false teaching as apostasy from true faith; and it is probably this that he understands as the "sin unto death" in vss 16f.[44] The singularity of the admonition in v 21 lies in the fact that

---

36   Ἐν τῷ before υἱῷ is omitted in many textual witnesses; in others Ἰησοῦ Χριστῷ is lacking.

37   Wilhelm Bousset, *Kyrios Christos*, tr. John Steely (Nashville: Abingdon, 1970), pp. 238f [178]. Since ἐν τῷ is missing in some MSS, it is doubtless a correction. The omission of Ἰησοῦ Χριστῷ in others is probably only an oversight of the scribe.

38   One may vacillate, to be sure. Cf. Holzmann's reflection: ". . . with the intention of being understood, no one can characterize two subjects in the same breath with ἀληθινός." Windisch also vacillates. However, a redactor who is compiling must be expected to write things an original author would not produce.

39   Schnackenburg thinks that the lack of the article before ζωή ("life") points to the fact "that this word was added as a genuine predicate which illuminates the context." I think it hardly calls for this consideration.

40   Ἑαυτούς for ἑαυτά following upon τεκνία is an understandable correction.

41   Φυλάσσειν occurs only here in 1 John. The word appears not infrequently elsewhere in the New Testament in the sense of "guard, protect." In John, however, it occurs only at 12:25; 17:12, but without ἑαυτούς ("yourselves"). This usage is also found in Greek literature; see Bauer s.v. 1c; likewise φυλάσσειν ἀπό is found in the New Testament only at Lk

the redactor, when he identifies the false teaching with the worship of false gods, condemns the false teaching simply as paganism. He is able to do that to the extent that he is acquainted with the characterization of the false teachers as antichrists (2:18–4:3), and that it can be said of them: ἐξ ἡμῶν ἐξῆλθαν, ἀλλ᾽ οὐκ ἦσαν ἐξ ἡμῶν ("they went out from us, but they were not of us,"

2:19), and αὐτοὶ ἐκ τοῦ κόσμου εἰσίν ("They are of the world," 4:5). He can therefore understand the false teaching only as apostasy from the true faith and thus call it "worship of idols," even though the heretics claim to be Christians.[45]

12:15; 2 Thess 3:3.

42 So used in Greek literature, in the LXX, and 1 Cor 12:2; Rev 9:20; see Bauer *s.v.*

43 Εἴδωλον is used in the sense of "false gods" in the LXX, in Judaism, in the New Testament at 1 Cor 8:4, 7; 1 Thess 1:9, and elsewhere; see Bauer *s.v.*

44 In the second edition Schnackenburg adopted the view of Nauck (*Die Tradition und der Charakter des ersten Johannesbriefes*) that the warning against εἴδωλα is simply a warning against sin. On Nauck's reading, false gods and sin are very closely related in the Qumran texts, and 1 Jn 5:21 is also to be understood from this perspective. Haenchen, "Neuere Literatur," pp. 21–4 [255–60], was already critical

of Nauck; then Braun, "Qumran und das Neue Testament," pp. 115f [I:304f] comments: "In Qumran the warning against idols is a warning against apostasy from the community with its strict observance; in ordinary Judaism the warning is against any heathen cultus; in 1 John there is a general warning against any taint of paganism in Christianity."

45 H. Braun, "Literar-Analyse," 288 [238], rightly considers it improbable that a second or third generation congregation would be warned against relapsing into paganism.

3 John

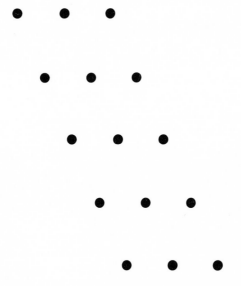

Prescript

1   **The elder to the beloved Gaius, whom I
     love in truth.**
     [RSV modified]

■ **1** The Third Epistle of John, like most early Christian letters, begins with a prescript, which is remarkably abrupt in contrast to other forms, indeed is incomplete. There is the customary mention of the sender and recipient, but the usual greeting (or wish) is missing.

The sender calls himself ὁ πρεσβύτερος ("the elder") without any further qualification. The term is used in this way in the Pastorals and in the letters of Ignatius. Who this "elder" is, is completely uncertain; it is certain only that the title designates the dignity and authority of the writer. It is improbable that the term is the title of an office; in that case, one would expect the text to read: ὁ πρεσβύτερος τῆς ἐκκλησίας ἐν . . . ("the elder of the church at . . .").[1] In an earlier period the term could mean simply the "old man,"[2] i.e. a senior to whom respect is due, with whom the author sustains a personal relationship. The use of the term ἀγαπητός ("beloved") for the addressee could be taken in support of this earlier meaning; the conclusion of the epistle (vss 12f) might

likewise be so understood. However, it is more likely that "the elder" designates the author as one of the πρεσβύτεροι ("presbyters") whom Papias (in Eusebius, *Hist. eccl.* 3.39.3f) calls the bearers and transmitters of the apostolic tradition.[3]

Nothing is known of the addressee, Gaius, from other sources.[4] Since the author reckons Gaius among "his" children in v 4, it is tempting to speculate that Gaius was converted to the Christian faith by "the elder." From v 15 it is perhaps to be inferred that he was a member of the congregation of which Diotrephes (vss 9f) claimed to be the leader, and that he formed the "center of a circle of friends" (Schnackenburg). The appellation "beloved" is a common characterization and form of

---

1   Πρεσβύτερος ("elder") is understood as the designation of an official by, e.g., Haenchen, "Neuere Literatur," 288–91 [307–11]: the πρεσβύτερος is the "bearer of a congregational office," the "praeses presbyterii." But above all by Ernst Käsemann, "Ketzer und Zeuge," 292–511. Käsemann is of the opinion that the author was once a presbyter of Diotrephes (mentioned in vss 9f), was excommunicated by Diotrephes because of heresy, but held on to his title as presbyter. This fanciful hypothesis is opposed, and rightly, by Haenchen, "Neuere Literatur," 277–81 [295–9]; Schnackenburg, pp. 299f; Günther Bornkamm, *TDNT* VI:671 n. 121 [671 n. 121].

2   The comparative force of πρεσβύτερος need not be retained; see Blass–Debrunner §244(2). Thus, Schnackenburg, Bornkamm and others translate it as *der Alte*, i.e., "the elder" ("elder" in English is not necessarily comparative).

3   Thus Bornkamm, *TDNT* VI:671 [671], "The elder with his wishes and works is outside any ecclesiastical constitution" (following Hans von Campenhausen, *Ecclesiastical Authority and Spiritual Power in the First Three Centuries*, tr. A. Baker [Stanford: Stanford University Press, 1969], 127 [132]). Werner Georg Kümmel, *Introduction to the New Testament*, tr. A. J. Matill, Jr. (Nashville: Abingdon, 1966), pp. 315f, also gravitates to this hypothesis. Willi Marxsen, *Einleitung in das Neue Testament* (Gütersloh: Bertelsmann, ⁴1964), 227, is undecided. Haenchen, "Neuere Literatur," 291 [310], thinks "that here the two fundamental meanings, 'elder as congregational office' and 'elder as bearer of the tradition,' were once combined." Schnackenburg, pp. 295–301, is detailed and very cautious on the question of authorship.

4   Gaius is a common name; to identify the Gaius here with any other Gaius in the New Testament (1 Cor

address among Christians.[5] Here, however, it has a special ring, since the author adds the affirmation: ὃν ἐγὼ ἀγαπῶ ἐν ἀληθείᾳ ("whom I love in truth"). The word ἀλήθεια ("truth") can be used in various senses, as v 3 immediately shows. In the combination ἀγαπᾶν ἐν ἀληθείᾳ ("to love in truth"), ἀλήθεια can only mean: in reality, authentically.[6] The clause replaces, as it were, what would otherwise be the customary greeting or wish in the prescript.

1:14; Acts 19:29; 20:4) would be arbitrary.

5   Cf., e.g., in the New Testament, Rom 1:7; 1 Cor 4:14; 10:14; 1 Petr 2:11.

6   Ἐν ἀληθείᾳ ("in truth") therefore has the sense of ἀληθῶς in Matt 14:33; Jn 1:47; 4:42, and elsewhere. The phrase ἀγαπᾶν ἐν ἀληθείᾳ ("love in truth") appears only here and in 2 Jn 1; however, it also appears in 1 Jn 3:18 in a special antithesis: μὴ ἀγαπῶμεν λόγῳ . . . ἀλλὰ ἐν ἔργῳ καὶ ἀληθείᾳ ("let us not love in word . . . but in deed and in truth"), where ἀλήθεια also means "reality." It can doubtless be said that the emphasis on the terms ἀγαπᾶν ("to love") and ἀλήθεια ("truth") is Johannine, without thereby saying anything significant about the question of authorship. It is arbitrary to identify the πρεσβύτερος ("the elder") with John the presbyter mentioned by Papias (Eusebius, *Hist. eccl.* 3.39.4) and even to see in him John the son of Zebedee; on this subject, see Haenchen, "Neuere Literatur," 267–9 [282–5], 289f [308f]. Schnackenburg, pp. 300f, is cautious: "On the whole, one is inclined to conclude that the question whether John the apostle and son of Zebedee is the author of the three Johannine letters cannot finally be settled on account of the complexity of the 'Johannine question,' but that one must at least postulate an eminent personality, from the 'Johannine circle,' perhaps a disciple of the apostle, who was responsible for the letters and who represents and maintains the 'Johannine tradition.' "

**Conduct with regard to
Itinerant Brethren**

2 Beloved, I pray that all may go well with
you and that you may keep well, as I
know it is well with your soul. 3 / For I
greatly rejoiced when some of the
brethren arrived and testified to the
truth of your life, as indeed you do
follow the truth. 4 / No greater joy can I
have than this, to hear that my children
follow the truth.

5 Beloved, it is a loyal thing you do when
you render any service to the brethren,
especially to strangers, 6 / who have
testified to your love before the church.
You will do well to send them on their
journey as befits God's service. 7 / For
they have set out for his sake and
have accepted nothing from the heathen.
8 / So we ought to support such men,
that we may be fellow workers in
the truth.

[RSV modified]

■ **2** The author chooses the opening mode of address, ἀγαπητέ ("beloved"), in accordance with the prescript. Following the vocative, the letter opens with a formulaic wish[1] for the well–being and health of the addressee.[2] The wish corresponds to the well–being of the addressee: καθώς ("corresponding to the fact that") εὐοδοῦταί σου ἡ ψυχή ("as I know it is well with your soul"). In this context, formulaic εὐοδοῦσθαι ("get along well") takes on a special nuance: it is not restricted here to the corporeal well–being of Gaius, but means the healthy condition of his "soul," as v 3 illustrates. Ψυχή ("soul") is certainly not to be understood in the sense of a dualism of body and soul, but refers simply to the person addressed.[3]

■ **3** The expression of joy in v 3 (as in 2 Jn 4) corresponds to the tradition of epistolary style.[4] The object of joy in this case is the praiseworthy conduct of Gaius, that is, his ἀλήθεια ("truth"). As in the case of the phrase immediately following, ἐν τῇ ἀληθείᾳ περιπατεῖν ("to walk in the truth"), "truth" can refer only to the conduct of Gaius that corresponds to the divine reality (or its revelation). The same thing can be said of the use of the term in vss 8, 12. Gaius' comportment has been reported

---

1 Such a wish as this is common at the beginning of private letters in late antiquity; cf., e.g., *P.Oxy.* XIV 1680.2ff; Loeb, *Select Papyri* I, nos. 111 and 112. Εὔχομαι ("I pray"), with which περὶ πάντων ("in all respects") goes, hardly refers to prayer, but is simply a wish in conformity with typical epistolary style. Cf. Robert Funk, "The Form and Structure of II and III John," *JBL* 86 (1967): 424–30.

2 Εὐοδοῦσθαι appears in the New Testament only here

and at Rom 1:10; 1 Cor 16:2. It is common in the LXX and papyri; see Bauer *s.v.*, and Schnackenburg, p. 321 n. 3, on ὑγιαίνειν in epistolary wishes. Cf. Funk, "The Form and Structure of II and III John," *JBL* 86 (1967): 425.

3 One could virtually translate, "your life," as in 1 Jn 3:16. Also cf. 1 Petr 1:9, where ὑμῶν σωτηρίαν ψυχῶν means simply, "your salvation."

4 See Bauer *s.v.* χαίρω 2. In Christian letters it is joy

to the author by means of the testimony of the brethren who came to him.[5] As emerges from vss 6f, these brethren are evidently missionaries. It is not to be concluded from their visit to Gaius, however, that the πρεσβύτερος ("elder") was the leader of a provincial missionary organization (Harnack). Their testimony corresponds to what the author is certain of in any case: καθὼς σὺ ἐν ἀληθείᾳ περιπατεῖς ("as indeed you do follow the truth").[6]

■ **4** Verse 4 explains the ἐχάρην λίαν ("I greatly rejoiced") of v 3: there is no greater joy for the author than to hear that his "children" lead their lives in the truth, as he had just said of Gaius in v 3.[7] Τέκνα ("children") as a designation of believers (1 John often uses τεκνία, "little children," instead) is common (Bauer, *s.v.* 2b). When the author speaks of "my children," it is natural to assume that he is referring to persons he himself has won to the faith; cf. Phil 2:22; 1 Cor 4:14; Gal 4:19.

■ **5** The author repeats the vocative "beloved" in v 5 and comes to the theme that is on his mind: the right conduct vis-à-vis itinerant brethren. Verse 5, in the first instance, is an admonition: Gaius ought to know that he acts "faithfully"[8] whenever he does anything for the brethren, especially strangers, and thus for those who are itinerant. It is to be concluded from v 7 that itinerant missionaries are involved.

■ **6** In v 6 praise and admonition are combined. Itinerant brethren have testified before the congregation on behalf of the love of Gaius,[9] which, in this case, naturally was demonstrated concretely as hospitality. The act of hospitality, in addition to other things, involves not only showing the guest the way and giving him directions, but also providing provisions for the journey.[10] In this respect, the praise is supplemented by the admonition: Gaius will do well to send the itinerant brethren on their way, equipped in a manner worthy of God.

■ **7** Verse 7 shows that the itinerant brethren are missionaries who have gone out ὑπὲρ τοῦ ὀνόματος ("for his

---

at the persistence or growth of the congregation addressed: Rom 16:19; 2 Cor 7:7, 13, 16; Phil 1:18; 1 Thess 3:9; Col 2:5. The γάρ ("for") is omitted after ἐχάρην ("I rejoiced") in several MSS, but may be original. Cf. Funk, "The Form and Structure of II and III John," *JBL* 86 (1967): 425ff.

5 Μαρτυρεῖν with the dative, "bear witness for," is frequent; see Bauer *s.v.* 1a; with τῇ ἀληθείᾳ ("for the truth") also Jn 5:33; 18:37.

6 In the first edition of his commentary, Schnackenburg translates the καθώς clause: "as you (indeed) really walk." The καθώς ("as") is probably understood correctly here, but not ἐν ἀληθείᾳ. The latter, in the second edition, is correctly rendered in my judgment as "in (the) truth." On the other hand, Schnackenburg now takes the καθώς-clause differently: "that is, that you walk. . . ." He thus takes the clause as indirect discourse, depending upon μαρτυρούντων ("testify"), and understands καθώς in the sense of ὡς or πῶς. Περιπατεῖν ("walk," as in 2 Jn 4) is common in a metaphorical sense; see Bauer *s.v.* 1a. Thus also 1 Jn 1:6f; 2:6, 11.

7 The variant χάριν instead of χαράν is certainly secondary, and could have been prompted by Pauline usages such as those in Rom 1:5; 1 Cor 3:10. Μειζότερος for μείζων is vulgar; see Blass–Debrunner § 61 (2); it appears only here in the New Testament. The ἵνα–clause (in place of τοῦ with the infinitive) is epexegetical, as often in John, e.g., Jn 15:2; 1 Jn 5:3; see Blass–Debrunner § 394.

8 Πιστὸν ποιεῖν means "act loyally"; see Bauer *s.v.* 1b. Ἐργάζεσθαι does not mean an official action, but a "voluntary charitable action," as Schnackenburg correctly interprets. Cf. Funk, "The Form and Structure of II and III John," *JBL* 86 (1967): 427f.

9 On μαρτυρεῖν with the dative, see above, n. 5. Ἐνώπιον ἐκκλησίας, i.e., "before the assembled congregation"; the article is lacking as is often the case in prepositional phrases (Blass–Debrunner § 255). The "church" (only here and in vss 9f in the Johannine writings) means the individual congregation, as often in Paul.

10 On this sense of προπέμπειν, see Bauer *s.v.* 2.

name's sake"), which can only mean "for Christ,"[11] i.e., to proclaim him. This is confirmed by the characterization: μηδὲν λαμβάνοντες ἀπὸ τῶν ἐθνικῶν ("accepting nothing from the heathen").[12] They thus do not resemble "heathen peripatetic philosophers (Cynics) nor the mercenary mendicant priests (of the Dea Syria [Syrian goddess])."[13] They are dependent, consequently, on the support of Christian brothers.

■ 8 The admonition is generalized in v 8: we, that is, we Christians, have the duty to extend hospitality or support to such itinerant missionaries.[14] The admonition contained in this generalization is not only made emphatic by the ἵνα–clause, but is also made plausible: ἵνα συνεργοὶ γινώμεθα τῇ ἀληθείᾳ ("that we may be fellow workers in the truth").[15] Ἀλήθεια ("truth") here, as in v 4, can only refer to the reality of God or its revelation.[16] Since γίνομαι can substitute for εἶναι, the sense need not be taken as "that we may become fellow workers"; nevertheless, what is probably intended is: "that we may prove ourselves to be . . .," as Schnackenburg translates.

11 Ὄνομα ("name") became a common designation for Christ at an early date; see Schnackenburg, p. 324 n. 7.
12 The ἐθνικοί are the "heathen," as in Matt 5:47; 6:7, or in this particular case, the heathen auditors of the proclamation.
13 So Schnackenburg, p. 324, who refers in n. 5 to illustrative examples.
14 See Bauer s.v. 1.
15 Συνεργεῖν ("work with") is common with the dative (of person); Bauer s.v. That the reference here is not to cooperative endeavor in something, but to personal relation to the truth (Schnackenburg), seems to me to be an erroneous notion. Roland Berg- meier, "Zum Verfasserproblem des II. und III. Johannesbriefes," ZNW 57 (1966):98, points to Ps. Clem. Hom. 17.19.7ff as parallel to συνεργοὶ . . . τῇ ἀληθείᾳ.
16 See above, on v 3.

Diotrephes as Opponent of the Elder

9 **I have written something to the church; but Diotrephes, who likes to put himself first, does not acknowledge my authority. 10/ So if I come, I will bring up what he is doing, prating against me with evil words. And not content with that, he refuses himself to welcome the brethren, and also stops those who want to welcome them and puts them out of the church.**

[RSV modified]

■ **9** Verses 9 and 10 are closely connected with vss 2–8. If, in vss 2–8, hospitality with regard to itinerant brethren was praised and required, now the conduct of Diotrephes with regard to these brethren is sharply censured. In this connection, the author makes reference to an earlier writing: ἔγραψά τι τῇ ἐκκλησίᾳ ("I have written something to the church").[1] We have no knowledge of this letter. It doubtless must have dealt with the theme of vss 3–8, i.e., the commendation of hospitality vis-à-vis itinerant brethren, since, according to v 10, it is precisely this that Diotrephes rejects.[2] Surely what is said of him, οὐκ ἐπιδέχεται ἡμᾶς ("he does not acknowledge us"), can only mean that rejection.[3] Whether he did not even lay the letter before a gathering of the congregation, or induced the congregation to reject it, cannot be determined. Diotrephes, of whom nothing is known otherwise, is called ὁ φιλοπρωτεύων αὐτῶν ("who likes to put himself first"), and thus the one who claims first position in the congregation (αὐτῶν, "among them"). The term φιλοπρωτεύων is attested elsewhere neither in the New Testament nor in non-Christian literature. It was perhaps created by the author, as a means by which he disparagingly avoids or replaces the real title of Diotrephes, i.e., ἐπίσκοπος ("bishop").[4] Since Diotrephes does not seem to be accused of being a false teacher, it must be a question of conflict between him and the author, evidently over congregational organization, as Harnack correctly saw long ago.[5] Harnack sees in Diotrephes "the first monarchical bishop we know," to whom are opposed the itinerant missionaries, who, for their part, de-

---

1   The variant ἄν instead of τί doubtless depends on the assumption that the letter in question was never really written ("I would have written to the church," instead of "I have written something . . .").

2   The letter can thus have been neither 1 John nor, as often assumed, 2 John.

3   The replacement of the singular by the plural (ἡμᾶς) here is hardly significant. In any case, it is not an editorial "we" any more than it is in vss 10 and 12. Ἐπιδέχεσθαι, which elsewhere means "receive (as a guest)" (as in v 10 immediately following), can here only have the sense "recognize."

4   This title for a congregational leader is met earlier in Phil 1:1, alongside πρεσβύτερος ("presbyter"); 1 Tim 5:17; Acts 14:23; etc.). The two titles are evidently used in the same sense in Tit 1:5–7. Cf. Bultmann, *Theology of the New Testament*, § 53.

5   Harnack, *Über den dritten Johannesbrief*. TU 15:3b (Leipzig: Hinrichs, 1897).

rive their authority from the πρεσβύτερος ("elder") as the leader of a missionary organization. The conflict between Diotrephes and the author is understood by other scholars as a conflict, at the same time, over right doctrine, with Diotrephes as an innovator and heretical teacher.[6] Ernst Käsemann[7] has reversed this thesis and probably justifiably claimed that Diotrephes was the representative of the developing orthodox ecclesiastical tradition, to whom the theological direction represented by the elder appeared to be heterodox. The reason was that this theology (like the Johannine literature generally) expressed the Christian faith in the conceptual apparatus of Gnostic thought.[8]

■ **10** The phrase, οὐκ ἐπιδέχεται ἡμᾶς ("he does not acknowledge us") of v 9, is described more concretely in v 10, where the author says he will "call to mind" works of Diotrephes, that is, he will bring them up for discussion during a visit now in prospect (v 14).[9] This means, of course, evil works as they are depicted by ἃ ποιεῖ λό- γοις πονηροῖς φλυαρῶν ἡμᾶς ("what he is doing, prating against me with evil words").[10] Thus they are irresponsible or even abusive words. His evil works, however, are not limited to that (καὶ μὴ ἀρκούμενος ἐπὶ τούτοις, "And not content with that"). Diotrephes also denies hospitality to (itinerant) brethren,[11] and not only that, he also prevents those who are willing from doing so, and excludes them from the congregation.[12] The present tense indicates the customary conduct of Diotrephes, but it does not specify when and how often Diotrephes has actually acted in this manner, nor do we learn, in particular, whether Gaius, who perhaps belonged to the congregation of Diotrephes, was also affected by it. If the author proposes to take Diotrephes to task on his visit, one is forced to conclude that the conduct of Diotrephes is not recognized by the congregation without opposition, and v. 15 probably shows that there were followers of the elder, or at least his line of thinking, in the congregation.[13]

---

6   It is so understood, for example, by H. Wendt in various publications; Walter Bauer, *Orthodoxy and Heresy in Earliest Christianity*, ed. R. A. Kraft and G. Krodel, Members of Philadelphia Seminar on Christian Origins (Philadelphia: Fortress Press, 1971) even characterizes Diotrephes as a major heretic. Cf. Haenchen, "Neuere Literatur," 270–7 [290–9], on the whole question.

7   Käsemann, "Ketzer und Zeuge," 292–311, [168–87]. Also cf. Käsemann's conception of the historical situation reflected in the Johannine writings in his work, *The Testament of Jesus: A Study of the Gospel of John in the Light of Chapter 17*, tr. Gerhard Krodel (Philadelphia: Fortress Press, 1968).

8   Although Käsemann may well be correct in holding that Diotrephes is the representative of the legitimate ecclesiastical tradition, to whom the Johannine literature must have appeared as suspiciously heretical, he has nevertheless carried this idea much too far with reference to 3 John. For, the theme of right doctrine is scarcely under discussion in 3 John, and Johannine terminology occurs only rarely, for instance in vss 11f. The view that the "elder" of 3 John was a presbyter in the congregation of Diotrephes

and that Diotrephes excommunicated this presbyter, who nevertheless retained his title as presbyter, is simply fanciful. In addition to Haenchen's discussion in "Neuere Literatur," also cf. G. Bornkamm, *TDNT* VI 671 n. 121; Schnackenburg, pp. 299f.

9   Ὑπομιμνῄσκω meaning to call to mind in an admonitory fashion appears also, e.g., in 2 Tim 2:14; 1 Clem 62:3.

10   Φλυαρεῖν ("bring unjustified charges against") appears only here in the New Testament; see Bauer *s.v.*

11   On ἐπιδέχεσθαι in a different sense here than in v 9, see above, p. 100 n. 3.

12   Ἐκβάλλω here can doubtless only mean excommunication, as in Jn 9:34f.

13   Schnackenburg, for example, also interprets it in this way.

Exhortation and Commendation of Demetrius

11 Beloved, do not imitate evil but imitate good. He who does good is of God; he who does evil has not seen God. 12/ Demetrius has testimony from every one, and from the truth itself; I testify to him too, and you know my testimony is true.

[RSV modified]

■ **11** The author addresses Gaius again as ἀγαπητέ ("beloved," as in vss 2 and 5) and warns him against following the bad example of Diotrephes, which does not necessarily prove that Gaius belonged to Diotrephes' congregation. For if the admonition not to do evil but to do good is an admonition to hospitality in accordance with v 10, as it doubtless is, it applies generally, irrespective of the congregation to which Gaius may have belonged. If, in spite of its reference to the concrete situation, the admonition as such has the ring of a general rule, this tone is enhanced by virtue of the two sentences appended without conjunction (asyndetically). The two sentences are reminiscent in form (i.e. antithetical parallelism) and in content of Johannine language and could be sentences out of the tradition of the Johannine school. Of course, the verb ἀγαθοποιεῖν ("to do good") appears only here in the Johannine writings, but ἐκ τοῦ θεοῦ ἐστιν ("to be out of God") sounds quite Johannine (cf. 1 Jn 3:10; 4:2–7; Jn 8:47).[1] The same can be said of the negative assertion, οὐχ ἑώρακεν τὸν θεόν ("has not seen God") (cf. 1 Jn 3:6).

■ **12** The admonition of v 11 is obliquely concretized in v 12, in the recommendation of a certain Demetrius to Gaius. Of Demetrius nothing is known from other sources. He could have belonged to the itinerant brethren, spoken of in vss 2–8. Perhaps he is the bearer of the present letter. His recommendation points to the fact that favorable testimony on Demetrius' behalf had been given by "every one" (that is, by everyone in question), indeed by the "truth" itself. In substance this can mean nothing different from the testimony of the brethren for the "truth" (of Gaius) in v 3. However, the "truth," therefore the divine reality or its revelation, is here personified.[2] The significance of this testimony is emphasized by the assertion that the author can also provide such testimony, and can appeal, in support of its validity, to the fact that Gaius knows him (καὶ οἶδας, "and you know").

---

1   For εἶναι ἐκ ("to be from"), which, although it denotes origin, means nature, also see 1 Jn 2:21.

2   So also in the quotation of Papias found in Eusebius, *Hist. eccl.* 3.39.3, to which Bergmeier, "Zum Verfasserproblem des II. und III. Johannesbriefes," 99, refers.

Closing Matters

13   I had much to write to you, but I would rather not write with pen and ink; 14 / I hope to see you soon, and we will talk together face to face.

15   Peace be to you. The friends greet you. Greet the friends, every one of them.

[RSV modified]

■ **13f** The assurance that the author could have written much more but rejects that option (as in 2 Jn 12) sounds formulaic and is reminiscent of Jn 20:30.[1] Here, however, it has a different motivation: in John the motivation is the superabundance of things to be written about, while here it is unnecessary to write more because the author will shortly see Demetrius personally and speak with him.[2]

■ **15** The closing wish is abrupt, as in 1 Petr 5:14: εἰρήνη ("peace").[3] It is followed by the closing greeting, as in Pauline, other Christian, and non–Christian letters.[4]

Those who send greetings are referred to as φίλοι ("friends"); this shows that the author stands in a circle of friends. And when the addressee is requested to greet the friends κατ' ὄνομα ("by name," i.e., individually[5]), it is evident that there is also a circle of friends in the congregation to which Gaius belongs. That appears to prove that the authority of Diotrephes is not recognized by the entire congregation (see above, on v 10).

1   On such formulae, see Bultmann, p. 697 n. 2 [540 n. 3] on Jn 20:30. Εἶχον (instead of ἔχων as in 2 Jn 12) denotes the duty or the possibility (Blass–Debrunner § 358); γράψαι (instead of γράφειν as in 2 Jn 12) "consequently, is natural" (Schnackenburg). (τὸ) μέλαν (literally "black") for ink is common; it appears in the New Testament only here and in 2 Jn 12; 2 Cor 3:3. Κάλαμος ("reed") for pen is likewise common, but appears only here in the New Testament.

2   Στόμα πρὸς στόμα λαλεῖν ("to talk mouth to mouth"), as in 2 Jn 12, is perhaps to be labelled an Old Testament formula; cf. Num 12:8; Jer 39:4. So, too, εἰρήνη σοι ("peace to you") in v 15 corresponds to the Old Testament–Jewish wish, in which "peace" (שָׁלוֹם) does not particularly mean "peace" but "well–being." As a wish of well–being (appearing in place of ἔρρωσο, which is customary in non–Christian letters), it is expanded in the Pauline letters and elsewhere in the New Testament by specifically Christian wishes.

3   See above, n. 2.

4   See Bauer, *s.v.* ἀσπάζομαι 1.

5   This usage is also met elsewhere; see Bauer (n. 4).

2 John

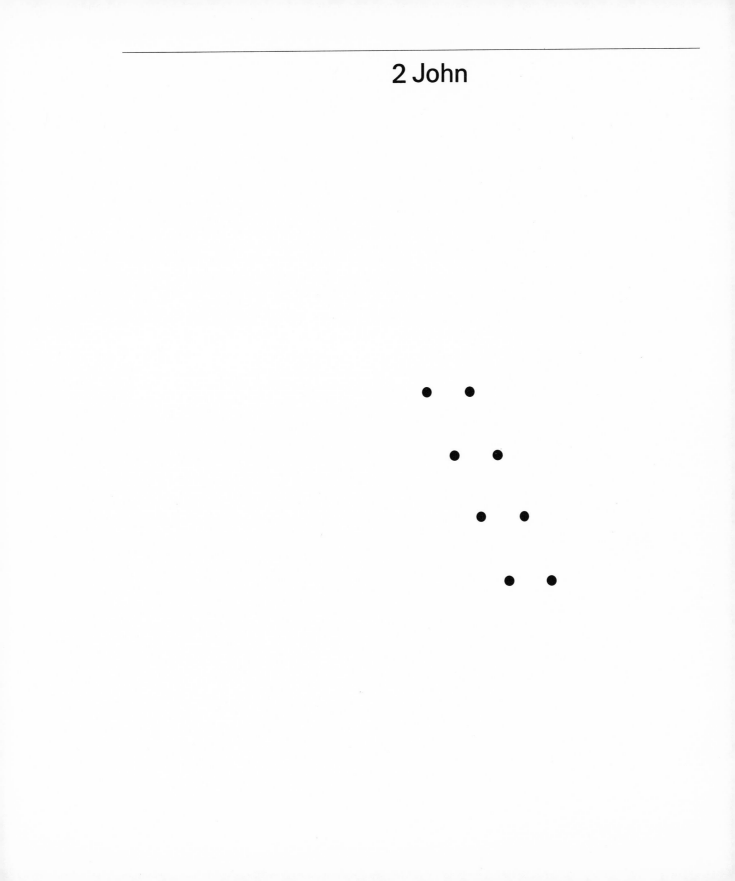

Prescript

1　The elder to an elect lady and her children,
　　whom I love in the truth, and not only
　　I but also all who know the truth,
　　2 / because of the truth which abides in
　　us and will be with us forever:

3　Grace, mercy, and peace will be with
　　us, from God the Father and from
　　Jesus Christ the Father's Son, in truth
　　and love.

[RSV modified]

The Second Epistle of John begins as a letter customarily does, with a prescript, which, unlike 3 John, contains the three usual parts: addressor, addressee, and greeting (or wish). All three parts are formed in ways peculiar to the epistle.

■ **1** The name used for the sender is ὁ πρεσβύτερος ("the elder"), as in 3 John. The question of who this elder is thereby arises, as it does in the case of 3 John, and it is to be answered with the same set of considerations and the same uncertainty.[1] But there is the question whether the epistolary form of 2 John is merely a fiction, in which the author made use of both 1 John and 3 John.[2] Just as the conclusion in vss 12f may be an imitation of 3 Jn 13f, so the designation of the alleged addressor by means of the simple phrase, "the elder," may also well be an imitation of 3 Jn 1.

There is the further difficulty of designation used for the addressee: ἐκλεκτῇ κυρίᾳ. Is one to translate, "to the elect lady"?[3] That ἐκλεκτή ("elect") is not a proper name follows from its customary use in the New Testament and is confirmed by v 13, where ἐκλεκτή is likewise employed as an adjective.[4] It is also clear

1　The often repeated conjecture concerning 2 John and 3 John, that the proper name has disappeared or been expunged, may be put down as fanciful. Yet it would be justified to a greater extent here than in 3 John, where a personal relation between author and those addressed is assumed; this would make it possible to dispense with any mention of the name (but see above). That the name alleged to have dropped out is Ἰωάννης ("John"), and the inference that the author is the elder mentioned by Papias, is not only without basis, but certainly also wrong. On the whole question, see Haenchen, "Neuere Literatur," 267–91 [282–311].

2　Martin Dibelius (RGG², 3:348) considers whether 2 John and 3 John are not really letters but fictions; Emanuel Hirsch (Studien zum vierten Evangelium. Text, Literarkritik, Entstehungsgeschichte [Tübingen: Mohr, 1936]) is of the opinion that they are fictional letters. On these views see Haenchen, "Neuere Literatur,"

pp. 281f [299f]. Also cf. Bergmeier, "Zum Verfasserproblem des II. und III. Johannesbriefes," 93–100.

3　So far as I know, all commentators so translate. Jülicher translates correctly as "to an elect lady" (Einleitung in das Neue Testament [Tübingen: J. C. B. Mohr, ⁷1931], p. 233; Eng. trans. of 1st ed., An Introduction to the New Testament, tr. J. P. Ward [London: Smith & Elder, 1904], p. 250).

4　Ἐκλεκτὴ κυρία ("elect lady") is only a circumlocution for ἐκκλησία ("church"); cf. 1 Petr 5:13, where ἡ (ἐν Βαβυλῶνι) συνεκλεκτή ("the elect lady [in Babylon]") stands for ἡ ἐκκλησία. Ἐκκλησία, like ἐκλεκτός, does not appear in John or 1 John; ἐκκλησία is found at 3 Jn 6ff.

that κυρία ("lady") is not an individual person, but a (or the) congregation, since she is addressed with her τέκνα ("children"), who can only be members of the congregation.[5] But is the "lady" addressed really a particular congregation? Why is it not then specified to which particular one the letter is addressed?[6] The conclusion, vss 12f, gives the impression, to be sure, that the writing is addressed to a specific congregation; but that only strengthens the suspicion that the epistolary character of 2 John is a fiction. It is therefore natural to assume that the author conceived his writing as a "catholic" letter, which the bearer would deliver to appropriate congregations from time to time. The author knew from 3 Jn 9f that there were itinerant brethren, who used to carry letters to individual congregations. That he himself visited other congregations, as the suspect conclusion in v 12 is perhaps designed to suggest to the reader, can only confirm this assumption.

The τέκνα ("children") are the members of the congregation to which the letter is delivered on a given occasion. Although they are characterized as οὓς ἐγὼ ἀγαπῶ ἐν ἀληθείᾳ ("whom I love in the truth"), this need not designate a personal tie, but that tie bestowed by virtue of a common Christian faith. "In truth" can simply mean: in reality, in a genuine manner, as in 1 Jn 3:18; 3 Jn 1.[7] But when the author continues: καὶ οὐκ ἐγὼ μόνος ἀλλὰ καὶ πάντες οἱ ἐγνωκότες τὴν ἀλή-

θειαν ("and not only I but also all who know the truth"), then "truth" must be the divine reality or its revelation, as in 1 Jn 1:8; 2:4. The "all" (πάντες) thus refers to those who, like the author, love the congregation addressed (on any particular occasion); the phrase thus expresses the community of all believers which has its basis in the "truth."

■ **2** Whether διὰ τὴν ἀλήθειαν . . . ("because of the truth . . .") in v 2 is intended to serve as the basis of ἀγαπῶ ("I love") in v 1, so that "and not only I but . . ." is to be understood as a parenthesis, or whether it is the motivation of "all who know the truth," can remain an open question. In any case, the meaning of ἀλήθεια ("truth"), which is characterized as μένουσα ἐν ἡμῖν ("abiding in us"), is precisely that of "truth" in v 1b. And the confidence is expressed that the gift of "truth" is granted to the Christian congregation forever.[8] That the "truth" is not simply a possession however, but must always be grasped anew as a gift, is shown by the independent sentence appended in v 2b: καὶ μεθ' ἡμῶν ἔσται εἰς τὸν αἰῶνα ("and will be with us forever"). This, too, is an expression of confidence, yet simultaneously an expression of hope. Confidence and hope belong together as a unity.

■ **3** The third and final part of the prescript follows in v 3. As a rule, this consists elsewhere of a health wish for those addressed, while here the expression of the common

---

5   Κυρία as the designation of a church (ἐκκλησία) is also met in Greek literature; see Bauer *s.v.* 2. The designation of Christians as τέκνα ("children") to characterize them as members or dependent, as in 3 Jn 4, appears also, e.g., at 1 Cor 4:14, 17; 2 Cor 6:13 and elsewhere, corresponding to Jewish usage; see Schnackenburg, p. 307 n. 2.

6   In all early Christian letters the designation of the addressee is preceded by the definite article and is thus specified, except, of course, in those letters addressed to individual persons, like 3 John and the Pastorals. The only exceptions are Ignatius' letters to the Trallians, Philadelphians, and Smyrneans, where, however, the ἐκκλησία is specified as οὔσῃ

ἐν . . . ("the church at . . ."). Similarly 1 Petr 1:1. It is surprising that Schnackenburg ignores the problem.

7   Ἐν ἀληθείᾳ would therefore here be synonymous with ἀληθῶς ("truly"); cf. Jn 1:47; 7:26; 8:31; 17:8). Schnackenburg agrees.

8   On μένειν ἐν, see p. 26 n. 9 on 1 Jn 2:6. If, in v 9, μένειν ἐν τῇ διδαχῇ (τοῦ Χριστοῦ) ("to abide in the doctrine [of Christ]") is spoken of in the same sense, a material relationship between "truth" and "doctrine" thereby emerges. Bergmeier, "Zum Verfasserproblem des II. und III. Johannesbriefes," 93–100, has correctly observed this point. However, "truth" and "doctrine" are not identical; for in

hope of v 2b is repeated: ἔσται μεθ᾽ ἡμῶν ("shall be with us").[9] However, the sentence takes on the tenor of a wish since the subject of ἔσται ("shall be") is an adaptation of the traditional greeting formula: χάρις, ἔλεος, εἰρήνη ("Grace, mercy, peace"),[10] as do the following phrases: παρὰ θεοῦ πατρός, καὶ κτλ. ("from God the father, and . . .").[11] There is the further addition of ἐν ἀληθείᾳ καὶ ἀγάπῃ ("in truth and love"), which appears superfluous. It is probably intended to characterize ἔσται μεθ᾽ ἡμῶν ("shall be with us") and prepare for vss 4–6, where ἀλήθεια ("truth") and ἀγάπη ("love")

are the dominant concepts. Ἀλήθεια is to be understood as the divine reality, as in vss 1b, 2. The entire prescript with its "full assurance" and dependence on traditional formulations may be an indication that 2 John comes from a relatively later period of Christian literature.

---

what follows upon v 1, "truth" is the object of knowledge, and this cannot be said of "doctrine." Also, one cannot very well speak of "walking in the doctrine," as he can of "walking in the truth" (3 Jn 3f).

9   That some witnesses read μεθ᾽ ὑμῶν ("with you") is an understandable correction, which transforms the sentence into the customary greeting formula.

10 Χάρις is to be understood as "grace" as in the customary greeting formula. It appears in 2 John only here, in 3 John not at all, in John only at 1:14, 16f. On the meaning of χάρις, see Bultmann, p. 74 n. 1 [49 n. 3] on 1:14. In Jas 1:1 and, for the most part, in the letters of Ignatius, the Greek wish χαίρειν takes the place of χάρις. In such formulas εἰρήνη does

not have the particular meaning, "peace," but "salvation," which corresponds to the Old Testament term שָׁלוֹם. Ἔλεος can mean "Grace" (of God); see Bultmann, TDNT II: 483–5 [480f]. In such wishes it is hardly differentiated from χάρις and εἰρήνη. It does not appear in John, 1 John, and 3 John. It is combined with εἰρήνη (which does not appear in 1 John) also in Gal 6:16; Jude 2, and all three are combined in the greetings in 1 Tim 1:2; 2 Tim 1:2.

11 In Paul and the Deutero-Paulines it is usually ἀπό rather than παρά.

Acknowledgment and Exhortation

4 I rejoiced greatly to find some of your children following the truth, just as we
have been commanded by the Father.
5/ And now I beg you, lady, not as
though I were writing you a new commandment, but the one we have had
from the beginning, that we love one
another. **6/** And this is love, that we
follow his commandments; this is the
commandment, as you have heard from
the beginning, that you follow love.

That 2 John is "carefully thought through and purpose-
fully constructed"[1] is to the point, insofar as everything
points to vss 7–11, the warning against heresy. For this
warning vss 4–6 are also preparation; in these verses are
combined *captatio benevolentiae* and exhortation leading up
to vss 7ff. The epistle is not original or theologically
independent. It consists essentially of traditional motifs
and reminiscences from 1 John.

■ **4** This letter, like 3 Jn 3, begins with an expression
of joy, which corresponds to older tradition.[2] In Christian
letters it is joy over the status of the addressees' Christian
faith. The formulation ἐχάρην λίαν ("I rejoiced
greatly") is met only here and in 3 Jn 3; in Paul the
formula is usually εὐχαριστῶ ("I give thanks") or
εὐχαριστοῦμεν τῷ θεῷ (μου) ("we give thanks to [my]
God"),[3] once εὐλογητὸς ὁ θεός . . . ("blessed be the
God . . .").[4] Even if the introductory formula sounds
conventional, that does not mean that the expression of
joy is not authentic.[5] That is even less the case here,

since the joy, for which the ὅτι–clause ("to find . . .")
provides the basis, is peculiarly limited by εὕρηκα ἐκ τῶν
τέκνων σου περιπατοῦντας κτλ. ("I found some of
your children walking . . ."). It thus cannot be said of all
members of the congregation that they lead their lives
"in truth."[6] But the author of the letter has "'found"some
who do.[7] It is dubious how ἐν ἀληθείᾳ ("in truth") is
to be understood. Since the article is missing, it can
scarcely be translated "in the truth," where "truth" is
the divine reality or its revelation, as in vss 1b, 2, but
must rather be understood, as is probably the case in
v 1a, in the sense of ἀληθῶς, "really, in an authentic
way," which is then explicated by the following καθώς–
clause ("just as . . .").[8] The ἐντολή ("commandment")
which "we have received" is, as v 5 shows, the love

---

1 So Haenchen, "Neuere Literatur," 287 [306].
2 See p. 97 on 3 Jn 3.
3 Thus Rom 1:8; 1 Cor 1:4; Phil 1:3; 1 Thess 1:2.
Likewise 2 Thess 1:3; Col 1:3.
4 Thus 2 Cor 1:3; likewise Eph 1:3; 1 Petr 1:3. Other
expressions of *captatio* occur in most of the letters of
Ignatius; Polycarp has συνεχάρην ὑμῖν ("I rejoice
with you").
5 No less so than in modern letters with "all best
wishes," and the like.
6 Περιπατεῖν ("to walk") in a figurative sense is common; cf. 1 Jn 1:6f; 2:6, 11, etc. Περιπατεῖν ἐν
ἀληθείᾳ also appears in 3 Jn 3.
7 Whether εὕρηκα ("I found") refers to a personal
meeting, either a visit of the author to the congregation or the reverse, cannot be certainly determined.
A possible meaning is: "I have imagined you to be
such" (Schnackenburg).
8 Schnackenburg points to Old Testament usages,
in which the ἐν ἀληθείᾳ of the LXX means "in

commandment, as in 1 Jn 2:7ff.[9] That we have received it παρὰ τοῦ πατρός ("through the Father") is understandable by itself, since Father and Son form a unity (v 3; 1 Jn 1:3, etc.); it is striking only insofar as one may miss the mention of Jesus Christ or perhaps καὶ τοῦ υἱοῦ αὐτοῦ ("and his Son"); but the υἱός ("son") is not expressly mentioned in 2 John and 3 John at all.

Since, according to vss 5f, the "commandment" is the love commandment, v 4 is the transition to vss 5f; at the same time, however, the restricted reference of the expression of joy permits the recognition that those "children" who are not acknowledged as "walking in the truth" are the gnosticizing heretics, against whom vss 7ff are directed. For the author knew from 1 John that false teaching and disregard of the love commandment go together.[10] And thus the exhortation to love in vss 4–6 also prepares for the polemic against false teachers in vss 7–11.

■ **5** The characterization of the love commandment in v 5[11] as a commandment which the congregation received ἀπ᾽ ἀρχῆς ("from the beginning") is an imitation of 1 Jn 2:7, except that the paradox of 1 Jn 2:8 is missing, viz., that the commandment is nevertheless a new command-

ment. That the commandment is not expressed as ἀγαπᾶν τὸν ἀδελφόν ("love the brother") as in 1 Jn 2:10, but as ἀγαπᾶν ἀλλήλους ("love one another," as also in 1 Jn 3:11, 23; 4:7, 11f) of course signifies no material difference.

■ **6** The definition of love in v 6a, by means of the ἵνα–clause, is strangely pedantic and unnecessary. In the definition, love is described as a περιπατεῖν κατὰ τὰς ἐντολὰς αὐτοῦ ("walking according to his commandments"), which is reminiscent of 1 Jn 2:3f, but where the text does not read "walk according to . . .," but "keep his commandments." Verse 6b is also superfluous; the "commandment" is again, as in v 5, characterized as one the readers heard "from the beginning";[12] the concluding ἵνα–clause is completely redundant. Whether the ἐν αὐτῇ ("in it") in this clause refers to the commandment or to love is uncertain, but makes no difference.

faithfulness." He likewise refers to comparable expressions found in the Qumran texts.

9 The commandments (ἐντολαί, v 6) are comprehended in the commandment (ἐντολή) to love. This interchange of plural and singular is also found in 1 Jn 2:3ff; see pp. 24ff.

10 See pp. 24ff.

11 On ἐρωτῶ σε ("I beseech you") in v 5, cf. Funk, "The Form and Structure of II and III John," *JBL* 86 (1967): 426f.

12 Ἀπ᾽ ἀρχῆς ("from the beginning") therefore is to be understood as in 1 Jn 2:7, 24; 3:11, thus the point within history when the Christian message was proclaimed and believed (differently than in 1 Jn 1:1; 2:13; see p. 9 n. 10 on 1 Jn 1:1). The reading of ἵνα before καθώς, represented by some witnesses, is probably secondary; on the other hand, ἵνα at the conclusion of v 6 is original.

Warning Against Heretical Teachers

7 For many deceivers have gone out into the world, men who will not acknowledge the coming of Jesus Christ in the flesh; such a one is the deceiver and the antichrist. 8/ Look to yourselves, that you may not lose what you have worked for, but may win a full reward. 9/ Any one who goes too far and does not abide in the doctrine of Christ does not have God; he who abides in the doctrine of Christ has both the Father and the Son. 10/ If any one comes to you and does not bring this doctrine, do not receive him into the house or give him any greeting; 11/ for he who greets him shares his wicked work.

[RSV modified]

■ **7** Verses 5f serve to prepare the reader for the warning against heretical teachers. The warning is identical with that in 1 Jn 2:18–27, 4:1–6, and the formulation of vss 7–9 is evidently dependent on these passages in 1 John. Individual variations can only demonstrate the secondary character of 2 John in relation to 1 John. The heretics are designated as πλάνοι ("deceivers") in v 7,[1] just as, in 1 Jn 2:26, they are called πλανῶντες ("those who deceive you"). That many of them "have gone out into the world" corresponds to the statement in 1 Jn 4:1, but with a different formulation: instead of ἐξεληλύθασιν εἰς τὸν κόσμον (1 Jn 4:1), it now reads ἐξῆλθον εἰς τὸν κόσμον (i.e., a change in tense).[2] Whence they have come does not, of course, have to be asked; if the question is raised at all, the answer can only be: from the antichrist. The κόσμος ("world") into which they have come is, as in 1 Jn 4:1, the world in the sense of the public sphere, in which they are active precisely as deceivers.[3]

The doctrine of the "deceivers" is characterized in substance as οἱ μὴ ὁμολογοῦντες κτλ. ("who do not acknowledge . . ."), as in 1 Jn 4:2, although the ἐληλυθότα ("has come") of 1 John is changed to ἐρχόμενον ("coming") in 2 John (change in tense). Naturally this cannot refer to the coming of Jesus Christ at his future parousia, since that is not a coming ἐν σαρκί ("in the flesh"), but ἐν δόξῃ ("in glory") (cf. Heb 4:13, etc.). Rather, the present tense of ἐρχόμενον ("coming") is a timeless characteristic of Jesus (as the one sent by God into the world), as in Jn 3:31; 6:14; 11:27. The motif of 1 Jn 2:18; 4:3, where the appearance of the heretics is interpreted in a historicizing manner as the coming of the antichrist,[4] is now utilized very awkwardly in this reference in the singular: οὗτός ἐστιν ὁ πλάνος καὶ ὁ ἀντίχριστος ("This is the deceiver and the antichrist"). Οὗτος ("This one") can only refer to ὁ μὴ ὁμολογῶν ("who does not acknowledge"). Οὗτος is probably to be understood as the predicate, with "the deceiver" and "the antichrist" as the subjects.[5]

---

1   Πλάνος ("deceitful") can be used as an adjective (as in 1 Tim 4:1) or as a noun (as in 2 Cor 6:8; Matt 27:63); cf. Bauer *s.v.* and Herbert Braun, *TDNT* 6: 229, 232f [235. 9–15].

2   The variant εἰσῆλθον is secondary.

3   Κόσμος thus does not mean "this world" here as it does in 1 Jn 2:15ff.

4   See pp. 35f on 1 Jn 2:18.

5   The reverse is also possible; see Schnackenburg, p. 313.

■ 8 The admonition which follows from v 7 is introduced in v 8 by the common formula βλέπετε ("take care," "be on guard")[6] with ἵνα μή ("lest") following.[7] The readers are admonished: ἵνα μὴ ἀπολέσητε ἃ εἰργάσασθε ("lest you lose what you have worked for").[8] The continuation, ἀλλὰ μισθὸν πλήρη ἀπολάβητε ("but may win a full reward"), is surprising, because it is a typical Jewish expression,[9] but is found neither in 1 John nor in John.[10] It is doubtless the case that μισθός ("reward") is ζωὴ αἰώνιος ("eternal life"; 1 Jn 2:25, etc.).

■ 9 Verse 9 indicates the significance of right confession in two sentences standing in antithetical parallelism, in obvious imitation of 1 Jn 2:23f. The negative side is given first: Πᾶς ὁ προάγων καὶ μὴ μένων κτλ. ("Any one who goes too far and does not abide . . ."). He who follows the heretical doctrine is characterized as one who goes too far,[11] and thus as one who goes beyond legitimate teaching, as μὴ μένων ("who does not abide") indicates. This could of course be said of those who, as Gnostics or gnosticizing Christians, strive for higher knowledge or think they have attained it. It is not said of a "deceiver" as such, but of all those who permit themselves to be deceived, as the πᾶς ("any one") indicates (as in 1 Jn 2:23 also). From the standpoint of the person, μένειν ("abide") means faithfulness.[12] That faithfulness consists in abiding in the διδαχὴ τοῦ Χριστοῦ ("doctrine of Christ") represents a distinction from 1 John, where the concept of didache is not met. But it is found in Jn 7:16f; 18:19.[13] With these passages in mind, τοῦ Χριστοῦ ("of Christ") may be taken as a subjective genitive; it is more probable, however, that "of Christ" is an objective genitive, since the author hangs everything on his christology, i.e., on the doctrine about Christ, as v 7 shows. Judgment is passed on the disciples of the heretical doctrine by the phrase, θεὸν οὐκ ἔχει ("does not have God"); this corresponds to 1 Jn 2:23, where it is said of "the one denying the Son," οὐδὲ τὸν πατέρα ἔχει ("he does not have the Father").[14] That means: he stands outside the fellowship of God.

The positive side of the antithesis is ὁ μένων ἐν τῇ διδαχῇ, οὗτος καὶ τὸν πατέρα καὶ τὸν υἱὸν ἔχει ("he who abides in the doctrine of Christ has both the Father and the Son"). This again corresponds to 1 Jn 2:24, from which the concept of μένειν ("abide"), i.e., faithfulness, is derived, as in the case of the negative side of the an-

---

6   Here the formula includes ἑαυτούς as in Mk 13:9. The formula is found in neither 1 John nor in John.

7   Βλέπετε μή with subjunctive is common (Mk 13:5; Matt 24:4, and elsewhere).

8   The well–attested reading εἰργάσασθε ("you have worked") is to be preferred to the reading ἠργασά-μεθα ("we have worked"), which admittedly is also well attested. The former alone fits the context (thus also Schnackenburg), while the latter would indicate that the author is the missionary responsible for the congregation addressed. One would then expect the author to address the readers as *his* children (thus Haenchen, "Neuere Literatur," 285 [304], correctly). On the other hand, the poorly attested reading ἀπολάβωμεν is secondary. The following ἀλλά–clause also does not fit with it.

9   See Schnackenburg, p. 314 n. 2. The variant ἀπολάβωμεν, like ἀπωλέσωμεν, is only poorly attested and certainly not original.

10   It occurs in a metaphorical sense, however, in Jn 4:36. Rev 3:11 is materially related: κράτει ὃ ἔχεις, ἵνα μηδεὶς λάβῃ τὸν στέφανόν σου ("hold fast what you have, so that no one may seize your crown").

11   Προάγειν in a metaphorical sense appears only here in the New Testament.

12   See p. 26 n. 9 on 1 Jn 2:6.

13   On the relationship between διδαχή and ἀλήθεια see pp. 108f n. 8. The formulation is reminiscent of 1 Jn 2:27, where the text speaks of the "teaching" (διδάσκειν) of the "anointing" (χρῖσμα), and where one also finds μένειν ἐν ("to abide in," viz., to abide in what the "anointing" has taught).

14   On ἔχειν τὸν θεόν see p. 39 n. 22 on 1 Jn 2:23.

tithesis. Now, however, "the Father" precedes "the Son." As always in 1 John and John, Father and Son belong together as a unity; cf., e.g., 1 Jn 2:23f; 5:10f.

■ **10f** The single original thing about the warning against heretics is the admonition respecting practical conduct vis-à-vis those heretics (vss 10f): fellowship with them must be severed. As a consequence, the hospitality[15] which was taken as obligatory elsewhere in primitive Christianity is not to be extended (μὴ λαμβάνετε αὐτὸν εἰς οἰκίαν, "do not receive him into the house") to itinerant heretics (εἴ τις ἔρχεται πρὸς ὑμᾶς κτλ., "if any one comes to you . . ."). Even the customary greeting is not to be extended to him (καὶ χαίρειν αὐτῷ μὴ λέγετε, "do not give him any greeting").[16] Since the greeting attests or establishes fellowship between the one greeting and the one greeted, the injunction to refuse the greeting has its special reason: he who greets him κοινωνεῖ τοῖς ἔργοις αὐτοῦ τοῖς πονηροῖς ("shares his wicked work").[17] Whether by "wicked work" the author understood specifically the spread of the heretical doctrine, or whether he included the moral conduct of the heretics, may remain an open question. Since heresy and disregard for the love commandment go together,[18] the latter is probably intended.[19]

---

15 Cf., for example, Rom 12:13; Heb 13:2; 1 Petr 4:9. Further, Schnackenburg, p. 316 n. 2.

16 Χαίρειν the common form of greeting (Bauer *s.v.* 2), occurs in the New Testament also at Acts 15:23; 23:26; Jas 1:1.

17 Κοινωνεῖν ("share or participate in") in the New Testament usually takes the dative (as often elsewhere; see Bauer *s.v.*), e.g. Rom 15:27; Gal 6:6; Phil 4:15; 1 Tim 5:22. Cf. especially the close parallel to 2 Jn 11 in 1 Tim 5:22: μηδὲ κοινώνει ἁμαρτίαις ἀλλοτρίαις ("do not participate in another man's sins").

18 See above on vss 5f and pp. 28f on 1 Jn 2:9–11; pp. 53f on 3:10f; pp. 65f on 4:7.

19 Matt 10:14 or Lk 10:10f comes to mind, where Jesus instructs his disciples to break off fellowship with those who do not receive his commandments and do not hear their words. But the situation is different. In 2 John it is a matter of false teachers, who represent themselves as Christians, with whom the Christian community is to have no fellowship.

Closing

> **12** Though I have much to write to you, I
> would rather not use paper and ink, but
> I hope to come to see you and talk
> with you face to face, so that our joy
> may be complete.
> **13** The children of your elect sister greet you.

■ **12** The conclusion of the letter is virtually verbally identical with the closing of 3 John. As a consequence, one cannot resist the suspicion that it is an imitation. When πολλὰ εἶχον γράψαι σοι ("I had much to write to you") is replaced by πολλὰ ἔχων ὑμῖν γράφειν ("having much to write to you"),[1] we have only a variation in expression. Since the epistle, unlike 3 John, is addressed to a congregation rather than an individual, σοι ("to you" [singular]) must naturally be replaced by ὑμῖν ("to you" [plural]). The replacement of ἀλλ' οὐ θέλω by οὐκ ἐβουλήθην κτλ. ("I would rather not . . .") is only an alternate way of saying the same thing. The same is true of the clauses beginning ἀλλὰ ἐλπίζω κτλ. ("but I hope . . ."), except that γενέσθαι πρὸς ὑμᾶς ("to come to you") in place of εὐθέως σε ἰδεῖν ("to see you soon") is a variant formula in which σε ("you" [singular]) has to be replaced, of course, by πρὸς ὑμᾶς ("to you" [plural]).[2] The sentence is expanded by means of ἵνα ἡ χαρὰ ἡμῶν πεπληρωμένη ᾖ ("so that our joy may be complete"), a clause in verbatim agreement with 1 Jn 1:4 and thus also obviously copied.[3]

■ **13** The closing greeting in v 13 forms the conclusion of the letter; cf. 3 Jn 15. In his formulation, the author reverts to the form of address in v 1; the subject of ἀσπάζεται ("greet") is now the τέκνα ("children"), i.e., the members of the congregation from which the author writes. The congregation is also characterized as ἐκλεκτή ("elect"), as in v 1; ἐκλεκτή is again used as an adjective.[4] The bond uniting the two congregations is expressed by the fact that the congregation addressed is designated as the ἀδελφή ("sister") of the congregation writing.[5]

---

1   Some witnesses read ἔχω for ἔχων; this can be either an error of hearing or of writing. Some witnesses read γράψαι for γράφειν; this is perhaps assimilation to the aorist ἐβουλήθην (Schnackenburg).

2   Some witnesses read ἐλθεῖν for γενέσθαι; there is no difference in meaning since γενέσθαι is often used in the sense, "to come" (see Bauer s.v. γίνομαι 4c).

3   Some witnesses have ὑμῶν ("your") instead of ἡμῶν ("our"), probably under the influence of ὑμῖν ("[see] you") and ὑμᾶς ("[talk with] you") in the preceding clause.

4   In some MSS ἐκκλησίας ("church") is added to τῆς ἐκλεκτῆς ("the elect"): an understandable addition. The addition of τῆς ἐν Ἐφέσῳ ("in Ephesus") naturally rests on the conjecture that Ephesus is the home congregation of the author.

5   In some late MSS, ἡ χάρις μετά σου (or μεθ' ὑμῶν) ("Grace be with you" [singular or plural]) is added on the analogy of the Pauline letters. The concluding ἀμήν ("Amen") is also found occasionally.

Bibliography
Indices

Bibliography

The basis for this bibliography is that of Bultmann himself, supplemented by that in Rudolf Schnackenburg, *Die Johannesbriefe (infra)*, xi–xxi. In addition, *New Testament Abstracts* and the *Elenchus Bibliographicus Biblicus* have been used extensively to verify references and to bring the bibliography up to date (late 1972). Bruce Metzger's *Index to Articles on the New Testament and the Early Church Published in Festschriften*, *JBL* Monograph Series 5 (Philadelphia: Society of Biblical Literature, 1951), has also been used, and David Scholer has kindly furnished more recent material from the forthcoming supplement to Metzger now being compiled by himself and Robert Karris. Several items in the bibliography, especially Edward Malatesta's *St. John's Gospel*, have also proved helpful in adding entries. The libraries of Harvard Divinity School, Weston College School of Theology, and the Episcopal Theological School have been invaluable resources for checking fugitive references. The work was begun by Eldon Jay Epp and completed by James Dunkly.

While it does not claim to be exhaustive, this list does purport to include all major commentaries and studies pertinent to the Johannine epistles published since 1900, together with the most important material from the nineteenth century. For earlier works, consult Schnackenburg's extensive compilation and James Moffatt's *Introduction to the New Testament*, *(infra)*, especially pp. 582f.

1. Commentaries

Bultmann uses only commentaries by Luther and Calvin published before 1800:

Luther, Martin
"Vorlesungen zum ersten Johannesbrief," in his *Werke* (Weimar: Bohlaus, 1883–   ), 20:599–801; 48:313–23 (supplement). ET, "Lectures on the First Epistle of St. John," tr. Walter A. Hansen, in *The Catholic Epistles*, Luther's Works, ed. Jaroslav Pelikan, vol. 30 (St. Louis: Concordia, 1967), 217–327.

Calvin, John
Commentarii in Novum Testamentum, ed. A. Tholuck (Berlin: Eichler, 1833–34, frequently reissued), 7:276–340.
Commentaries on the Catholic Epistles, tr. John Owen (Grand Rapids: Eerdmans, 1948), 156–275, 456–461.

The Gospel according to St. John 11–21 and The First Epistle of John, tr. T. H. L. Parker, Calvin's New Testament Commentaries, ed. David W. Torrance and Thomas F. Torrance, vol. 5 (Edinburgh: Oliver & Boyd; Grand Rapids: Eerdmans, 1961), 227–315.
See also Bengel, *Gnomon Novi Testamenti*, below.

The following are the principal modern commentaries, including pertinent sections of major one-volume works on the whole Bible. The entries are arranged chronologically.

Lücke, Friedrich
Commentar über die Briefe des Evangelisten Johannes (Bern: Weber, ²1836).
A Commentary on the Epistles of St. John, tr. with additional notes by Thorleif Gudmundson Repp, The Biblical Cabinet 15 (Edinburgh: Clark, 1837).

Köstlin, Karl Reinhold
Der Lehrbegriff des Evangeliums und der Briefe Johannis und die verwandten neutestamentlichen Lehrbegriffe (Berlin: Bethge, 1843).

Hilgenfeld, Adolf
Das Evangelium und die Briefe Johannis, nach ihrem Lehrbegriff dargestellt (Halle: Schwetschke, 1849).

Mayer, Georg Karl
Commentar über die Briefe des Apostels Johannes (Vienna: Braumüller, 1851).

Düsterdieck, Friedrich
Die drei johanneischen Briefe, mit einem vollständigen theologischen Commentare (Göttingen: Dieterich, 1852–54), 2 vols.

Erdmann, David
Primae Joannis epistolae argumentum, nexus et consilium. Commentatio exegetica (Berlin: Wiegandt & Grieben, 1855).

Ebrard, Johannes Heinrich August
Die Briefe Johannis, Biblischer Commentar über sämmtliche Schriften des Neuen Testaments 6, 4 (Königsberg: Unzer, 1859).
Biblical Commentary on the Epistles of St. John, in Continuation of the Work of Olshausen. With an Appendix on the Catholic Epistles, and an Introductory Essay on the Life and Writings of St. John, tr. W. B. Pope, Clark's Foreign Theological Library, 3rd series, 8 (Edinburgh: Clark, 1860).

Bengel, Johann Albrecht
Gnomon Novi Testamenti (Stuttgart: Steinkopf, 1860), 991–1016. ET, *Gnomon of the New Testament*, tr. Charlton T. Lewis and Marvin R. Vincent

(Philadelphia: Perkinpine & Higgins, 1864), 2: 782–822; reprinted as *New Testament Word Studies* (Grand Rapids: Kregel, 1971). Latin original first published in 1742.

Bisping, August

Erklärung der sieben katholischen Briefe, his Exegetisches Handbuch zum Neuen Testament 8 (Münster: Aschendorff, 1871).

Jelf, William Edward

A Commentary on the First Epistle of St. John (London: Longmans, Green, 1877).

Rothe, Richard

Der erste Brief Johannis praktisch erklärt, ed. K. Mühlhäusser (Wittenberg: Koelling, 1878).

Haupt, Erich

Der erste Brief des Johannes. Ein Beitrag zur biblischen Theologie (Colberg: Jancke, 1870). ET, *The First Epistle of St. John. A Contribution to Biblical Theology*, tr. with an introduction by W. B. Pope, Clark's Foreign Theological Library, n.s. 64 (Edinburgh: Clark, 1879).

Huther, J. E.

Kritisch-exegetisches Handbuch über die drei Briefe des Apostel Johannes, KEK 14 (Göttingen: Vandenhoeck & Ruprecht, ⁴1880). ET, *Critical and Exegetical Handbook to the General Epistles of James, Peter, John, and Jude*, tr. from 3rd German ed. by Paton J. Gloag, D. B. Croom, and Clarke H. Irwin, with a preface and supplementary notes by Timothy Dwight, Meyer's Commentary on the New Testament 10 (New York: Funk & Wagnalls, 1887).

Wolf, Carl August

Ein exegetischer und praktischer Commentar zu den drei Briefen St. Johannis (Leipzig: Kössling, 1881).

Plummer, Alfred

The Epistles of St. John, with Notes, Introduction and Appendices, Cambridge Bible for Schools and Colleges (Cambridge: At the University Press, 1884).

Plummer, Alfred

The Epistles of St. John, with Notes, Introduction and Appendices, Cambridge Greek Testament (Cambridge: At the University Press, 1886).

Lias, J. J.

The First Epistle of St. John (London: Nisbet, 1887).

Westcott, Brooke Foss

The Epistles of St. John: The Greek Text with Notes and Essays (London: Macmillan, ³1892; reprinted Abingdon: Marcham Manor, 1966); reprint has introductory essay by F. F. Bruce, "Johannine Studies Since Westcott's Day," lix–lxxvii.

Poggel, Heinrich

Der zweite und dritte Brief des Apostels Johannes geprüft auf ihren kanonischen Charakter, übersetzt und erklärt (Paderborn: Schöningh, 1896).

Karl, Wilhelm

Johanneische Studien I. Der erste Johannesbrief (Freiburg: Mohr–Siebeck, 1898).

Weiss, Bernhard

Die drei Briefe des Apostel Johannes, KEK 14 (Göttingen: Vandenhoeck & Ruprecht, ⁶1900).

Calmes, T.

Épîtres Catholiques, Apocalypse, traduction et commentaire (Paris: Bloud, 1905).

Belser, Johannes Evangelist

Die Briefe des heiligen Johannes (Freiburg: Herder, 1906).

Schmiedel, Paul Wilhelm

Evangelium, Briefe und Offenbarung des Johannes nach ihrer Entstehung und Bedeutung, Religionsgeschichtliche Volksbücher 1,12 (Tübingen: Mohr–Siebeck, 1906). ET, *The Johannine Writings*, tr. Maurice A. Canney (London: Black, 1908).

Holtzmann, H. J.

Evangelium, Briefe und Offenbarung des Johannes, rev. Walter Bauer, Hand–Commentar zum Neuen Testament 4 (Tübingen: Mohr–Siebeck, ³1908).

Camerlynck, Achille

Commentarius in Epistolas Catholicas, Commentarii Brugenses (Bruges: Beyaert, 1909).

Findlay, George G.

Fellowship in the Life Eternal (London: Hodder & Stoughton, 1909; reprinted Grand Rapids: Eerdmans, 1955).

Bauer, Walter

Die katholischen Briefe des Neuen Testaments, Religionsgeschichtliche Volksbücher 1, 20 (Tübingen: Mohr–Siebeck, 1910).

Brooke, A. E.

A Critical and Exegetical Commentary on the Johannine Epistles, International Critical Commentary (Edinburgh: Clark, 1912, frequently reprinted).

Law, Robert

The Tests of Life. A Study of the First Epistle of St. John (Edinburgh: Clark, ¹1909, ²1909, ³1914).

Baumgarten, Otto

"Die Johannes–Briefe," in *Die Schriften des Neuen Testaments*, ed. Wilhelm Bousset and Wilhelm Heitmüller (Göttingen: Vandenhoeck & Ruprecht, ³1918), 4:185–228.

Gore, Charles

The Epistles of St. John (London: John Murray; New York: Scribner, 1920).

Loisy, Alfred

Le quatrième Évangile, les Épîtres dites de Jean (Paris: Nourry, 1921).

Ritter, Karl Bernhard

Die Gemeinschaft der Heiligen. Eine Auslegung des Ersten Briefes St. Johannis (Hamburg: Hanseatische Verlagsanstalt, 1924).

Strack, Hermann L., and Paul Billerbeck

Kommentar zum Neuen Testament aus Talmud und Midrasch. Bd. 3: *Die Briefe des Neuen Testaments und die Offenbarung Johannis* (Munich: Beck, 1926); Johannine epistles, 776–779.

von Häring, Theodor

Die Johannesbriefe (Stuttgart: Calwer, 1927).

Büchsel, Friedrich

Die Johannesbriefe, Theologischer Handkommentar zum Neuen Testament 17 (Leipzig: Deichert, 1933).

Chaine, Joseph
Les Épîtres Catholiques: La seconde épître de saint Pierre, les épîtres de saint Jean, l'épître de saint Jude, Études bibliques (Paris: Gabalda, 1939).

Horn, Fritz
Der erste Brief des Johannes (Munich: Kaiser, 1931).

Oehler, Wilhelm
Das Wort des Johannes an die Gemeinde (Gütersloh: Bertelsmann, 1936).

Wrede, Wilhelm
"Der erste Johannesbrief, der zweite Johannesbrief, der dritte Johannesbrief" in *Die katholischen Briefe*, tr. with commentary by Max Meinertz and Wilhelm Vrede, Die Heilige Schrift des Neuen Testamentes, ed. Fritz Tillmann, 9 (Bonn: Hanstein, ⁴1932), 143–192.

Lauck, Willibald
Das Evangelium und die Briefe des heiligen Johannes, Die Heilige Schrift für das Leben erklärt 13 (Freiburg: Herder, 1941).

Dodd, C. H.
The Johannine Epistles, The Moffatt New Testament Commentary (London: Hodder & Stoughton, 1946).

de Ambroggi, Pietro
Le Epistole Cattoliche di Giacomo, Pietro, Giovanni e Giuda, La Sacra Bibbia, ed. S. Garofalo (Turin and Rome: Marietti, ²1949; reprinted 1957).

Charue, André
"Les Épîtres de S. Jean," in *La Sainte Bible*, ed. Louis Pirot and Albert Clamer (Paris: Letouzey & Ané, ¹1938, ²1946, ³1951), 12:503–564.

Windisch, Hans
Die Katholischen Briefe, rev. Herbert Preisker, Handbuch zum Neuen Testament 15 (Tübingen: Mohr–Siebeck, 1951).

Michl, Johann
Die Katholischen Briefe, Regensburger Neues Testament 8, 2 (Regensburg: Pustet, 1953).

Bonsirven, Joseph
Épîtres de Saint Jean, Verbum salutis 9 (Paris: Beauchesne, ²1954).

Ross, Alexander
The Epistles of James and John, New International Commentary on the New Testament (London: Marshall, Morgan & Scott; Grand Rapids: Eerdmans, 1954).

Grant, Frederick C.
The Gospel of John and the Epistles of John in the King James Version, with Introduction and Critical Notes, Harper's Annotated Bible Series 13–14 (New York: Harper, 1956); no. 13 (Jn 1–12) and no. 14 (Jn 13–21 and Johannine epistles) are bound together in vol. 2 of the entire set.

Asmussen, Hans
Wahrheit und Liebe. Eine Einführung in die Johannesbriefe. Die urchristliche Botschaft 22 (Hamburg:

Furche, ³1957).

Hauck, Friedrich
Die Kirchenbriefe, Das Neue Testament Deutsch 10 (Göttingen: Vandenhoeck & Ruprecht, ⁸1957).

Wilder, Amos N.
"The First, Second, and Third Epistles of John: Introduction and Exegesis," in *The Interpreter's Bible*, ed. George Buttrick *et al.* (Nashville and New York: Abingdon, 1957), 12:207–313.

Braun, F.-M.
Les Épîtres de saint Jean, La Sainte Bible (Paris: Cerf, ²1960), 195–243; the first part of the volume is *L'Évangile de saint Jean*, by D. Mollat.

Bonnard, Pierre
La première Épître de Jean. Nouvelle traduction, introduction et notes, Série biblique (Neuchâtel and Paris: Delachaux & Niestlé, 1961).

Schneider, Johannes
Die Briefe des Jakobus, Petrus, Judas und Johannes: Die Katholischen Briefe, Das Neue Testament Deutsch 10 (Göttingen: Vandenhoeck & Ruprecht, ⁹1961).

von Speyr, Adrienne
Die katholischen Briefe. II: Die Johannesbriefe (Einsiedeln: Johannes, 1961).

Alexander, Neil
The Epistles of John. Introduction and Commentary, Torch Bible Commentaries (London: SCM, 1962).

Grant, Frederick C.
"The Epistles of John," in *Nelson's Bible Commentary, based on the Revised Standard Version* (New York: Nelson, 1962), 7:347–63.

Johnston, George
"I, II, III John," in *Peake's Commentary on the Bible*, ed. Matthew Black and H. H. Rowley (London: Nelson, 1962), 1035–40.

Kohler, Marc
Le coeur et les mains. Commentaire de la première épître de Jean (Neuchâtel: Delachaux & Niestlé, 1962).

Guy, Harold A.
The Gospel and Letters of John (London: Macmillan; New York: St. Martin's, 1963).

Gaugler, Ernst
Die Johannesbriefe, Auslegung neutestamentlicher Schriften 1 (Zürich: EVZ, 1964).

Schlatter, Adolf
Die Briefe und das Offenbarung des Johannes ausgelegt für Bibelleser, his Erläuterungen zum Neuen Testament 10 (Stuttgart: Calwer, 1965).

Williams, R. R.
The Letters of John and James, The Cambridge Bible Commentary on the New English Bible (Cambridge: At the University Press, 1965).

de Jonge, M.
De brieven van Johannes, De Prediking van Nieuwe Testament (Nijkerk: Callenbach, 1968).

Rennes, Jean
La première épître de Jean (Geneva: Labor et Fides, 1968).

Vawter, Bruce

"The Johannine Epistles," in *The Jerome Biblical Commentary*, ed. Raymond E. Brown, Joseph A. Fitzmyer, and Roland E. Murphy (Englewood Cliffs, N. J.: Prentice-Hall, 1968), 404–13.

Russell, Ralph

"1, 2 and 3 John," in *A New Catholic Commentary on Holy Scripture*, ed. R. C. Fuller *et al.* (London: Nelson, 1969), 1257–62.

Bruce, F. F.

The Epistles of John. Introduction, Exposition and Notes (London: Pickering & Inglis; Old Tappan, N. J.: Revell, 1970).

Gärtner, Bertil E.

"Johannesbreven," in Bo Reicke and Bertil E. Gärtner, *De Katolska Breven* (Stockholm: Verbum, 1970), 111–223.

Moody, Dale

The Letters of John (Waco, Tex.: Word, 1970).

Schnackenburg, Rudolf

Die Johannesbriefe. Herders Theologischer Kommentar zum Neuen Testament 13, 3 (Freiburg: Herder, ⁴1970).

Shepherd, Massey H., Jr.

"The First Letter of John," in *The Interpreter's One-Volume Commentary on the Bible*, ed. Charles M. Laymon (Nashville and New York: Abingdon, 1971), 935–39.

"The Second Letter of John," *ibid.*, 940.

"The Third Letter of John," *ibid.*, 941.

2. Studies

The principal monographs and articles published since 1900 are given here, with a selection of earlier material. Articles on the Johannine epistles from encyclopedias, dictionaries, and the like are given here rather than in the preceding section. Strictly philological articles are omitted, unless they are restricted to the usage of the Johannine epistles. Entries are arranged alphabetically by author.

del Alamo, Mateo
"El 'Comma Joaneo,' " *Estudios Bíblicos* 2 (1943): 75–105.

del Alamo, Mateo
"Los 'Tres testificantes' de la primera Epístola de S. Juan, V, 7," *Cultura Bíblica* 4 (1947): 11–14.

Alfaro, J.
"Cognitio Dei et Christi in 1 Jo.," *Verbum Domini* 39 (1961): 82–91.

de Ambroggi, Pietro
"La teologia delle Epistole di S. Giovanni," *Scuola Cattolica* 76 (1946): 35–42.

Argyle, A. W.
"1 John iii.4f," *ExpT* 64 (1953–54): 62–3.

de Ausejo, S.
"El concepto de 'carne' aplicado a Cristo en el IV Evangelio," *Estudios Bíblicos* 17 (1958): 411–27.

Ayuso Marazuela, Teófilo
"Nuevo estudio sobre el 'Comma Ioanneum,' " *Biblica* 28 (1947): 83–112, 216–35; 29 (1948): 52–76.

Bacon, Benjamin Wisner
The Fourth Gospel in Research and Debate (New York: Moffatt, Yard, 1910).

Bardy, Gustave
"Cérinthe," *Revue Biblique* 30 (1921): 344–73.

Bartlet, J. Vernon
"The Historical Setting of the Second and Third Epistles of St. John," *JTS*, o.s. 6 (1905): 204–16.

Bauer, Walter
"Johannesevangelium und Johannesbriefe," *ThR*, n.s. 1 (1929): 135–60.

Bauer, Walter
Rechtgläubigkeit und Ketzerei im ältesten Christentum, ed. Georg Strecker, Beiträge zur historischen Theologie 10 (Tübingen: Mohr–Siebeck, 1964). ET, *Orthodoxy and Heresy in Earliest Christianity*, tr. Philadelphia Seminar on Christian Origins, ed. Robert A. Kraft and Gerhard Krodel (Philadelphia: Fortress, 1971).

Bauernfeind, Otto
"Die Fürbitte angesichts der 'Sünde zum Tode,' " in *Von der Antike zum Christentum: Untersuchungen als Festgabe für Viktor Schultze zum 80. Geburtstag am 13. Dezember 1931 dargebracht von Greifswalder Kollegen* (Stettin: Fischer & Schmidt, 1931), 43–54.

Behler, G. M.
" 'Nous avons cru en l'amour' (1 Jn 4, 16)," *La Vie Spirituelle* 119 (1968): 296–318.

Belser, Johannes Evangelist
"Erläuterungen zu I Joh.," *ThQ* 95 (1913): 514–31.

Belser, Johannes Evangelist
"Zur Textkritik der Schriften des Johannes," *ThQ* 98 (1916): 145–84.

Bergmeier, Roland
"Zum Verfasserproblem des II. und III. Johannesbriefes," *ZNW* 57 (1966): 93–100.

Bettencourt, E.
"A Escatologia no Evangelho e nas Epístolas de São João," *Revista de Cultura Bíblica* 3 (1959): 179–92.

Beyer, H. W.
Review of *Festgabe für Adolf Jülicher* (Tübingen: Mohr–Siebeck, 1927) in *ThLZ* 54 (1929): 606–17; see Bultmann, "Analyse," below. Bultmann's essay is criticized by Beyer in cols. 612f.

Birley, Hugh H.
"The Use of the Word *ZOE* in the Gospel and Epistles of St. John," *Theology* 33 (1936): 105–07.

Bludau, Augustinus
"Die 'Epistula ad Parthos,' " *Theologie und Glaube* 11 (1919): 223–36.

Bludau, Augustinus
Die ersten Gegner der Johannesschriften, Biblische Studien 22, 1–2 (Freiburg: Herder, 1925).

Bogaert, P.-M.
"Structure et message de la Première Épître de saint Jean," *Bible et Vie Chrétienne* 83 (1968): 33–45.

Boismard, M.-É.
"The First Epistle of John and the Writings of Qumran," in *John and Qumran*, ed. James H. Charlesworth (London: Chapman, 1972), 156–65.

Boismard, M.-É.
"La connaissance de Dieu dans l'Alliance Nouvelle d'après la première lettre de S. Jean," *Revue Biblique* 56 (1949): 365–91.

Boismard, M.-É.
"Je ferai avec vous une alliance nouvelle," *Lumière et Vie* 8 (1953): 94–109.

Boismard, M.-É
"La literatura de Qumran y los escritos de S. Juan," *Cultura Bíblica* 12 (1955): 250–64.

Bonsirven, Joseph
"La théologie des épîtres johanniques," *Nouvelle Revue Théologique* 62 (1935): 920–44.

Bornkamm, Günther
"πρεσβύς, κτλ.," in *ThWNT* 6:651–683, esp. 670–72; *TDNT* 6:651–83, esp. 670–72.

Bott, J. C.
"De notione lucis in scriptis S. Johannis Apostoli," *Verbum Domini* 19 (1939): 81–90, 117–22.

Braun, F.-M.
"L'eau et l'esprit," *Revue Thomiste* 49 (1949): 5–30.

Braun, F.-M.
Jean le théologien et son Évangile dans l'église ancienne,

Études bibliques (Paris: Gabalda, 1959); survey of critical issues in the Johannine epistles (pp. 27–41).

Braun, F.-M.
"Le péché du monde selon saint Jean," *Revue Thomiste* 65 (1965): 181–201.

Braun, Herbert
"Literar-Analyse und theologische Schichtung im ersten Johannesbrief," *ZThK* 48 (1951): 262–92, reprinted in his *Gesammelte Studien zum Neuen Testament und seiner Umwelt* (Tübingen: Mohr–Siebeck, 1962), 210–42.

Braun, Herbert
"Qumran und das Neue Testament: Ein Bericht über 10 Jahre Forschung (1950–1959)," *ThR* 28 (1962–63): 97–234; 29 (1963–64): 142–76, 189–260; 30 (1964–65): 1–38, 89–137; reprinted as *Qumran und das Neue Testament* (Tübingen: Mohr–Siebeck, 1966), 2 vols., the most important section of which is 1:290–306 for the Johannine epistles.

Bresky, Bennona
Das Verhältnis des zweiten Johannesbriefes zum dritten. (Münster: Aschendorff, 1906).

Briggs, R. C.
"Contemporary Study of the Johannine Epistles," *Review and Expositor* 67 (1970): 411–22.

Brooke, A. E.
"John, Epistles of," *Dictionary of the Apostolic Church*, ed. James Hastings (Edinburgh: Clark; New York: Scribner, 1916–18), 1:643–48.

Brooks, O. S.
"The Johannine Eucharist. Another Interpretation," *JBL* 82 (1963): 293–300.

Brown, Raymond E.
"John, Epistles of St.," in *New Catholic Encyclopedia* (New York: McGraw-Hill, 1967), 7:1078–80.

Brown, Raymond E.
"The Qumran Scrolls and the Johannine Gospel and Epistles," *Catholic Biblical Quarterly* 17 (1955): 403–19, 559–74; reprinted in *The Scrolls and the New Testament*, ed. Krister Stendahl (New York: Harper, 1957), 182–207, and in Brown, *New Testament Essays* (Milwaukee: Bruce, 1965), 102–31 [paperback edition (Garden City, N. Y.: Doubleday, 1968), 138–73].

Bruns, J. Edgar
"A Note on John 16:33 and I John 2:13–14," *JBL* 86 (1967): 451–53.

Büchsel, Friedrich
Der Begriff der Wahrheit in dem Evangelium und den Briefen des Johannes, BFTh 15, 3 (Gütersloh: Bertelsmann, 1911).

Büchsel, Friedrich
"Zu den Johannesbriefen," *ZNW* 28 (1929): 235–41.

Bultmann, Rudolf
"Analyse des ersten Johannesbriefes," in *Festgabe für Adolf Jülicher* (Tübingen: Mohr–Siebeck,

1927), 138–58; reprinted in his *Exegetica*, ed. Erich Dinkler (Tübingen: Mohr–Siebeck, 1967), 105–23.

Bultmann, Rudolf
Das Evangelium Johannes, KEK 2 (Göttingen: Vandenhoeck & Ruprecht, 18 1964); *Ergänzungsheft* (1966). ET, *The Gospel of John: A Commentary*, tr. G. R. Beasley–Murray, with R. W. N. Hoare and J. K. Riches (Oxford: Blackwell; Philadelphia: Westminster, 1971).

Bultmann, Rudolf
"Johannesbriefe," *RGG*³ 3:836–39, with bibliographic note on *Auslegungsgeschichte* by Wilfrid Werbeck, 839–840.

Bultmann, Rudolf
"Johannesevangelium," *RGG*³ 3:840–850, with bibliographic note on *Auslegungsgeschichte* by Wilfrid Werbeck, 850–51.

Bultmann, Rudolf
"Die kirchliche Redaktion des ersten Johannesbriefes," in *In Memoriam Ernst Lohmeyer*, ed. Werner Schmauch (Stuttgart: Evangelisches Verlagswerk, 1951), 189–201; reprinted in Bultmann's *Exegetica*, ed. Erich Dinkler (Tübingen: Mohr–Siebeck, 1967), 381–91.

Bultmann, Rudolf
"Die Theologie des Johannes–Evangelium und der Johannes–Briefe," in his *Theologie des Neuen Testaments* (Tübingen: Mohr–Siebeck, 1952–55, 5 1965), 354–445. ET, "The Theology of the Gospel of John and the Johannine Epistles," in his *Theology of the New Testament*, tr. Kendrick Grobel (London: SCM; New York: Scribner, 1952–55), 2: 1–92.

Bultmann, Rudolf
Review of Schnackenburg, *Die Johannesbriefe*² (*q.v. supra*), in *ThLZ* 92 (1967): 273–75.

Caird, George B.
"John, Letters of," in *The Interpreter's Dictionary of the Bible*, ed. George A. Buttrick (Nashville and New York: Abingdon, 1962), 2: 946–52.

Chapman, John
"The Historical Setting of the Second and the Third Epistles of St. John," *JTS*, o.s. 5 (1904): 357–68, 517–34.

Chapman, John
John the Presbyter and the Fourth Gospel (Oxford: Clarendon, 1911).

Charlesworth, James H., ed.
John and Qumran (London: Chapman, 1972); principally, but not entirely, devoted to the Fourth Gospel.

Chmiel, J.
Lumière et charité d'après la première épître de Saint Jean. (Rome: Institut Pontifical des Recherches Ecclesiastiques, 1971).

Clapperton, J. Alexander
"Τὴν Ἁμαρτίαν (1 John iii.4)," *ExpT* 47 (1935–36): 92–3.

Clavier, Henri

"Notes sur un mot-clef du johannisme et de la sotériologie biblique: ἱλασμός," *Novum Testamentum* 10 (1968): 287–304.

Clemen, Carl
"Beitäge zum geschichtlichen Verständnis der Johannesbriefe," *ZNW* 6 (1905): 271–81.

Conzelmann, Hans
" 'Was von Anfang war,' " in *Neutestamentliche Studien für Rudolf Bultmann zu seinem siebzigsten Geburtstag am 20. August 1954*, Beihefte zur ZNW 21 (Berlin: Töpelmann, 1954, ²1957), 194–201.

Cooper, E. J.
The Consciousness of Sin in I John," *Laval Théologique et Philosophique* 28 (1972): 237–48.

Coppens, Joseph
"Miscellanées bibliques. LII. 'Agapè et 'Agapân dans les Lettres johanniques," *Ephemerides Theologicae Lovanienses* 45 (1969): 125–27.

Corsani, Bruno
"Studi sulla I Epistola di Giovanni," *Protestantesimo* 23 (1968): 82–93.

Dammers, A. H.
"Hard Sayings — II," *Theology* 66 (1963): 370–72; on 1 Jn 5:16ff.

Denney, James
"He that Came by Water and Blood," *Expositor*, 7th series, 5 (1908): 416–28.

Dibelius, Martin
"Johannesbriefe," *RGG²* 3:346–349.

von Dobschütz, Ernst
"Johanneische Studien I," *ZNW* 8 (1907): 1–8.

Dobson, J. H.
"Emphatic Personal Pronouns in the New Testament," *Bible Translator* 22 (1971): 58–60.

Dodd, C. H.
"The First Epistle of John and the Fourth Gospel," *Bulletin of the John Rylands Library* 21 (1937): 129–56.

Dölger, Franz Josef
"*Domina Mater Ecclesia* und die 'Herrin' im zweiten Johannesbrief," in his *Antike und Christentum*, Band 5 (Münster: Aschendorff, 1936), 211–17.

Drumwright, Huber
"Problem Passages in the Johannine Epistles: A Hermeneutical Approach," *Southwestern Journal of Theology* 13 (1970): 53–64.

Eichholz, Georg
"Der 1. Johannesbrief als Trostbrief und die Einheit der Schrift," *Evangelische Theologie* 5 (1938): 73–83.

Eichholz, Georg
"Erwählung und Eschatologie im 1. Johannesbrief," *Evangelische Theologie* 5 (1938): 1–28.

Eichholz, Georg
"Glaube und Liebe im 1. Johannesbrief," *Evangelische Theologie* 4 (1937): 411–37.

Feuillet, André
" 'Dieu est amour,' " *Esprit et Vie* 81 (1971): 537–48.

Feuillet, André
"Les épîtres johanniques," in André Robert and André Feuillet, *Introduction à la Bible. Tome II: Nouveau Testament* (Tournai: Desclée, 1959), 685–708. ET, "The Johannine Epistles," in Robert and Feuillet, *Introduction to the New Testament*, tr. Patrick W. Skehan *et al.* (New York: Desclée, 1965), 669–89.

Feuillet, André
"Étude structurale de la première épître de saint Jean. Comparaison avec le quatrième évangile. La structure fondamentale de la vie chrétienne selon saint Jean," in *Neues Testament und Geschichte. Historisches Geschehen und Deutung im Neuen Testament. Oscar Cullmann zum 70. Geburtstag*, ed. Heinrich Baltensweiler and Bo Reicke (Zürich: Theologischer Verlag; Tübingen: Mohr–Siebeck, 1972), 307–27.

Feuillet, André
Le Mystère de l'amour divin dans la théologie johannique, Études bibliques (Paris: Gabalda, 1972).

Filson, Floyd V.
"First John: Purpose and Message," *Interpretation* 23 (1969): 259–76.

Findlay, George G.
"The Preface to the First Epistle of John," *Expositor*, 4th series, 7 (1893): 97–108.

Findlay, George G.
"Studies in the First Epistle of John" in *Expositor* as follows:
"1. The Advocate and the Propitiation," 6th series, 8 (1903): 321–44.
"2. The True Knowledge of God," 6th series, 8 (1903): 455–67; 9 (1904): 36–46.
"3. The Old and New Commandment," 6th series, 9 (1904): 226–40; 10 (1904): 30–36.
"4. The Filial Character and Hope," 6th series, 10 (1904): 149–60, 175–86.
"5. The Inadmissibility of Sin," 6th series, 10 (1904): 313–20, 451–60.
"6. Christian Heart Assurance," 6th series, 12 (1905): 380–400.

Francis, Fred O.
"The Form and Function of the Opening and Closing Paragraphs of James and I John," *ZNW* 61 (1970): 110–26.

Franke, A. H.
Das alte Testament bei Johannes (Göttingen: Vandenhoeck & Ruprecht, 1885).

Freed, Edwin D.
"Variations in the Language and Thought of John," *ZNW* 55 (1964): 167–97.

Funk, Robert W.
"The Form and Structure of II and III John," *JBL* 86 (1967): 424–30.

Galtier, Paul
"Le chrétien impeccable (I Jean III, 6 et 9)," *Mélanges de Science Religieuse* 4 (1947): 137–54.

Giardini, F.
"La rinuncia cristiana nel Vangelo e nelle Lettere di S. Giovanni," *Rivista di Ascetica e Mistica* 10

(1965): 224–39.

Gibbins, H. J.
"The Problem of the Second Epistle of St. John,"
Expositor, 6th series, 12 (1905): 412–24.

Gibbins, H. J.
"The Second Epistle of St. John," *Expositor*, 6th
series, 6 (1902): 228–36.

Giblet, J.
" 'Mundus' in Evangelio et Epistolis Sancti Joannis," *Collectanea Mechliniensia*, n.s. 19 (1949):
525–32.

Gloag, Paton James
Introduction to the Johannine Writings (London: Nisbet, 1891); Johannine epistles, 215–80.

Greiff, A.
"Die drei Zeugen in 1 Joh. 5, 7f.," *ThQ* 114
(1933): 465–80.

Guy, Harold A.
"1 John i. 1–3," *ExpT* 62 (1950–51): 285.

Haenchen, Ernst
"Neuere Literatur zu den Johannesbriefe,"
ThRund 26 (1960): 1–43, 267–91; reprinted in his
*Die Bibel und Wir: Gesammelte Aufsätze, Zweiter
Band* (Tübingen: Mohr–Siebeck 1968), 235–311.

Häring, Theodor
"Gedankengang und Grundgedanke des ersten
Johannesbriefs," in *Theologische Abhandlungen.
Carl von Weizsäcker zu seinem siebzigsten Geburtstage
11. Dezember 1892 gewidmet* (Freiburg: Mohr–
Siebeck, 1892), 171–200.

von Harnack, Adolf
Über den dritten Johannesbrief, TU 15,3b (Leipzig:
Hinrichs, 1897).

von Harnack, Adolf
"Das 'Wir' in den Johanneischen Schriften," *SAB*
(1923): 96–113.

von Harnack, Adolf
"Zur Textkritik und Christologie der Schriften
des Johannes," *SAB* (1915): 534–73; reprinted in
*Studien zur Geschichte des Neuen Testaments und der
alten Kirche. I: Zur neutestamentlichen Textkritik*, Arbeiten zur Kirchengeschichte 19 (Berlin and Leipzig: de Gruyter, 1931), 105–52.

Harris, J. Rendel
"The Problem of the Address in the Second Epistle of John," *Expositor*, 6th series, 3 (1901): 194–
203.

Heise, Jürgen
Bleiben. Menein in der Johanneischen Schriften, Her-
meneutische Untersuchungen zur Theologie 8
(Tübingen: Mohr–Siebeck, 1967).

Henle, Franz Anton
*Der Evangelist Johannes und die Antichristen seiner
Zeit* (Munich: Stahl, 1884).

Héring, Jean
"Y a-t-il des aramaïsmes dans la première épître
johannique?" *Revue d'Histoire et de Philosophie
Religieuses* 36 (1956): 113–21.

Herkenrath, Josef
"Sünde zum Tode," in *Aus Theologie und Philo-

sophie: Festschrift für Fritz Tillmann zu seinem 75.
Geburtstag (1. November 1949)*, ed. Theodor Stein-
büchel und Theodor Müncker (Düsseldorf: Pat-
mos, 1950), 119–38.

Higgins, A. J. B.
"The Words of Jesus According to St. John,"
Bulletin of the John Rylands Library 49 (1967): 363–
86.

Hirsch, Emmanuel
Studien zum vierten Evangelium, Beiträge zur historischen Theologie II (Tübingen: Mohr–Siebeck,
1936).

Holtzmann, H. J.
"Das Problem des ersten johanneischen Briefes in
seinem Verhältniss zum Evangelium," *Jahrbuch
für protestantische Theologie* 7 (1881): 690–712; 8
(1882): 128–52, 316–42, 460–85.

Horner, J.
"Introduction to the Johannine Epistles," *Southwestern Journal of Theology* 13 (1970): 41–51.

Hoskyns, Edwyn
"The Johannine Epistles," in *A New Commentary
on Holy Scripture Including the Apocrypha*, ed. Charles
Gore, Henry Leighton Goudge, and Alfred Guil-
laume (New York: Macmillan, 1928), part III,
pp. 658–73.

Howard, Wilbert Francis
Christianity according to St. John, Studies in Theology (London: Duckworth, 1943).

Howard, Wilbert Francis
"The Common Authorship of the Johannine Gospel and Epistles," *JTS*, o. s. 48 (1947): 12–25;
reprinted in his *The Fourth Gospel in Recent Criticism
and Interpretation*, rev. C. K. Barrett (London:
Epworth, ⁴1955), 282–96.

Howard, Wilbert Francis
*The Fourth Gospel in Recent Criticism and Interpreta-
tion*, rev. C. K. Barrett (London: Epworth, ⁴1955).

Humbert, A.
"L'observance des commandements dans les
écrits johanniques," *Studia Moralia* 1 (1963): 187–
219.

James, A. G.
"Jesus Our Advocate: A Free Exposition of I John
II. 1, 2," *ExpT* 39 (1927–28): 473–75.

Jochums, Heinrich
*Im Kampf wider der Irrlehrer. Betrachtungen zum 1.
Johannesbrief*, Aktuelle Fragen 17 (Wuppertal–
Elberfeld: Verlag und Schriftenmission der Evan-
gelischen Gesellschaft für Deutschland, 1968).

Johnston, George
"I, II, III John," in *Peake's Commentary on the Bible*,
ed. Matthew Black and H. H. Rowley (London:
Nelson), 1035–40.

Johnston, George
"The Will of God: V. In I Peter and I John,"
ExpT 72 (1960–61): 237–40.

Jones, Peter Rhea
"A Structural Analysis of I John," *Review and
Expositor* 67 (1970): 433–44.

de Jonge, M.
" 'Geliefden, laten wij elkander liefhebben, want de liefde is uit God' (I Joh. 4:7)," *Nederlands Theologisch Tijdschrift* 22 (1967–68): 352–67.

de Jonge, M.
"The Use of the Word ΧΡΙΣΤΟΣ in the Johannine Epistles," in *Studies in John Presented to Professor Dr. J. N. Sevenster on the Occasion of His Seventieth Birthday*, Supplements to Novum Testamentum 24 (Leiden: Brill, 1970), 66–74.

Joüon, Paul
"1 Jean 2, 16: ἡ ἀλαζονεία τοῦ βίου. 'La présomption des richesses,' " *Recherches de Science Religieuse* 28 (1938): 479–81.

Joüon, Paul
"Le verbe ἀναγγέλλω dans saint Jean," *Recherches de Science Religieuse* 28 (1938): 234–36.

Käsemann, Ernst
Jesu letzter Wille nach Johannes 17 (Tübingen: Mohr–Siebeck, 1966). ET, *The Testament of Jesus. A Study of the Gospel of John in the Light of Chapter 17*, tr. Gerhard Krodel (Philadelphia: Fortress, 1968).

Käsemann, Ernst
"Ketzer und Zeuge. Zum johanneischen Verfasserproblem," *ZThK* 48 (1951): 292–311; reprinted in his *Exegetische Versuche und Besinnungen I* (Göttingen: Vandenhoeck & Ruprecht, 1960), 168–87.

Katz, Peter
"The Johannine Epistles in the Muratorian Canon," *JTS*, n.s. 8 (1957): 273–74.

Keppler, P. W.
"Geist, Wasser und Blut. Zur Erklärung von I. Joh. 5, 6–13 (ev. Joh. 19, 34)," *ThQ* 68 (1886): 3–25.

De Keulenaer, Jules
"De I Joannis II, 15–17," *Collectanea Mechliniensia*, n.s. 6 (1932): 189–90.

De Keulenaer, Jules
"De interpretatione I Joannis I, 5–10," *Collectanea Mechliniensia*, n.s. 13 (1939): 279–82.

De Keulenaer, Jules
"De interpretatione I Joannis IV, 7–21," *Collectanea Mechliniensia*, n.s. 5 (1931): 639–43.

De Keulenaer, Jules
"De interpretatione prologi I Joannis (I, 1–4)," *Collectanea Mechliniensia*, n.s. 6 (1932): 167–73.

Kilpatrick, George D.
"Two Johannine Idioms in the Johannine Epistles," *JTS*, n.s. 12 (1961): 272–73.

Kittler, R.
"Erweis der Bruderliebe an der Bruderliebe?! Versuch der Auslegung eines 'fast unverständlichen' Satzes im 1. Johannesbrief," *Kerygma und Dogma* 16 (1970): 223–28.

Klein, Günter
" 'Das wahre Licht scheint schon! Beobachtungen zur Zeit– und Geschichtserfahrung einer urchristlichen Schule," *ZThK* 68 (1971): 261–326.

Klöpper, A.
"1. Joh. 5, 6–12," *Zeitschrift für wissenschaftliche Theologie* 43 (1900): 378–400.

Klöpper, A.
"Zur Lehre von der Sünde im 1. Johannesbrief, Erläuterung von 5, 16–fin.," *Zeitschrift für wissenschaftliche Theologie* 43 (1900): 585–602.

Knopf, Rudolf
"Katholische Briefe," *RGG*¹ 3:1016–1030; Johannine epistles, 1024–28.

König, A.
"Is die Weerhouer al uit die Weg Geruim?" *Nederduits Gereformeerde Teologiese Tydskrif* 11 (1970): 36–44.

Kragerud, Alv
Der Lieblingsjünger im Johannesevangelium (Oslo: Osloer Universitätsverlag, 1959).

Kubo, Sakae
"I John 3:9: Absolute or Habitual?" *Andrews University Seminary Studies* 7 (1969): 47–56.

Kümmel, Werner Georg
Einleitung in das Neue Testament (Heidelberg: Quelle & Meyer, ¹⁴1965), §§31–32; based on the work of Paul Feine and Johannes Behm. ET, *Introduction to the New Testament*, tr. A. J. Mattill, Jr. (Nashville and New York: Abingdon, 1966), §§ 31–32.

Künstle, Karl
Das Comma Ioanneum auf seine Herkunft untersucht (Freiburg: Herder, 1905).

Lazure, Noël
"La convoitise de la chair en I Jean, ii, 16," *Revue Biblique* 76 (1969): 161–205.

Lazure, Noël
Les valeurs morales de la théologie johannique (Évangile et Épîtres), Études bibliques (Paris: Gabalda, 1965).

Leconte, R.
"Jean (Épîtres de saint)," in *Dictionnaire de la Bible: Supplément*, ed. Louis Pirot (Paris: Letouzey et Ané, 1928–), 4:797–815.

Lee, G. M.
"1 John i. 1–3," *ExpT* 62 (1950–51): 125.

Lemonnyer, A.
"Comma johannique," in *Dictionnaire de la Bible: Supplément*, ed. Louis Pirot (Paris: Letouzey et Ané, 1928–), 2:67–73.

Lightfoot, Joseph Barber
"St. Paul and the Three," in his *Dissertations on the Apostolic Age*, published by Trustees of the Lightfoot Fund (London and New York: Macmillan, 1892), 46–134.

Lindskrog, Christian
Fortolkning til første Johannesbrev (Copenhagen: Gyldendal, 1941).

Lohmeyer, Ernst
"Über Aufbau und Gliederung des ersten Johannesbriefes," *ZNW* 27 (1928): 225–63.

Luthardt, Christoph Ernst
De primae Joannis epistolae compositione (Leipzig:

1860).

Lyonnet, Stanislaus
"De natura peccati quid doceat Novum Testamentum. V. De scriptis Ioanneis," *Verbum Domini* 35 (1957): 271–78.

Malatesta, Edward
The Epistles of St. John. Greek Text and English Translation Structurally Arranged, Polyglot Editions "Berardi" for the Study of the Holy Scriptures (Fano: Typis Paulinis, 1967).

Malatesta, Edward
St. John's Gospel 1920–1965. A Cumulative and Classified Bibliography of Books and Periodical Literature on the Fourth Gospel, Analecta Biblica 32 (Rome: Pontifical Biblical Institute, 1967), esp. pp. 50–51.

Mangenot, E.
"Jean (Première Épître de Saint)," in *Dictionnaire de la Bible*, ed. F. Vigouroux (Paris: Letouzey & Ané, 1907–12) 3:1192–99.

Mangenot, E.
"Jean (Seconde Épître de Saint)," in *Dictionnaire de la Bible*, ed. F. Vigouroux (Paris: Letouzey & Ané, 1907–12), 3:1199–1201.

Mangenot, E.
"Jean (Troisième Épître de Saint)," in *Dictionnaire de la Bible*, ed. F. Vigouroux (Paris: Letouzey & Ané, 1907–12), 3:1201–03.

Manson, Thomas Walter
"Entry into Membership of the Early Church," *JTS*, o.s. 48 (1947): 25–33.

Marty, Jacques
"Contribution à l'étude des problèmes johanniques: Les petites épîtres 'II et III Jean,'" *Revue de l'Histoire des Religions* 91 (1925): 200–11.

Menoud, Philippe–H.
"Johannesbriefe," in *Biblisch–historisches Handwörterbuch*, ed. Bo Reicke and Leonhard Rost (Göttingen: Vandenhoeck & Ruprecht, 1964) 2:874–75.

Michel, Otto
"Johannesbriefe," in *Calwer Bibellexikon*, ed. Theodor Schlatter (Stuttgart: Calwer, ²1967), 671–73.

Michl, Johann
"Der Geist als Garant des rechten Glaubens," in *Vom Wort des Lebens. Festschrift für Max Meinertz zur Vollendung des 70. Lebensjahres 19. Dezember 1950*, ed. Nikolaus Adler, Neutestamentlichen Abhandlungen, Ergänzungsband 1 (Münster: Aschendorff, 1951), 142–51.

Minear, Paul S.
"The Idea of Incarnation in First John," *Interpretation* 24 (1970): 291–302.

Moe, Olaf
"Das Priestertum Christi im NT ausserhalb des Hebräerbriefs," *ThLZ* 72 (1947): 335–38.

Moffatt, James
An Introduction to the Literature of the New Testament (Edinburgh: Clark, ³1918, reprinted 1961), 475–82 (2–3 Jn), 582–619 (1 Jn, Johannine tradition).

Especially helpful for earlier bibliography.

Moody, Dale
"The Theology of the Johannine Letters," *Southwestern Journal of Theology* 13 (1970): 7–22.

Moore, W. E.
"1 John iv. 12a," *ExpT* 65 (1953–54): 29–30.

Mouroux, J.
"L'expérience chrétienne dans la première épître de s. Jean," *Vie Spirituelle* 78 (1948): 381–412.

Mussner, Franz
"Eine neutestamentliche Kurzformel für das Christentum," *Trierer Theologische Zeitschrift* 79 (1970): 49–52.

Mussner, Franz
ΖΩΗ: *Die Anschauung vom 'Leben' im 4. Evangelium unter Berücksichtigung der Johannesbriefe. Ein Beitrag zur biblischen Theologie*, Münchener Theologische Studien 1, 5 (Munich: Zink, 1952).

Nagl, Erasmus
"Die Gliederung des ersten Johannesbriefes," *Biblische Zeitschrift*, o.s. 16 (1922–25): 77–92.

Nauck, Wolfgang
Die Tradition und der Charakter des ersten Johannesbriefes zugleich ein Beitrag zur Taufe im Urchristentum und in der alten Kirche, Wissenschaftliche Untersuchungen zum Neuen Testament 3 (Tübingen: Mohr–Siebeck, 1957).

Neufeld, Vernon H.
The Earliest Christian Confessions, New Testament Tools and Studies 5 (Leiden: Brill; Grand Rapids: Eerdmans, 1963); see "The Homologia in the Gospels and Letters of John," 69–107.

Noack, Bent
"On I John ii. 12–14," *NTS* 6 (1959–60): 236–41.

Nunn, H. P. V.
"The First Epistle of St. John," *Evangelical Quarterly* 17 (1945): 296–303.

Oggioni, C.
La dottrina della carità nel Quarto Vangelo e nella Prima Lettera di Giovanni, Pontificia Facultas Theologica Mediolanense 3 (Alba: Editiones Paulinae, 1953); also in *Scrinium Theologicum* 1 (1953): 221–93.

Omodeo, A.
Il quarto Evangelo e le lettere attribuite a Giovanni (Bari:Laterza, 1931).

O'Neill, J. C.
The Puzzle of 1 John. A New Examination of Origins (London: SPCK, 1966).

Pecorara, G.
"De verbo 'manere' apud Johannem," *Divus Thomas* 40 (1937): 159–71.

Percy, Ernst
Untersuchungen über den Ursprung der johanneischen Theologie zugleich ein Beitrag zur Frage nach der Entstehung des Gnostizismus (Lund: Gleerup, 1939).

Phythian–Adams, W. J.
"The New Creation in St. John," *Church Quarterly Review* 144 (1947): 52–75.

Piper, Otto A.
"I John and the Didache of the Primitive

Church," *JBL* 66 (1947): 437–51.

Polhill, John B.

"An Analysis of II and III John," *Review and Expositor* 67 (1970): 461–71.

de la Potterie, Ignace

"La connaissance de Dieu dans le dualisme eschatologique d'après I Jn, II, 12–14," in *Au service de la parole de Dieu. Mélanges offerts à Monseigneur André-Marie Charue* (Gembloux: Duculot, 1968), 77–99.

de la Potterie, Ignace

"L'impeccabilité du chrétien d'après 1 Jn 3, 6–9," in *L'Évangile de Jean. Études et problèmes*, Recherches bibliques 3 (Bruges: Desclée, 1958), 161–77; reprinted in de la Potterie and Stanislaus Lyonnet, *La vie selon l'Esprit. Condition du chrétien*, Unam Sanctam 55 (Paris: Cerf, 1965), 197–216. ET, "The Impeccability of the Christian According to I Jn 3, 6–9," in de la Potterie and Stanislaus Lyonnet, *The Christian Lives by the Spirit*, tr. John Morriss (Staten Island: Alba House, 1971), 175–96.

de la Potterie, Ignace

" 'Naître de l'eau et naître de l'Esprit.' Le texte baptismal de Jn 3, 5," *Sciences Ecclésiastiques* 14 (1962): 417–43; reprinted in de la Potterie and Stanislaus Lyonnet, *La vie selon l'Esprit. Condition du chrétien*, Unam Sanctam 55 (Paris: Cerf, 1965), 31–63. ET, " 'To Be Born Again of Water and the Spirit'—The Baptismal Text of John 3, 5," in de la Potterie and Stanislaus Lyonnet, *The Christian Lives by the Spirit*, tr. John Morriss (Staten Island: Alba House, 1971), 1–36.

de la Potterie, Ignace

"L'onction du chrétien par la foi," *Biblica* 40 (1959): 12–69; reprinted with additions in de la Potterie and Stanislaus Lyonnet, *La vie selon l'Esprit. Condition du chrétien*, Unam Sanctam 55 (Paris: Cerf, 1965), 107–67. ET, "Anointing of the Christian by Faith," in de la Potterie and Stanislaus Lyonnet, *The Christian Lives by the Spirit*, tr. John Morriss (Staten Island: Alba House, 1971), 79–143.

de la Potterie, Ignace

" 'Le péché, c'est l'iniquité' (I Jn 3, 4)," *Nouvelle Revue Théologique* 78 (1956): 785–97; revised in de la Potterie and Stanislaus Lyonnet, *La vie selon l'Esprit. Condition du chrétien*, Unam Sanctam 55 (Paris: Cerf, 1965), 65–83. ET, " 'Sin Is Iniquity' (I Jn 3, 4)," in de la Potterie and Stanislaus Lyonnet, *The Christian Lives by the Spirit*, tr. John Morriss (Staten Island: Alba House, 1971), 37–55.

Prunet, Oliver

La morale chrétienne d'après les écrits johanniques (Évangile et Épîtres), Études d'Histoire et de Philosophie Religieuses 47 (Paris: Presses Universitaires, 1957).

Riemens, Johannes

De Beteekenis van den eersten brief van Johannes in het historisch–kritisch onderzoek naar den oorsprong van het vierde Evangelie (Utrecht: Kemink, 1869).

Riggenbach, Eduard

Das Comma Iohanneum: Ein nachgelassenes Werk, BFTh 31, 4 (Gütersloh: Bertelsmann, 1928).

Robinson, J. A. T.

"The Destination and Purpose of the Johannine Epistles," *NTS* 7 (1960–61): 56–65; reprinted in his *Twelve New Testament Studies*, Studies in Biblical Theology, 1st series, 34 (London: SCM, 1962), 126–38.

Rogers, Lawrence M.

"I John i.9," *ExpT* 45 (1933–34): 527.

Romaniuk, Kasimir .

" 'Die vollkommene Liebe treibt die Furcht aus.' Eine Auslegung von 1 Jo 4, 17–18," *Bibel und Leben* 5 (1964): 80–84.

Sabatier, A.

"Jean (Épîtres et Evangile de)," in *Encyclopédie des Sciences Religieuses*, ed. F. Lichtenberger (Paris: Fischbacker, 1880), 7:177–93.

Salmond, S. D. F.

"Epistles of John," in *A Dictionary of the Bible*, ed. James Hastings (Edinburgh: Clark, 1902–04), 2:728–42.

Salom, A. P.

"Some Aspects of the Grammatical Style of I John," *JBL* 74 (1955): 96–102.

Schenke, Hans-Martin

"Determination und Ethik im ersten Johannesbrief," *ZThK* 60 (1963): 203–15.

Schlatter, Adolf

Die Sprache und Heimat des vierten Evangelisten, BFTh 6, 4 (Gütersloh: Bertelsmann, 1902).

Schlier, Heinrich

"Die Bruderliebe nach dem Evangelium und den Briefen des Johannes," in *Mélanges bibliques en hommage au R. P. Béda Rigaux*, ed. Albert Descamps and André de Halleux (Gembloux: Duculot, 1970), 235–45; reprinted in his *Das Ende der Zeit. Exegetische Aufsätze und Vorträge III* (Freiburg: Herder, 1971), 124–135.

Schlögl, Nivard

"Der erste Johannesbrief," *Zeitschrift für Katholische Theologie* 38 (1914): 617–27.

Schmiedel, Paul W.

"John, Son of Zebedee," in *Encyclopaedia Biblica*, ed. T. K. Cheyne and J. Sutherland Black (London: Black, 1899–1903), 2:2503–62.

Schnackenburg, Rudolf

"Johannesbriefe," in *Lexikon für Theologie und Kirche*, ed. Josef Höfer and Karl Rahner (Freiburg: Herder, ²1957–68), 5:1099–1100.

Schnackenburg, Rudolf

"Neue Arbeiten zu den johanneischen Schriften," *BZ*, n.s. 11 (1967): 303–07; 12 (1968): 141–45, 306–11; 13 (1969): 134–45.

Schnackenburg, Rudolf

"Der Streit zwischen dem Verfasser von 3. Johannesbrief und Diotrephes und seine verfassungsgeschichtliche Bedeutung," *Münchener Theologische Zeitschrift* 4 (1953): 18–26.

Schnackenburg, Rudolf
"Zum Begriff der 'Wahrheit' in den beiden kleinen Johannesbriefen," *BZ*, n.s. 11 (1967): 253–58.

Schwartz, Eduard
"Johannes und Kerinthos," *ZNW* 15 (1914): 210–19.

Schweizer, Eduard
"Der Kirchenbegriff im Evangelium und den Briefen des Johannes," in *Studia Evangelica: Papers presented to the International Congress on "The Four Gospels in 1957" held at Christ Church, Oxford, 1957*, ed. Kurt Aland, F. L. Cross, *et al.*, TU 73 (Berlin: Akademie–Verlag, 1959), 363–81; cf. Schweizer, *Gemeinde und Gemeindeordnung im Neuen Testament*, Abhandlungen zur Theologie des Alten und Neuen Testaments 35 (Zürich: Zwingli, 1959), sections 11–12. ET, "The Concept of the Church in the Gospel and Epistles of St. John," in *New Testament Essays. Studies in Memory of Thomas Walter Manson (1893–1958)*, ed. A. J. B. Higgins (Manchester: Manchester University Press, 1959), 230–45; cf. Schweizer's *Church Order in the New Testament*, tr. Frank Clarke, Studies in Biblical Theology, 1st series, 32 (London: SCM, 1961), sections 11–12.

Schweizer, Eduard
"Zum religionsgeschichtlichen Hintergrund der 'Sendungsformel' Gal 4 4f, Röm 8 3f, Joh 3 16f, 1 Joh 4 9," *ZNW* 57 (1966): 199–210; reprinted in his *Beiträge zur Theologie des Neuen Testaments* (Zürich: Zwingli, 1970), 83–95.

Schwertschlager, Rudolf
Der erste Johannesbrief in seinem Grundgedanken und Aufbau (Coburg: Tageblatt–Haus, 1935).

Seeberg, Reinhold
"Die Sünden und die Sündenvergebung nach dem ersten Brief des Johannes," in *Das Erbe Martin Luthers und die gegenwärtige theologische Forschung. Theologische Abhandlungen D. Ludwig Ihmels zum siebzigsten Geburtstage 29. O. 1928 dargebracht von Freunden und Schülern*, ed. Robert Jelke (Leipzig: Doerffling & Franke, 1928), 19–31.

Segalla, G.
"L'esperienza cristiana im Giovanni," *Studia Patavina* 18 (1971): 299–342.

Segond, A.
"1re Épître de Jean, chap. 5: 18–20," *Revue d'Histoire et de Philosophie Religieuses* 45 (1965): 349–51.

Sevenster, G.
"Remarks on the Humanity of Jesus in the Gospel and Letters of John," in *Studies in John Presented to Professor Dr. J. N. Sevenster on the Occasion of His Seventieth Birthday*, Supplements to Novum Testamentum 24 (Leiden: Brill, 1970), 185–93.

Shutt, R. J. H.
"1 John iv. 12a," *ExpT* 64 (1952–53): 239–40.

Simpson, J. G.
"The Message of the Epistles: The Letters of the Presbyter, *ExpT* 45 (1933–34): 486–90.

Škrinjar, A.
"De divisione epistolae primae Joannis," *Verbum Domini* 47 (1969): 31–40.

Škrinjar, A.
"De unitate epistolae 1J," *Verbum Domini* 47 (1969): 83–95.

Škrinjar, A.
"Differentiae theologicae 1 Jo et Jo," *Verbum Domini* 41 (1963): 175–85.

Škrinjar, A.
"Errores in epistola I Jo impugnati," *Verbum Domini* 41 (1963): 60–72.

Škrinjar, A.
"Maior est Deus corde nostro," *Verbum Domini* 20 (1940): 340–50.

Škrinjar, A.
"Prima Epistola Johannis in theologia aetatis suae," *Verbum Domini* 46 (1968): 148–68.

Škrinjar, A.
"Theologia Epistolae IJ comparatur cum philonismo et hermetismo," *Verbum Domini* 46 (1968): 224–34.

Škrinjar, A.
"Theologia primae epistolae Joannis," *Verbum Domini* 42 (1964): 3–16, 49–60; 43 (1965): 150–80.

Smit Sibinga, J.
"I Johannes tegen de achtergrond van de teksten van Qumran," *Vox Theologica* 29 (1958–59): 11–14.

Smit Sibinga, J.
"A Study in I John," in *Studies in John Presented to Professor Dr. J. N. Sevenster on the Occasion of His Seventieth Birthday*, Supplements to Novum Testamentum 24 (Leiden: Brill, 1970), 194–208.

Soltau, Wilhelm
"Die Verwandtschaft zwischen Evangelium Johannis und dem 1. Johannesbrief," *Theologische Studien und Kritiken* 89 (1916): 229–33.

Songer, Harold S.
"The Life Situation of the Johannine Epistles," *Review and Expositor* 67 (1970): 399–409.

Spicq, Ceslaus
"La justification du charitable (1 Jo 3,19–21)," *Biblica* 40 (1959): 915–27.

Spicq, Ceslaus
"Notes d'exégèse johannique. La charité est amour manifeste," *Revue Biblique* 65 (1959): 358–370.

Stagg, Frank
"Orthodoxy and Orthopraxy in the Johannine Epistles," *Review and Expositor* 67 (1970): 423–32.

Stemberger, Günter
La symbolique du bien et du mal selon saint Jean, Parole de Dieu (Paris: Seuil, 1970).

Stevens, George B.
The Johannine Theology. A Study of the Doctrinal Contents of the Gospel and Epistles of the Apostle John (New York: Scribner, 1894).

Stockmeyer, Immanuel

Die Struktur des ersten Johannesbriefes (Basel: Schneider, 1873).

Strathmann, Hermann
"Johannesbriefe," in *Evangelisches Kirchenlexikon* (Göttingen: Vandenhoeck & Ruprecht, 1956–61), 2:363–65.

Suitbertus a S. Joanne a Cruce, P.
"Die Vollkommenheitslehre des ersten Johannesbriefes," *Biblica* 39 (1958): 319–33, 449–70.

Šurjanský, Antonius Johannes
De mysterio Verbi incarnati ad mentem B. Ioannis Apostoli libri tres. Vol. I: Introductio et liber primus, Lateranum, n.s. 7, 1–4 (Rome: Lateran, 1940).

Synge, F. C.
"I John 3, 2," *JTS*, n.s. 3 (1952): 79.

Thiele, Walter
"Beobachtungen zum Comma Iohanneum (I Joh 5, 7f.)," *ZNW* 50 (1959): 61–73.

Thiele, Walter
Wortschatzuntersuchungen zu den lateinischen Texten der Johannesbrief, Vetus Latina. Aus der Geschichte der lateinischen Bibel 2 (Freiburg: Herder, 1958).

Thompson, P. J.
"Psalm 119: a possible Clue to the Structure of the First Epistle of John," *Studia Evangelica, Vol. II: Papers Presented to the Second International Congress on New Testament Studies Held at Christ Church, Oxford, 1961: Part I: The New Testament Scriptures*, ed. F. L. Cross, TU 87 (Berlin: Akademie–Verlag, 1964), 487–92.

Thornton, T. C. G.
"Propitiation or Expiation? Ἱλαστήριον and Ἱλασμός in Romans and 1 John," *ExpT* 80 (1968–69): 53–55.

Thornton-Duesbery, J. P.
"1 John i. 9," *ExpT* 45 (1933–34): 183–84.

Thüsing, Wilhelm
"Glaube an die Liebe. Die Johannesbriefe," in *Gestalt und Anspruch des Neuen Testaments*, ed. Josef Schreiner (Würzburg: Echter, 1969), 282–98.

Tilden, Elwyn E., Jr.
"The First Epistle of John," *Interpretation* 4 (1950): 193–201.

Tomoi, Kozue
"The Plan of the First Epistle of John," *ExpT* 52 (1940–41): 117–19.

Trépanier, B.
"Contribution à une recherche de l'idée de témoin dans les écrits johanniques," *Revue de l'Université d'Ottawa* 15 (1945): 5*–63*.

Trudinger, Paul
"Concerning Sins, Mortal and Otherwise. A Note on 1 John 5, 16–17," *Biblica* 52 (1971): 541–42.

Uttendoerfer, Pastor
"Ein Kennzeichen dafür, dass wir aus der Wahrheit sind. Versuch einer Auslegung des Abschnittes 1. Joh. 3, 18–24," *Neue Kirchliche Zeitschrift* 11 (1900): 985–1002.

Vedder, Henry C.

The Johannine Writings and the Johannine Problem (Philadelphia: Griffith & Rowland, 1917).

Vénard, L.
"Épîtres de S. Jean," in *Dictionnaire de Théologie Catholique*, ed. A. Vacant, E. Mangenot, and É. Amann (Paris: Letouzey & Ané, 1924–50), 8: 584–593 [part of his article "Jean (Saint)," 8:537–593].

Vicent Cernuda, Antonio
"Engañan la oscuridad y el mundo; la luz era y manifiesta lo verdadero. (Esclarecimento mutuo de Jn 1,9; 1 Cor 7,31; 1 Jn 2,8 y 17)," *Estudios Bíblicos* 27 (1968): 153–75, 215–32.

Walder, Ernest
The God of Love. A Literary Research into the Origin and Meaning of S. John's Epistles (London: Williams & Norgate, 1927).

Ward, R. A.
"The Theological Pattern of the Johannine Epistles," *Southwestern Journal of Theology* 13 (1970): 23–39.

Weiss, Konrad
"Orthodoxie und Heterodoxie im 1. Johannesbrief," *ZNW* 58 (1967): 247–55.

Wendt, H. H.
"Der 'Anfang' am Beginne des I Johannesbriefes," *ZNW* 21 (1922): 38–42.

Wendt, H. H.
"Die Beziehung unseres ersten Johannesbriefes auf den zweiten," *ZNW* 21 (1922): 140–46.

Wendt, H. H.
Die Johannesbriefe und das johanneische Christentum (Halle/Saale: Buchhandlung des Waisenhauses, 1925).

Wendt, H. H.
"Zum ersten Johannesbrief," *ZNW* 22 (1923): 57–79.

Wendt, H. H.
"Zum zweiten und dritten Johannesbrief," *ZNW* 23 (1924): 18–27.

Wennemer, Karl
"Der Christ und die Sünde nach der Lehre des ersten Johannesbriefes," *Geist und Leben* 33 (1960): 370–376.

Westcott, Brooke Foss, and Hort, Fenton John Anthony
"The Divisions of the First Epistle of St. John: Correspondence Between Drs. Westcott and Hort," ed. A. Westcott, *Expositor*, 7th series, 3 (1907): 481–93.

Wiesinger, A.
"Der Gedankengang des ersten Johannesbriefes," *Theologische Studien und Kritiken* 72 (1899): 575–81.

von Wilamowitz-Moellendorff, Ulrich
"Lesefrüchte," *Hermes* 33 (1898): 513–533; no. XXI, pp. 529–31, is pertinent to the Johannine epistles.

Willmering, H.
"The Epistles of St. John," in *A Catholic Commen-*

tary on Holy Scripture, ed. Bernard Orchard *et al.* (London: Nelson, 1953), 1185–90.

Wilson, W. G.
"An Examination of the Linguistic Evidence Adduced against the Unity of Authorship of the First Epistle of John and the Fourth Gospel," *JTS*, o.s. 49 (1948): 147–56.

Wohlenberg, G.
"Glossen zum ersten Johannesbrief," *Neue Kirchliche Zeitschrift* 12 (1901): 581–83, 746–48; 13 (1902): 233–40, 632–45.

Wurm, Alois
Die Irrlehrer im ersten Johannesbrief, Biblische Studien 8,1 (Freiburg: Herder, 1903).

Zahn, Adolf
De notione peccati, quam Iohannes in prima epistola docet, commentatio (Halle: Mühlmann, 1872).

Zahn, Theodor
"Johannes der Apostel," in *RE*[3] 9:272–85. ET, "John the Apostle," in *The New Schaff–Herzog Encyclopedia of Religious Knowledge*, ed. Samuel Macauley Jackson (New York and London: Funk & Wagnalls, 1908–12), 6:202–07.

Zerwick, Maximilian
"Veritatem facere," *Verbum Domini* 18 (1938): 338–42, 373–77.

3. Reviews

The principal reviews of Bultmann, *Die drei Johannesbriefe*, are as follows:

P. Block, *Svensk Teologisk Kvartalskrift* 46 (1970): 61–63.

Günther Bornkamm, *Evangelische Kommentare* 1 (1968): 347–48.

C. Brütsch, *Theologische Zeitschrift* 24 (1968): 470–71.

Bruno Corsani, *Protestantesimo* 23 (1968): 82–93.

Gerhard Krodel, *Lutheran World* 15 (1968): 151.

Robert Kysar, *Interpretation* 22 (1968): 499–502.

W. Pesch, *Trierer Theologische Zeitschrift* 78 (1969): 185–86.

Karl Hermann Schelkle, *Theologische Quartalschrift* 148 (1968): 482.

Rudolf Schnackenburg, *ThLZ* 94 (1969): 586–87.

J. N. Sevenster, *Nederlands Theologisch Tijdschrift* 22 (1968): 449–51.

D. Moody Smith, Jr., *JBL* 88 (1969): 120–21.

R. H. Smith, *Concordia Theological Monthly* 41 (1970): 61–62.

Indices*

1. Passages

a / Old Testament and Apocrypha

Gen
18:19	45(8)

Lev
4:2ff	86(9)

Num
12:8	103(2)
15:22ff	86(9)

Deut
32:4	21(31)

Josh
24:14	21(31)
24:7	10

2 Sam
8:15	45(8)

Job
34:8	12(21)

Ps
14:2	45(8)

LXX Ps
31:1	50(26)
50:4	50(26)

Pr
28:13	21(26)

Jer
39:4	103(2)

Amos
2:10f	10

Nah
9:8,38	21(31)

Wisd Sol
5:8	34(24)

b / Old Testament Pseudepigrapha and Other Jewish Literature

Pesahim
116b	10

Philo
De migr. Abr.
122	22(36)

1QS	28(25)

Sota
48a	86(9)

Test Dan
6:2	22(36)

Test Lev
3:5	22(36)
5:6	22(36)

Test Napht
2:10	20(21)

c / New Testament

Matt
5:8	49(24)
5:9	46(10),48
5:10ff	54(47)
5:47	99(12)
6:24	20
7:23	50(26)
10:14	114(19)
11:27 par.	47(14)
12:18	67(13)
12:33	59(83)
13:41	50(26)
14:55	96(6)
19:28	46(9)
23:12	50(26)
24:4	113(7)
24:11,24	62
24:12	50(26)
25:46	73
27:63	112(1)

Mk
1:11	67(13)
3:28	87(17)
9:7	67(13)
12:44	34(25)
13:5	113(7)
13:9	113(6)
13:22	62
13:32 par.	47(14)

Lk
6:44	59(83)
10:10f	114(19)
12:15	90(41)
23:24	86(5)
24:39	9(11)

Jn
1:1	9
1:8	36(6)
1:12	59(80), 84(26)
1:13f	33
1:14	9,11
1:14,16f	109(10)
1:14,18	67
1:18	68
1:29	23(38), 51(29)
1:47	96(6), 108(7)
2:5	57(60)

*Numbers in parentheses following page citations for this volume refer to footnotes.

■

Ref	Page
2:23	59(80)
3:3,7	46(9)
3:5	46(9)
3:6	33
3:9	67(10)
3:15	40(27),83
3:16	47(14), 51(30), 66,67
3:16f	23(38)
3:17	67
3:18	59(80),67
3:18,36	40(28)
3:19	16,28(21), 33,74
3:20f	19(17)
3:29	14(30)
3:31	34(26), 36(6),112
3:33	82
4:14	34(30)
4:23	36(4)
4:24	66
4:34	34(29)
4:35	87(15)
4:36	113(10)
4:42	71(7) 96(6),
4:42f	23(38)
5:23	38(16)
5:24	28(21), 40(28), 55,74
5:25	36(4)
5:33	98(5)
5:37	48
5:45	49
6:14	112
6:29	59(77)
6:53–56	20(25)
6:63	80(4)
6:69	37(9)
7:7	33
7:13	73(9)
7:16f	113
7:26	108(7)
7:28	48
8:12	17
8:14	48
8:19	38(16)
8:23	36(6)
8:29	58(73)
8:31	108(7)
8:32	19
8:42	89(31)
8:44	219,51,5
8:47	64,102

■

Ref	Page
9:34f	101(12)
9:41	20(24)
11:24f	36(4)
11:25f	40(28)
11:25	83,90
11:27	112
11:55	49(25)
12:25	90(41)
12:31	33
12:35	29(27)
12:43	33
12:44f	38(16)
12:47	23(38)
13:15	26(12)
13:18	36(6)
13:24	58(75)
13:33	22(34)
13:34	27,27(14), 28(28), 54(44)
13:35	17
14:1ff	40(28),48
14:6	19,80(60), 83,90
14:7	38(16)
14:9	38(16)
14:10f	20(21)
14:13	57(60)
14:15,21	25(3), 27(14)
14:16,26	22(36)
14:17	64(17)
14:23	47(14)
14:27	14(29)
14–16	80(5)
15:2	98(7)
15:10	25(3), 27(14),72
15:11	14(29)
15:12	28(28), 54(44)
15:12,17	58(75)
15:16	57(60)
15:18f,24	33
15:19	48
15:20	54(47)
15:22,24	20(24)
15:23	38(16)
15:26	22(26), 64(17)
16:3	39(16),48
16:7	22(36)
16:11	33
16:13	64(17)
16:20–24	14(28)
16:23f,26	85(2), 86(6)

■

Ref	Page
16:33	32,63(14), 83
17:1,5,24	49
17:3	38,84
17:6,16	14(29)
17:8	108(7)
17:11,12,15	89
17:12	90(41)
17:13	14(28) (29)
17:14	33
17:15	32,73
17:24–26	40(28)
18:19	113
18:36	33,34(26)
18:37	19,64, 98(5)
19:11	20(24)
19:28	14(30)
19:34b,35	20(25), 81(8)
19:38	73(9)
20:19	73(9)
20:24ff	9(11)
20:30	103
20:31	83,84(24)
21:17	57(65)

Acts

Ref	Page
2:23	50(27)
10:35	45(8)
14:23	100(4)
15:9	22(32)
15:23	114(16)
17:27	9
19:29	95(4)
20:4	95(4)
21:24,26	49(25)
23:26	114(16)
24:18	49(25)

Rom

Ref	Page
1:5	98(7)
1:7	96(5)
1:8	110(3)
1:10	97(2)
2:12	50(27)
3:23	23(38)
3:25	23(37)
4:4f	59
4:7	50(26)
5:1	58(69)
6:4	19(19)
6:19	50(26)
8:4	19(19)
8:15	73(9)
8:17–19	49
8:34	22(36)

■

Ref	Page
10:9f	62(9)
12:2	49
12:13	114(15)
12:19	26(13)
13:11f	28(21)
14:15	19(19)
15:27	114(17)
16:19	97(4)

1 Cor

Ref	Page
1:4	110(3)
1:9	21(31)
1:14	95(4)
1:20	28(21)
2:6,8	28(21)
3:3	19(19)
3:10	98(7)
3:19	33
4:14	96(5),98
4:14,17	108(5)
5:10	33
5:11	31(4)
7:29,31	28(21)
7:31	33,34
8:1	37
8:4,7	91(43)
9:21	50(27)
10:13	21(31)
10:14	96(5)
12:2	91(42)
15:43ff	49
16:2	97(2)

2 Cor

Ref	Page
1:3	110(4)
1:21	37(12)
3:3	103(1)
3:18	49
4:2	19(19)
5:19	23(88)
6:8	112(1)
6:13	108(5)
6:14	50(26)
7:1	22(32), 26(13)
7:7,13,16	97(4)
10:2	19(19)

Gal

Ref	Page
4:19	22(34),98
6:6	114(17)
6:11	31(4)
6:16	109(10)

Eph

Ref	Page
1:3	110(4)
1:21	28(21)
2:2	33
2:3	34(23)
4:18	89(32)
5:8	19(19)

■

Ref	Page
5:8–14	28(21)
5:26	22(32)
6:12	28(21)
6:16	32

Phil

Ref	Page
1:1	100(4)
1:3	110(3)
1:5	12(21)
1:18	97(4)
2:22	98
3:21	49
4:6	86(5)
4:15	114(17)

Col

Ref	Page
1:3	110(3)
1:21	89(32)
2:5	97(4)
3:3f	48
3:4	49

1 Thess

Ref	Page
1:2	110(3)
1:9	89,91(43)
3:9	97(4)
5:4–10	28(21)
5:21	61

2 Thess

Ref	Page
1:3	110(3)
2:1–12	36(3)
2:3,7,8,9	50
2:11	64(18)
3:3	32,89(26), 90(41)

1 Tim

Ref	Page
1:2	109(10)
1:9	50(26)
2:6	23(38)
4:1	112(1)
5:17	100(4)
5:22	88,114 (17)

2 Tim

Ref	Page
1:2	109(10)
2:14	101(9)
4:10	33

Tit

Ref	Page
1:5–7	100(4)
2:12	34(23)
2:14	22(32), 50(26)
3:5	46(9)

Phlmn

Ref	Page
6	12(21)
19,21	31(4)

Heb

Ref	Page
1:9	50(26)
2:17	23(37)
4:13	112

ὁμολογεῖν
39,43,59,62,69,70ff,
78
ὀφείλειν
26

παιδία
11,31
παλιγγενεσία
46
παράκλητος
22
παρουσία
44,72
παρρησία
43,44f,58,69,72,85
πατήρ
12f,15,31,47,71
πείθειν
56
περιπατεῖν
14,17,19,21,26
πιστεύειν
59,61,69,70f,76,77f,
82
πίστις
59,77f,79ff
πλανάτω
51
πλάνοι
41
πλεονεξία
47
πληροῦσθαι
14
πλησίον
28
πνεῦμα
59f,70,80,81f
τῆς ἀληθείς ⎱ s.v.
τῆς πλάνης ⎰ πνεῦμα
τοῦ θεοῦ
πνεύματα
61f
πονηρός
32,63,77,89
πρῶτος
75

σκάνδαλον
28
σκοτία
27f
σπέρμα
52f

σπλάγχνα
56
σωτήρ
71

τελειοῦν
72f
τελειοῦσθαι
68f
τέκνα
47f,53
τεκνία
11,22,51
τηρεῖν
25,88
τηρεῖν τὰς ἐντολάς
51

ὕδωρ
79
υἱός
12f,83
υἱός τοῦ θεοῦ
83

φανερωθῆναι
8,44,48,50,67f
φόβος
73
φυλάσσειν
90
φύσις
46
φῶς
16,27f

χαρά
13f
χρῖσμα
37,41,60,80

ψευδοδιδάσκαλοι
62
ψεύδεσθαι
21
ψεῦδος
37,41
ψευδοπροφῆται
62
ψεύστης
18f,22,25,38,51,76
ψηλαφᾶν
9

ὥστε
51

3. Subjects

Aeons
28(21)
Almsgiving
56(52)
Anointing
37,41,80
Antichrist
35f,38,60,61,62,63,112
Antithetical parallelism
39,52,65,82(11),83,102,113
Apocalyptic
35f

Baptism
37,37(12),46(9),80f
Belief
70
Believe
71(9),59,61
Believing
69
Brethren, Itinerant
101,102,108
Brother
28f,54

Cain
54
Catholicism, Early
2
Cerinthus
38(17)
Children
22,98,108(5),115
Christology
7ff,12f,20,22,36,38ff,51,55,
62,67,79f,83,113
Commandment
14,16,27,54,58f,70,77,110f
Commandments
13,25
Confess
59(78),78
Confession
21,21(28),62(9),69,70ff,
79ff,113
Confidence
43,44f,58,69,72f,85f
Cynics
99
Cyprian
81

Darkness
17,18(13),27f
Deceivers
41,112
Demetrius
102
Demonstrative, Followed by
ἵνα
72(1),83
Followed by ὅτι
83(16)
Demonstrative Anticipatory
13(27),24(1),54(43),83(16)
With ἵνα 15(1)
With ὅτι 15(1)
Devil
32f,50f,52,54,67
See Satan
Diotrephes
95(1),100f,101(8),102
Docetics
38(17)
Docetism
62
Dualism
17,17(8),18(13),19,33(18),
38f,97
Dualistic
46(9)

Ecclesiastical Redaction
44(1)
Ecclesiastical Redactor
20,20(25),21,23,30,44,50,
68,72f,83
Epexegetical ἵνα
58(74),98(7)
Ephesus
115(4)
Eschatological Event
9,10f,38f,47,48,67
Eschatology
27,30,40
Eternal Life
40

Faith
43,58f,59,71,76,77f,79ff,80
False Prophets
62,63
False Teachers
27,28,35ff,40f,47,49f,51,
60(84),64,68,76,79f,111
False Teaching
21,30,32,43,44,61f,63,65ff,
66,90f

137

Designer's Notes

In the design of the visual aspects of *Hermeneia*, consideration has been given to relating the form to the content by symbolic means.

The letters of the logotype *Hermeneia* are a fusion of forms alluding simultaneously to Hebrew (dotted vowel markings) and Greek (geometric round shapes) letter forms. In their modern treatment they remind us of the electronic age as well, the vantage point from which this investigation of the past begins.

The Lion of Judah used as a visual identification for the series is based on the Seal of Shema. The version for *Hermeneia* is again a fusion of Hebrew calligraphic forms, especially the legs of the lion, and Greek elements characterized by the geometric. In the sequence of arcs, which can be understood as scroll-like images, the first is the lion's mouth. It is reasserted and accelerated in the whorl and returns in the aggressively arched tail: tradition is passed from one age to the next, rediscovered and re-formed.

"Who is worthy to open the scroll and break its seals . . ."
Then one of the elders said to me
"weep not; lo, the Lion of the tribe of David,
the Root of David, has conquered,
so that he can open the scroll and
its seven seals."
Rev. 5:2, 5

To celebrate the signal achievement in biblical scholarship which *Hermeneia* represents, the entire series will by its color constitute a signal on the theologian's bookshelf: the Old Testament will be bound in yellow and the New Testament in red, traceable to a commonly used color coding for synagogue and church in medieval painting; in pure color terms, varying degrees of intensity of the warm segment of the color spectrum. The colors interpenetrate when the binding color for the Old Testament is used to imprint volumes from the New and vice versa.

Wherever possible, a photograph of the oldest extant manuscript, or a historically significant document pertaining to the biblical sources, will be displayed on the end papers of each volume to give a feel for the tangible reality and beauty of the source material.

The title page motifs are expressive derivations from the *Hermeneia* logotype, repeated seven times to form a matrix and debossed on the cover of each volume. These sifted out elements will be seen to be in their exact positions within the parent matrix. These motifs and their expressional character are noted on the following page.

Horizontal markings at gradated levels on the spine will assist in grouping the volumes according to these conventional categories.

The type has been set with unjustified right margins so as to preserve the internal consistency of word spacing. This is a major factor in both legibility and aesthetic quality; the resultant uneven line endings are only slight impairments to legibility by comparison. In this respect the type resembles the hand written manuscript where the quality of the calligraphic writing is dependent on establishing and holding to integral spacing patterns.

All of the type faces in common use today have been designed between 1500 A.D. and the present. For the biblical text a face was chosen which does not arbitrarily date the text, but rather one which is uncompromisingly modern and unembellished so that its feel is of the universal. The type style is Univers 65 by Adrian Frutiger.

The expository texts and footnotes are set in Baskerville, chosen for its compatibility with the many brief Greek and Hebrew insertions. The double column format and the shorter line length facilitate speed reading and the wide margins to the left of footnotes provide for the scholar's own notations.

Kenneth Hiebert, Designer

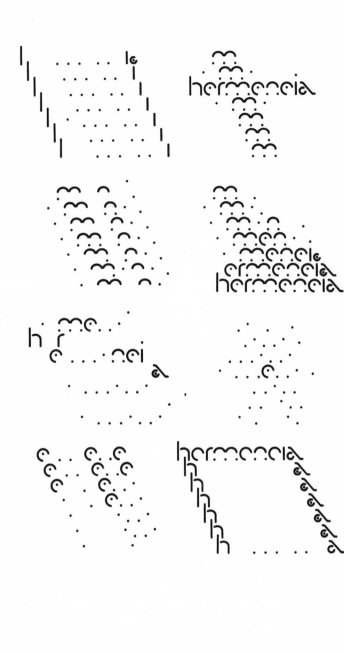

Category of biblical writing,
key symbolic characteristic,
and volumes so identified

1
Law
(boundaries described)
  Genesis
  Exodus
  Leviticus
  Numbers
  Deuteronomy

2
History
(trek through time and space)
  Joshua
  Judges
  Ruth
  1 Samuel
  2 Samuel
  1 Kings
  2 Kings
  1 Chronicles
  2 Chronicles
  Ezra
  Nehemiah
  Esther

3
Poetry
(lyric emotional expression)
  Job
  Psalms
  Proverbs
  Ecclesiastes
  Song of Songs

4
Prophets
(inspired seers)
  Isaiah
  Jeremiah
  Lamentations
  Ezekiel
  Daniel
  Hosea
  Joel
  Amos
  Obadiah
  Jonah
  Micah
  Nahum
  Habakkuk
  Zephaniah
  Haggai
  Zechariah
  Malachi

5
New Testament Narrative
(focus on One)
  Matthew
  Mark
  Luke
  John
  Acts

6
Epistles
(directed instruction)
  Romans
  1 Corinthians
  2 Corinthians
  Galatians
  Ephesians
  Philippians
  Colossians
  1 Thessalonians
  2 Thessalonians
  1 Timothy
  2 Timothy
  Titus
  Philemon
  Hebrews
  James
  1 Peter
  2 Peter
  1 John
  2 John
  3 John
  Jude

7
Apocalypse
(vision of the future)
  Revelation

8
Extracanonical Writings
(peripheral records)